THE NEW AMERICAN REVOLUTION

ALSO BY TAMMY BRUCE

*The Death of Right and Wrong: Exposing
the Left's Assault on Our Culture and Values*

*The New Thought Police:
Inside the Left's Assault on Free Speech and Free Minds*

TAMMY BRUCE

THE NEW AMERICAN REVOLUTION

Using the Power of the Individual
to Save Our Nation from Extremists

wm

WILLIAM MORROW
An Imprint of HarperCollinsPublishers

HarperCollins books may be purchased for educational, business, or sales promotional use. For information please write: Special Markets Department, HarperCollins Publishers, 10 East 53rd Street, New York, NY 10022.

FIRST EDITION

Printed on acid-free paper

Library of Congress Cataloging-in-Publication Data

Bruce, Tammy.
   The New American Revolution : using the power of the individual to save our nation from extremists / by Tammy Bruce.—1st ed.
      p. cm.
   Includes bibliographical references and index.
   ISBN 978-0-06-072621-8

   1. United States—Politics and government—2001– 2. Radicalism—United States.
3. Culture conflict—United States. 4. National characteristics, American.
5. Individuality—United States.   I. Title.

E902.B78 2005
305.8'00973—dc22   2005044390

05 06 07 08 09 JTC/RRD 10 9 8 7 6 5 4 3 2 1

For the New American
The phoenix out of the ashes of September 11, 2001

CONTENTS

1 The New American Revolution   1

2 The New Radical Individual   36

3 Politics and the Individual   62

4 The Sleeping Beauty of America   92

5 Individualism in the Palm of Your Hand   120

6 Tearing Down the Institutions   148

7 Know Your Enemy: Unmasking the Left   183

Epilogue: The Elephants in the Room   215

Acknowledgments **244**

Appendix Tool Chest 1:
Continuing the Revolution **245**

Appendix Tool Chest 2:
Reading into the New American Revolution **262**

Notes **272**
Index **277**

THE NEW AMERICAN REVOLUTION

1

The New American Revolution

Citizens, by birth or choice, of a common country, that country has a right to concentrate your affections. The name of American, which belongs to you in your national capacity, must always exalt the just pride of patriotism more than any appellation derived from local discriminations.

—GEORGE WASHINGTON, Farewell Address, 1796

The reelection of George W. Bush on November 2, 2004, was a confirmation of what began on September 11, 2001—a New American Revolution.

That national election was not simply a culmination of the changing of our nation, but a *continuation* of that change in the most personal and individual ways. One by one, person by person, there has been a shift in how Americans view themselves and what we're willing to put up with.

We're tired of cleaning up the world's messes. We're tired of waiting for Europe to deal with terrorists and tyrants. We took it upon ourselves to deal with them in the only way possible—with righteous vengeance and preemptive action.

The American Left complains that we have no right to be the world's police force. On the contrary. We've been the world's janitor for almost a century, and after September 11, it became obvious it's better, safer, and more productive to change things instead of cleaning up after the mess.

I contend our DNA changed on September 11. As the years pass and we adjust to what has been called the "New Normal," we may not think about those tragic events every day, but we have been forever changed personally. We no longer take our freedom for granted. We looked into the face of a savage and realized evil does exist. We now understand that beasts nurtured by the rest of the world don't care about justice, compassion, or freedom.

We finally understand at our very core that tomorrow is not guaranteed. We "get it" that decisions we make today will shape the world of tomorrow. With all at stake, our individual consciousness as Americans and our responsibility to the future are now irreversible.

Despite the results manifesting all around us, the depth of this change and its consequences have gone largely unrecognized. Americans, even under attack, have been principally a people desirous of being left alone, reticent to go to war.

In the last century, more than half a million Americans died fighting two world wars brought to us by the fascist hubris of Europe and Asia. Now a new century revealed the face of a new savage from the Middle East. There is a point, even for the most restrained, when enough is enough.

I contend September 11 was the beginning of America's tipping point. The subsequent exposure of the deep depravity of the American Left reinforced what is now a New American Revolution.

After that consuming tragedy in 2001, the American Left wallowed in its favorite self-obsessed "It's all our fault!" jingle. The Hate America First crowd, ranging from Michael Moore to Bill Maher to Sean Penn, whined that the only way America could deal with terrorism was to fix "why they hate us."

Instead, the power of the individual American emerged. It became apparent that the Left's decades-long effort to condition us to hate this country is failing. The strength of the American character survives. Instead of worrying about the hurt feelings of the Inner Child of Islamist terrorists, we decided to invade their countries, kill or capture the tyrants and terrorists, and liberate the people who for far too long had suffered under despotic regimes.

Our transformation from a passive, guilt-ridden nation drowning in Leftist moral relativism was actually already in motion when we elected George W. Bush president in 2000.

The defeat of Al Gore that year was a message from a nation that ultimately was deeply disgusted by Bill Clinton. We realized we had a choice about whom we wanted to emulate—a man so easily able to lie, betray, and harm those closest to him, or someone who was, at his core, decent.

When the chips were down, we came through, wanting a better role model. And thank God we did. Much of the rhetoric on both sides of the political spectrum was that the 2004 election was the most important in our lifetime. Little did we know that it was actually the 2000 election that would determine the course of our world.

Eating Our Spinach

George W. Bush was the right man at the right time. He, like us, is a product of a time when Americans had to decide to put up or shut up. On September 10, 2001, George W. Bush and this nation as a whole were very much like a Popeye who had sworn off spinach.

You see, the American Individual is a Regular Guy with a Special Power. For Popeye, his secret was spinach. For us, it is something invisible and infused in our very being—understanding of and love for freedom and liberty. We are the world's first descendants of an *idea*. We are the only place on earth where identity is not based in the mass identity of geography. Instead, we are the stewards of an idea rooted in individualist freedom and opportunity.

And yet, because of decades of Leftist hectoring, America toward the end of the twentieth century had begun to doubt itself and its greatness. In my first two books, *The New Thought Police* (*NTP*) and

The Death of Right and Wrong (DRW), I chronicle our successful brainwashing by the American Left. We were slowly succumbing to the lie that America was a racist, sexist, homophobic place. American values and culture were the scourge of the world, socialism was the wave of the future, and Americans were conditioned to look away.

We began to allow multiculturalism and moral relativism to win the day.

When I wrote those books I had no idea how near we were to a New American Revolution. But I should not have been surprised. Americans have always come through; even if only when pushed to the edge, we always, sooner or later, make the right choices. We eventually eat our spinach.

We are living examples of our surprising power—the American Dream. Like our nation, it is larger than ourselves, but requires and expects each of us to make the most of being free. Every day Americans put into practice the idea of liberty and its necessary machinery—capitalism.

Our spinach is Hopes and Dreams. And not just for ourselves, but for our children. It is living a dream every day with a sort of hope everyone else in the world can only imagine. The power of this idea, the transformative effect of personally knowing the American Dream, is indeed a secret power because it is a modest thing unless under threat. It is the unseen thing that gives us strength to emerge from our regular American lives to save the world.

We are underestimated as Popeye can be underestimated. Yes, we live lives at home that don't necessarily expose the heroics at our core—heroics immortalized by the Greatest Generation of soldiers who saved the world during World War II.

When I say on September 10 we were the reflection of Popeye who had sworn off spinach, I'm speaking of the impact of the Leftist message on our nation.

We had slipped into lazily accepting the scourge of multiculturalism, which is meant to keep the American culture—the American Dream—at bay. Our compassion had been manipulated to the point where we believed, falsely, that Internationalists should take care of the world. We had succumbed to the Thought Police, and looked away from the moral relativism enveloping our courts and culture. We were saturated with the Leftist politics of victimhood, entitlements, and hate.

We were almost beaten as Popeye is often almost beaten until he remembers to reach for that can of spinach. On September 11 we, too, remembered to reach for ours, and the process has changed us forever. Not only did it wake us up to the dangerous lies of the Left, but it reminded us, irrevocably, of what we're made of and who we are.

Our greatness perturbs many in the world for a variety of reasons, not the least of which is that it reminds the mediocre of, well, their mediocrity. So, we acquiesced to the Left's command that we pretend to be like everyone else. More concerned with hurting others' feelings, we retreated. Any show of strength or, God forbid, superiority, is to be avoided lest we make another country feel bad about itself.

And how best to make others feel better about themselves than to deny our own greatness, the Left malevolently insists. The Leftists taught us to hate ourselves so that other people and nations could feel adequate.

America was well on her way to being destroyed by this benign neglect. Our turning inward at the insistence of Leftists worldwide allowed the disease of Islamic Fascism to spread, and self-styled Men of God to assert themselves.

Winning the Culture War

This is the core of our culture war—a war now finally being lost by Leftists and Fascists worldwide. They're losing not only because they're depraved, but because Americans once again have proven that we will not be brainwashed or bullied into a silent cowardice.

The New American Revolution is the individual waking up from the cultural and political coma the Left so carefully cooked up. It is the intensely personal realization that if we continue to play the games of American Leftist extremists, there will be no future for our children.

The success and strength of this nation also shines a big fat light on the failure and depravity of the Left—the Socialists and Marxists, and unfortunately today's Democrat party, who rely on victimhood and hopelessness. The American frame of mind is their deadly kryptonite, a light that they would prefer to snuff out.

September 11, with all its horror, righted our perspective. President Bush, a true product of our generation, knew America needed to take a different track or else all would be lost. The savages of the world and the American Left had grown used to the soft and weak, embodied by Bill Clinton.

Bin Laden relied on all Americans being just like Monica Lewinski's sloppy and distracted boyfriend. Instead, he got Popeye on a full can of spinach.

Taking America Back

In the pages that follow, I'll detail for you how and why we've changed, and how this New American Revolution has intensified the cultural civil war we're enduring to this day.

Recognizing, embracing, and understanding the intense and deeply personal revelations of the last few years will help each one of us recognize the enemy at home and abroad.

And we've finally had enough, enough to the point where the inherent American fear of not being liked is eclipsed by our love for this nation and our duty to protect her. And for a nation built on ideas, while we love the land on which our nation rests, our passion to defend our nation means we're defending the ideas of freedom, liberty, and democracy.

That means an end to putting up with tyrants in the name of "security," or dealing with terrorist Fascists in the name of "diplomacy."

We see now, as we did twice in the last century, that a passive, compassionate American face presented to the rest of the world is not enough. Corruption and a sordid ugliness will prevail, intent on leaving no innocent untouched—including our children.

And while we are a patient people, the moment it becomes clear that it's us or them, American passion, courage, and bravery guarantee that enemies of this nation will not survive.

Or—as the U.S. Marines make clear—with America you have no greater friend, and no worse enemy.

Our tendency to respond only when attacked cost the United States five hundred thousand lives in World War II, and the world fifty-three million lives. September 11 did what even Pearl Harbor did not—it caused us to decide that waiting to be killed by Fascists around the world would not do. Our need to be liked has been eclipsed by our love for our children. Gone are the days where we feel compelled to make the world feel better about itself.

We now refuse to bow to the Left's insistence that tyrants be allowed to rule because, as French President Jacques Chirac argues, democracy is "cultural" and "Western." We know that oppression is like a cancer—if left untreated it will spread beyond where it originated and consume the whole body.

Ignoring the cancer of oppression that feeds terrorism is now unacceptable. It is now more unacceptable than being called a racist. It is more unacceptable than not being liked. It is, indeed, more unacceptable than having to face the truth about facing down the enemy within our own nation—the American Left.

Despite an unprecedented attack on this nation by our Leftist enemies—both within and outside the country—the New Radical Individual sent an undeniable message on election day that we are taking this nation back. We are taking it back from nihilistic Leftists who work feverishly to erase God from the public square, perpetuate the isolationist failure of multiculturalism, and further the death of right and wrong.

The Triumph of the Individual

We would know on November 2, 2004, if the Individual would prevail or if the Individual would be crushed by the likes of George Soros, Michael Moore, Dan Rather, John Kerry, and every other Malignant Narcissist out there who wants you silenced.

As we now thrillingly know, the triumph was enjoyed by the Individual. We sent an undeniable message that our vote, our very sense of self, was not for sale or susceptible to bullying. This was no small feat, because the attacks from the Left were relentless.

Major media, Internet networks, Leftist pod-people, Gestapos from every liberal special-interest group, and more than a few Marxists and atheists made it their life's mission to search and destroy the heart and soul of America.

Billionaire George Soros pledged to spend his entire fortune to defeat George W. Bush. Michael Moore received the support of Europe and an American film distributor to smear this nation and the president with *Fahrenheit 911*. Dan Rather, Mary Mapes, and a few other desperate souls at CBS News were so obsessed with themselves and their worldview, they presented fabricated documents as "news" to vilify a sitting president during a time of war.[1]

The New American Revolution describes more than the newfound passion and freedom of America's so-called conservatives. It is a cultural shift that has revealed the American Left for all it is—hypocritical, fascistic, and self-loathing.

From Howard Dean to Jesse Jackson, actress Cameron Diaz to U.N. nuclear weapons watchdog Mohammad El-Baradei, Elton John to Jacques Chirac, the Left insisted the 2004 election and the choices Americans were making were about life and death. And they were right. This was and is a struggle for the future of this nation, and once again Americans have embraced hope and freedom, to the chagrin of our enemies within.

In 2004, every hat had a rabbit. Every rhetorical gun was deployed. Every Chicken Little was recruited by the Left. The Left even dared to register "Mary Poppins" and "Dick Tracy" to vote in Ohio. Fortunately for us, Ohioan election officials noticed those two and a few other nonexistent people had been registered. For the Democrats, it was indeed going to be the Supercalifragilistic election, whatever it took.

The president and, by proxy, all conservatives and people of faith were compared to Hitler.

Nothing was out-of-bounds, nothing off-limits. Fortunately for us, the American spirit of hope, optimism, and individuality prevailed. As we reflect, it seems extraordinary we survived such an obscene onslaught of lies and hatred.

While it was exhausting and most of us are thankful it's over, something remarkable and beautiful happened in the process of our defending the American way of life. We demanded the return of values—which have made this great nation the best place on earth.

That rendezvous with our better selves confirmed there was no turning back. It ensured our actions and attitudes were not simply moments in time. It confirmed there was a New American Revolution on the march—one that would not be stopped.

As is typical of Americans, our revolution was not born out of a desire for one, or out of a thirst for conflict and division. During the twentieth century the enemy brought the fight to us. In fact, our isolationist position kept us in check for far too long, as Asia suffered under the cruel boot of the Japanese invaders and London withstood a year of nightly bombings by the Nazis. As we slept and ate and played, and turned away, millions died.

America still owes an apology to all those who suffered because of our selfish inaction. My generation realizes that we have learned our lesson, and it will never happen again.

Now, here at home in the twenty-first century, an enemy brought war to us, and once again it was only after years of decent Americans looking the other way. We waited until they brought this nation to the brink and tried to push it over the edge. We waited until enough was enough. Once again the giant has awakened, and I'm not speaking of Michael Moore or Teddy Kennedy.

Real Heroes Versus Real Fascists

The New American Revolution is epitomized by the leadership of George W. Bush. We see our renewed commitment to freedom exemplified by Secretary of State Condoleezza Rice. Fallen hero Pat Tillman stands for our all volunteer military and their personal sacrifice for freedom. Colorado Congressman Tom Tancredo leads the fight to secure our nation's borders. The entire Cheney family, Dick, Lynn, Mary, and Elizabeth, work to make this nation all it can be.

Mel Gibson commits almost his entire personal fortune and reputation to make a film about Christ because he knows it's the right thing to do. He does so even though many claimed it would end his career and ruin him personally. He knew otherwise, and now so do the rest of us.

Roger Ailes soldiers on, despite constant attacks by moonbats on the Left who cannot abide any sign of dissent and alternative points of view. Because Ailes's vision with the Fox News Channel provides something other than Leftist party propaganda, Americans and people the world over are finding they're not alone. Yes, Virginia, not everyone has a Che Guevara T-shirt.

Cultural hero-writers like David Horowitz, Michelle Malkin, Thomas Sowell, and Mark Steyn push on, writing and working to remind us all of the truth. Race relations, immigration, the American character, freedom, and liberty are made clear by these people. As a result, the Left hates them.

In a time when American heroes are born, and we more easily recognize the courageous and strong for what they are, what does the Left offer this nation and the world?

Their Ideal Men (and occasional Women) include:

University of Colorado "ethnic studies" professor Ward Churchill. On the day after the September 11 terrorist massacre of innocent Americans, this man sat down and wrote a now infamous article comparing the victims of the attack to Adolf Eichmann, the architect of the Holocaust.[2]

While Americans in general are repulsed by the antics of this disgusting man, the Left has embraced him as the Second Coming. Liberal scholar Noam Chomsky calls Churchill's "achievements of inestimable value." HBO talk host Bill Maher fawns over him as they discuss "the blood on America's hands." While some speaking engagements were canceled, more poured in, with Leftist attendees providing standing ovations for screeds that condemn this nation.

In his article, Churchill declares the victims in the World Trade Center disaster worked for the "engine of profit" and applauded the nature of their deaths with, "If there was a better, more effective, or in fact any other way of visiting some penalty befitting their participation upon the little Eichmanns inhabiting the sterile sanctuary of the twin towers, I'd really be interested in hearing about it."

Regardless of what happens to Churchill (a man worthy of being resented for the simple fact his existence smears a heroic historical last name), the Left Elite have again exposed themselves for what they are—a cult of misery, victimhood, and hate.

Failed Democrat presidential candidate Howard Dean, also known to conservatives as the gift that keeps on giving. Dean is a man who represents all the hate, all the division, and all that's wrong with today's Democrat Elite. This is a man whose identity is based on opposing the war in Iraq, while spending tens of millions of dollars to lose all but one of the Democrat party presidential primaries. And yet, inexplicably, he is elevated as the chair of the Democrat party.

As the Democrat machine continues to claim they're the party of love and inclusion, here's the sort of comment that garnered Dean the top post: "I hate the Republicans and everything they stand for, but I admire their discipline and their organization."

And once he was ensconced as leader of the Love and Tolerance party, Dean's tune did not change. At a speech in Kansas to Democrat activists he had this to say:

> Moderate Republicans can't stand these people [conservatives], because they're intolerant. They don't think tolerance is a virtue. . . . I'm not going to have these Right-wingers throw away our right to be tolerant.

Do you think Dean understands the irony of condemning other people because they're not tolerant enough? Probably not. He concluded his speech by describing Democrat "values," and then announced, "This is a struggle of good and evil. And we're the good."

Well, thank goodness for that clarification! It's odd when even Dean feels the need to assure his own activists that they're not the evil ones.

For technical reasons electing Dean to head the party is perplexing. You don't select the biggest Democrat loser to design the strategy to win elections. Choosing Dean to lead the party during the New American Revolution is the equivalent of putting O. J. Simpson in charge of a battered women's shelter—stupid, disastrous, and doomed to fail. But it also tells you a great deal about the people making the decision, doesn't it?

The elevation of Dean, however, may not be as strange as it seems on the surface. In fact, it confirms for us who now controls the Democrat party—George Soros. While I go into detail later about the serious danger Soros poses for our nation, it's important to note that Soros attended only one fund-raiser for a candidate during 2004. That candidate was Howard Dean.

Make no mistake—Dean is Soros's boy, and so is the party itself. In fact, in December 2004, Eli Pariser, the head of MoveOn.org's PAC, sent out an e-mail to supporters with a message to the "professional election losers" who run the Democrat party: "We bought it, we own it, we're going to take it back."

And who helped MoveOn.org "buy" the party? Their major funder, of course—George Soros.

When Zell Miller wrote his book *A National Party No More*, I'm sure even he had no idea it would ultimately be reduced to the party of one man and his half dozen Leftist foot soldiers.

What a shame for everyone who remembers the glorious history of the party of Roosevelt, Truman, and Kennedy.

And **Lynne Stewart,** the darling of the American Left, is a lawyer who embodies the collaboration between the American Left and Islamist Fascists. You can't look at the crimes of Lynne Stewart and still say with a straight face that the Left is composed of loyal, patriotic Americans. (For the most comprehensive details about operatives with the American Left and those who support them, visit www.discoverthenetwork.org.)

In 2005, veteran "civil rights" lawyer Stewart was convicted of helping her imprisoned terrorist client, a radical Egyptian sheik, to smuggle messages of violence to his terrorist foot soldiers on the outside. She represents everything reprehensible in this nation, and exemplifies why we should consider the American Left our internal enemy.

Karl Rove,
International Man of Mystery

While New York Democrat **Congressman Maurice Hinchey** may not be as dangerous as Stewart, he's the perfect example of how deeply disturbed the Democrat Elite really are. Responding to the CBS forged-memo disaster regarding the president's National Guard service, Hinchey offered one of the most paranoid conspiracy theories this side of Area 51. At a forum about Social Security, Congressman Hinchey accused the Bush administration of manipulating the media and then said he believed Bush adviser Karl Rove planted the fake documents with CBS News.

He then said the following (seriously):

> I have no proof, but if the documents originated at the White House, then it would fit the pattern of the White House manipulating the media. And if it did originate in the White House, then it must have come from the most brilliant, most Machiavellian of all of them, Karl Rove.[3]

In other words, Hinchey's theory is very much as Dan Rather described the documents themselves, fake but accurate. He has no proof, but it sounds good. It fits with what he'd like to believe about the White House, so if it did happen, he's saying it did, because, gee, there could be a chance it's true, and if not, well, it should be.

Yeah, that's the ticket.

Hinchey is in good company when it comes to bizarre conspiracy theories about how the world is under the spell of one man—and it's not Austin Powers.

Walter Cronkite, the venerable CBS newsman, flew the first Karl-Rove-Controls-the-World trial balloon on CNN's *Larry King Live*. On October 29, 2004, just days before the election, King asked Cronkite to comment on the appearance on a new bin Laden tape that threatened Americans with more death and destruction if we did not bend to his will.

Here is how the man, once described as the Most Trusted Man in America, responded:

> So now the question is basically right now, how will this affect the election? And I have a feeling that it could tilt the election a bit. In fact, I'm a little inclined to think that Karl Rove, the political manager at the White House, who is a very clever man, he probably set up bin Laden to this thing. The advantage to the Republican side is to get rid of, as a

principal subject of the campaigns right now, get rid of the whole problem of the al Qaqaa explosive dump. Right now, that, the last couple of days, has, I think, upset the Republican campaign.[4]

I would expect that sort of paranoid conspiracy-mongering to be limited to state hospitals. The fact that the Dems sent Cronkite out to float that balloon, and that he would agree to do it, shows you how much contempt these people have for us.

Cronkite expects Americans to be so dense that we would not only believe American leadership would do that, but we'd also believe that bin Laden was under Karl Rove's spell, too!

The murderous conspiracies don't stop there. While Roger Ailes is working to bring a variety of points of view back into the media spotlight, Eason Jordan, CNN's chief news executive, made clear his opinion of the U.S. military.

Jordan, you should recall, admitted in April 2003 that CNN had been ignoring stories of Saddam Hussein's crimes against his own people in order to keep the CNN Baghdad office open.[5] This explains why Castro allowed CNN to open a bureau in Havana. After all, with friends like CNN, who needs Joseph Goebbels?

In February 2005, at the World Economic Forum in Davos, Switzerland, this man, whose Baghdad bureau admittedly looked away from torture and murder victims so they would benefit, accused the U.S. military of deliberately targeting journalists. First reported by a blogger who taped the forum where the comments were made, the story eventually forced Jordan to resign his post.

Virtually ignored by the mainstream media (MSM), it was yet again bloggers—once scorned as regular people sitting around in their pajamas—who made sure the story received the attention it was due. They refused to let it be buried. These Media Minutemen (and women!) offer a perfect example of the New American Revolution having its way with the Old Guard, the Old Rules, while exacting a price for the same old lies.

And whether they do it in their jammies, three-piece suits, evening gowns, or Casual Friday garb, it's all a good thing.

While the emerging conspiracy theories are so absurd they can be amusing, it's important to recognize the seriousness of their advent. Genocidal socialist and fascist regimes have always devolved into wild paranoiac conspiracy theories to control populations and rise to power. Paranoid conspiracies drove Stalin and his murder of at least twenty million Russians. We also will never forget how Hitler and his fascist compatriots in Italy and France promulgated Jew-hatred with hysterical rantings of bizarre conspiracies.

It's one thing for talk about Jews, Karl Rove, or Martians controlling the world to be the center point of scary campfire stories, or as middle-of-the-night discussions between the disturbed and marginal. Make no mistake—it is a very bad sign for these sorts of theories to emerge in the MSM, and to be promoted by Democrat and national liberal leaders. It is a significant sign of the monster they're morphing into, and the historical attachment they have to the emergence of fascism.

For too long the Leftist status quo, with their control of the MSM, feared nothing because they had no one to answer to. The Leftists' outlets were the only way to reach the majority of the American people, while the targets—you and me—had no way to respond in real time or with any comparable power of reach. Courtesy of bloggers and radio talk show hosts, a cadre of which I am proud to be among, now we do.

Even for the more passive American, the remarkable difference between what the Right and Left are offering this nation is striking. Up until now I have tended to classify other liberals as separate from the Left. With the obvious meltdown of the liberal establishment and desolation it offers the country, I'm finding it more difficult to find excuses for liberals and Democrats who continue to actively support the party and its henchmen.

There is now no excuse for ignoring the consumption of the Democrat party leadership by appeasers of death-loving Fascists bent on destroying this nation. But even that wouldn't satisfy them—the New American Revolution has come about in part because we know the terrorist death cultists also would love to murder our children.

Ask parents in Beslan, Russia. Hundreds escorting their children to the first day of elementary school watched mostly Arab Islamist terrorists take them all hostage and then shoot their children in the back as they tried to escape.

It's becoming obvious there are many reasons why the Democrat party as a whole is in such disarray. At the core of their problem is the fact that there is simply no there there. It's as though a sommelier walks up to you with a wonderful bottle of 1947 Chateau Margaux. The bottle itself looks good but you notice the cork is out, and it's actually empty.

The sommelier goes on and on about how wonderful the wine is, how it is known to be the best, talks about its history and how wonderful it will be. He expects you to buy it, but completely ignores the fact that the bottle is empty. He supposes you won't notice, that you will be dazzled by the idea and tricked by the fact that in the past the bottle had been full.

In many ways, he's simply ignoring the fact that the wine is gone. For him, it is the past he's hanging on to, and hopes you are as well. Being able to deal with reality, with the change in circumstance, is simply too much, too difficult to acknowledge. Without that bottle he's lost, his job is gone, and he'll have nothing to speak of, nothing to sell.

Unfortunately for us, we live in a world where that sommelier— the Left—does not respond well when confronted with the truth of the matter and his hopeless situation.

Americans, however, are already reminding the world that we are not like everyone else and will not acquiesce to violence. In other words, America is not Spain.

"True Democrats"

I do enjoy the e-mail I receive from listeners, readers, and those who catch my appearances on Fox News. While the majority are supportive and great to read, every now and then I receive a piece of hate mail that perfectly illustrates just how far gone Leftists really are.

For the life of me, I don't understand why someone would take time out of their life to send an e-mail to a stranger they despise, but then again, incoherence is a hallmark of today's so-called liberals.

Those from members of the Party of Love, Inclusion, and Tolerance (aka Democrats) usually cut right to the chase with their hate and disdain. Robert's diatribe is a perfect example. In the months prior to the 2004 election, he apparently caught my radio program and just couldn't contain himself. He started his e-mail with "Are you confused or are you just stupid? Just because you write two books and are a Fox contributor does not mean you have brains . . ."

Suddenly hearing strains of "neener neener neener" in the background, I read on as the tone turns quite a bit more menacing:

> " . . . I am a Democrat who loves to fight back, not a 'treehugger,' but one who will spit in the face of you and your Republican listeners. I will do it with my knowledge, my beliefs, and my fists, something you and your listeners lack . . ."

Without a beat, Robert moves from a personal insult to threats of violence against Republicans and my listeners. After declaring that my opinion about the Democrat party "makes him sick," Robert then apparently decided that he would like to cast himself and other Democrats like him as scarier than Al Qaeda as he insists, "Tell Ashcroft that the only group he and his administration needs to worry about are the Democrats . . ."

Fascinating, isn't it? Robert's inference is unmistakeable—I am to send a message to the then–Attorney General of the United States, one of the men leading the Homeland Security effort, that Democrats are to be more feared than that other group at the top of the list—Al Qaeda. Now even I wouldn't make that suggestion, but it's striking that there's a Democrat who not only thinks so, but felt comfortable putting it into writing.

Make no mistake, his is the mentality the Left's campaign of hatred has manifested. And how does he sign off?

> *"From Kerry to Hillary, damn it is going to be so funny watching your kind just fade away!! True Democrat, Robert*
> *PS. G.W. the only Bush I do not like . . . now I can add you to the same category!!"*

Robert sent this e-mail to me prior to the 2004 election. Clearly, he was as deluded about the outcome of that event as he is about Democrat omnipotence.

Yes, unfortunately, these days Robert is a "True Democrat." This is what the party has sunk to and why this nation gave President Bush an undeniable victory. I share this particular e-mail with you because it has all the elements I see in most of the letters I receive from today's "Democrats." They are violently hostile. And, almost without fail, they inject a little misogyny, which is quite revealing.

Unfortunately, Robert is typical and reflective of what today's Leftist leaders have created in their frenzy to demonize conservatives, while simultaneously brainwashing their own constituents. This man exhibits virtually every symptom of groupthink, and it has manifested in a sort of hate that compels him to strike out.

While my life is not interrupted by this sort of tripe, the problem is that people like Robert are lost and their deluded hate infects the national discourse.

The work of Leftist special-interest groups condemns their constituencies to lives of frustration and hatred in part because they do not understand why no one will hear them. Their victimization grows as they become increasingly alienated from society, which they see as "stupid" and worthy of humiliation and violence. People who disagree with them also become something other than human.

Robert's e-mail exemplifies all of these problems. Disturbingly, he uses a phrase that I've seen more and more in the e-mails I receive from the hate-filled Left. Over the past few years, as MoveOn.org and the other Soros-funded organizations spread their message comparing the president to Hitler, the "your kind" reference began to appear quite frequently.

Keep in mind what "your kind" implies. To be of a "kind" indicates that I am not "of" the accuser's kind. In other words, I am not completely human, simply because I choose to think for myself and reject the Left's groupthink. It shouldn't be surprising—this is the natural and expected result of the venom and hate spewed for so long by leaders throughout the Democrat party and the Left.

And yet, not one Democrat party leader stands up and says, "Wait a minute, listen to yourselves, while we disagree with the Republicans and the president, we need to reject the ugliness of what's happening."

Instead, the rhetoric continues and so does the threats of violence, which turned to actual acts of violence against some people.

Desperate Democrats

It's par for the course for Fascists to turn to violence when they cannot win through peaceful public persuasion. They never have, and never can. Intimidation through violence is a tactic the Left has always eventually resorted to. Why? Because people everywhere naturally reject plans that include human enslavement—both mentally and physically. As the Left finds it cannot win power through legitimate means, the nature of its leadership gravitates automatically to the use of violence and intimidation.

When Leftist leadership, as we've seen in our nation, rallies its foot soldiers with hate and fear, the emergence of Brownshirts is inevitable. We are not yet at the point of Germany's Kristallnacht* courtesy of the Nazis, but we must acknowledge the direction of the Democrat party and its hijacking by malevolent Leftists.

You see, the Left truly believes that people are evil and need to be controlled for their own good. The projection is obvious, but when you believe you have sole possession of the truth, the end begins to justify the means. Whether it be Russia, Germany, or Italy, intimidation, violence, and terrorism were all used by Leftists and their fascist brethren to gain power.

Here it is no different. While the episodes I note for you, if taken alone, may seem isolated or ineffective, it's important to see this in the broader historical context of the use of violence by every Leftist regime in history. Americans have a choice—coerced change by the thuggery offered by the Left, or the sort of revolutionary change at the core of the American spirit—through hope and optimism for the future, recognizing our unique responsibility in the world, as flame-holders for freedom and liberty.

While we have seen violence exacted as "political expression" in fascist countries, I don't think any of us expected it to become a tactic by what has been a major political party in the United States as soon as it has. The reaction to the election of 2004 not only indicated how desperate the Democrat party has become, it revealed an actual element of the underlying nature of its machinery.

By being void of ideas, the least it exposes is how liberal leadership has abandoned its supporters by stirring them up into a hate frenzy. Apparently the Dems have found out that their own people won't ask them what's going on, what's the plan, or the increasingly important question, "How did Fascists take over our party?" when being told there's a bogeyman out to get them.

Barry M. Seltzer insisted he was exercising his "political expression" when he was arrested on charges he nearly ran down U.S. Rep. Katherine Harris and a group of her supporters with his car.[6]

*For more background on the early formative tactics of the Nazis, visit the Jewish Virtual Library at http://www.jewishvirtuallibrary.org/jsource/Holocaust/kristallnacht.html.

Congresswoman Harris and some volunteers for her 2004 reelection campaign were on the sidewalk when witnesses told police a silver Cadillac sped through an intersection and hurtled onto the sidewalk, heading straight toward Harris. At the last moment, the car swerved and drove off.

Witnesses took the license plate number, which police tracked to Seltzer. When approached by police at his home, Seltzer declared, "I intimidated them with my car," he was quoted as telling police. "I was exercising my political expression."[7]

Elsewhere in the country in the lead-up to the election the Democrats' insistence that Republicans were intimidating voters and would try to "steal" the election was clearly a case of projection; gunshots were fired into Bush-Cheney '04 offices in West Virginia, Florida, and Tennessee; windows were broken in West Virginia, and campaign staffers threatened.

Republican offices in the Seattle area; Spokane, Washington; Canton, Ohio; Fairbanks, Alaska; and Edwardsville, Illinois, were also burglarized and/or vandalized. In the Canton, Ohio, break-in, a Bush-Cheney '04 staffer was forced to lock herself in an office while the break-in was in progress. The GOP office in Gallatin County, Montana, was vandalized twice in less than a week.

In Orlando, Florida, Democrat activists and union members stormed the local Bush-Cheney headquarters, and the ensuing melee resulted in a broken arm and other physical injuries to at least two Republican campaign workers. The liberal protesters justified their actions—including ramming the head of one of the workers into an office door—by blaming President Bush's "negative campaign."

Do not think these events are flukes, or simply juvenile preelection tactics to intimidate voters. This is not a symptom of the decline of the entire American electoral system. Nothing comparable occurred at Democrat party headquarters or to liberal activists. In actuality, the resort to violence, base intimidation, and crime is classic fascism, and is the emerging result of the meltdown of the Democratic party and the exposure of the actual face of its leadership.

All pretense was gone when on November 5, 2004, three days after the election, a mob of vandals attacked the North Carolina Republican party headquarters, causing smoke damage, breaking windows, and leaving vulgar messages, police said. Also, the mob left a burned effigy depicting the president. In addition to the vandalism, police reported several spent fireworks, poster boards with slogans, and spray-painted expletives on the walls. Police also noted it appeared that the vandals tried to put incendiary devices *inside* the building.

This group was found after a police officer reported seeing about one hundred people wearing masks and gloves walking down a street near the headquarters.

"The people who did this are sick," said Kevin Howell, communications director for the state Republican party. "People don't understand that debate and elections are part of the process. This isn't how you act."[8]

Howell is right; it's not how decent people act, but it is increasingly how Fascists masquerading as "Democratic Activists" behave.

The worst among them have taken control of the machine, co-opting the name of the party. Liberals and young people who identify as "Leftist" because it seems romantic are the most at risk. They're being egged on by a leadership that has no ideas, no vision, but plenty of fear and loathing.

When your own party leadership tells you that Republicans are "evil" and you are "good," in what exactly do you think that will result? It is clear the Dems will continue to lose ground politically and socially. Because they do not understand what has happened and where we're headed, their failure will only become more intense, and so will their rhetoric.

Soros Loser

George Soros may have failed in his immediate effort to personally unseat President Bush in 2004, but do not think this man is finished. Soros remains a primary enemy of the New American Revolution and this nation as a whole as he continues to work feverishly to wipe away the values we all hold so dear.

Do not dismiss him—despite the monumental losses of 2004 for Soros and his ilk, he managed to take over the Democrat party because he remains its Sugar Daddy.

A few things became crystal clear during the 2004 election—decent Americans have had enough of the hate and divisions sown by the Left. It's worth noting here the differences between the agenda of the losers and the goals of the winners. I'm not speaking of the candidates themselves, but the men running for the highest office in the land do mirror the core attitude of their supporters.

What the deterioration of the American Left shows us is that our goal is not just to be an "individual"—you can be that *and* driven by hate and money and Malignant Narcissism, and still be lost. The individualism I speak of is only worthwhile, only effective, only real when based in the core ideas of our Founding Fathers and the American Ideal.

Soros made himself quite the player in 2004. He declared that defeating George W. Bush was the central focus of his life. He pledged his "entire fortune" to do it.[9] In fact, a year before the election, Soros had already spent fifteen million in his attempt to subvert and eclipse the votes of the people. That's a lot of money. Soros is the billionaire hedge fund manager turned Leftist organizer. His obsessions include what he terms "open societies."

In a November 2003 *Washington Post* interview, Soros introduced the comparison of Bush to Hitler, with which Leftists the world over still promulgate. In that interview he declared the White House was guided by a "supremacist ideology," and "America, under Bush, is a danger to the world. . . . When I hear Bush say, 'You're either with us or against us,' it reminds me of the Germans. . . . My experiences under Nazi and Soviet rule have sensitized me."[10]

When asked by *Hemispheres* magazine if he was using his wealth to meddle in national affairs, he noted, "Of course what I do could be called meddling because I want to promote an open society. An open society *transcends national sovereignty* [emphasis mine]."[11]

At least now we know what this Hungarian-born U.S. citizen means by "open societies"—a world without the United States so the rest of us can feel important again. It's a sort of Affirmative Action for nations. Make no mistake—without the nature of the United States—liberty, democracy, and freedom—to serve as a beacon, the rest of the world would collapse under the weight of modern-day Marxists who dream of smashing pesky individualism.

Despite Soros spending an estimated twenty million dollars (What? Not the "whole" fortune!?), individual Americans made it clear they could not be bought or brainwashed. Soros gave millions and became the largest donor to the attack-dog group MoveOn.org, pledged ten million to "America Coming Together," and millions more to the Center for American Progress, a new liberal think tank that is financing the likes of Bush-hating pundit Eric Alterman, and headed by former Clinton chief of staff John Podesta.[12]

As Americans, we looked at the Men of the DNC Calendar, saw George Soros, and we did not like it. We had two very distinct choices—an America that makes us proud, influenced by the commonsense values of Christianity, the rule of law, justice, and freedom; or an America divided by false hate, isolation, victimhood, and self-loathing.

George Soros, who as noted earlier has effectively bought the Democrat party, promotes mass immigration into the United States; finances antigun lawsuits and lobbyists; demands voting rights for felons; seeks the abolition of capital punishment; exacerbates Palestinian unrest; and promotes doctor-assisted suicide, drug legalization, and "Global Government."

It's also worth noting that the only reason the world exists now is because the United States has not been under the boot of a world driven by either spineless appeasers or megalomaniacal despots. Make no mistake, "Global Government" is merely a euphemism for a world without the United States as we know it. Soros and other Leftists want that world because it is the only place where the Malignant Narcissist will finally rule.

Malignant Narcissism Manifest

In my book DRW, I describe elements in the canon of the psychological underpinnings of "projection" by Malignant Narcissists. The definition of projection from orthodox psychology texts explains this as projecting one's own unconscious or undesirable characteristics onto an opponent—for example, an aggressive man who accuses other people of being hostile or a cheat who is sure that everyone else is dishonest. Or, as noted earlier, violent vandals pointing the finger at others.

I bring this up because of Soros's obsession with President Bush and his bizarre analogy of our president with Jew-hating, country-destroying, control-freak Hitler.

Consider his own remarkable admission: Soros, who is Jewish, in a speech to Jewish Funders Network, astoundingly blamed the cause of anti-Semitism on Israel and then on himself.[13]

After blaming Israel and the U.S. for causing anti-Semitism and citing the Malaysian prime minister's statement that the "Jews rule the world by proxy," Soros then confessed: "I'm also very concerned about my own role because the new anti-Semitism holds that the Jews rule the world. As an unintended consequence of my actions, I also contribute to that image."[14]

Immediately after Soros's remarks, Michael Steinhardt, the man who invited him to speak, took the podium and had this to say by way of an explanation (and Freudian slip) of the billionaire Leftist's apparent disdain for Jews: "George Soros does not think Jews should be hated any more than they deserve to be."[115]

That certainly clears everything right up.

The Godless God

We all know, however, there is something else at the core of Soros's hatred for the American ideals embodied in the president. Soros is indeed our most and best example of a Malignant Narcissist.

Soros, like others obsessed and filled with hate for people of faith, is a self-proclaimed atheist. He is godless. As the theory of Malignant Narcissism commands, in his struggle to belong, Soros must make society look like him. It must be godless, and having a man in the White House who looks to something beyond himself—God—Soros is reminded and made frantic by the fact that he—Soros—is not the person around whom everything revolves.

The only thing that makes Soros even more dangerous than every other Malignant Narcissist out there is that he has seven billion dollars with which to do considerable damage.

Not convinced? Consider Soros's own words about his opinion of himself:

"If truth be known, I carried some rather potent messianic fantasies with me from childhood, which I felt I had to control, otherwise they might get me in trouble," he once wrote. When asked to elaborate on that passage by *The Independent*, Soros said, "It is a sort of disease when you consider yourself some kind of God, the creator of everything, but I feel comfortable about it now since I began to live it out."[16]

Soros's hatred of Christian America as represented by President Bush is more understandable under the rubric of Malignant Narcissism. A man who thinks he is God cannot abide having anyone, let alone the president of the United States, be answerable to a god other than Soros himself.

Eighty-five percent of Americans identify as Christian. A full 96 percent of Americans celebrate Christmas. Personally, while I believe in God (not the George Soros version—but the one with that troublemaking son, Jesus), I do not identify as a Christian, and yet it is impossible for any American who is honest with himself not to recognize that it is Christian values that have made our lives worth living.

On November 2, 2004, Americans in part said they wanted a president who sincerely believed in God. Not only am I not threatened by that, I for one want a man or woman in the White House who feels there *is* something greater than himself to answer to. As leader of the free world, he (or she!) should have the comfort and support of God in making decisions that change the world every day.

Part of America's birth is the result of the tyranny and havoc wreaked in Europe by men who also considered themselves divine. We have seen what manifests when the true God is removed, and man himself becomes omnipotent. Ranging from the Romans to the French Revolution to the Soviet Union and Stalin—genocide becomes the order of the day.

Whether or not some voters considered the history of atheistic states when they voted, they at least saw the difference in the humanity of the men running for office, and the people surrounding them.

Why I Support George W. Bush

As a Democrat and a pro-choice feminist, it is indeed time for me to explain why I support our Republican president and why every other self-respecting and decent Democrat should do the same.

The morphing of the Democrat party into a team of threatening Brownshirts burning effigies and trying to burn down buildings makes the decision a no-brainer. It's not difficult to see how this is not the Roosevelt or Kennedy version of the Democrat party. Kennedy dispatched the National Guard to put down roving mobs determined to intimidate people who were different.

Today, Democrats have *become* the mob.

In Kennedy's time, black people were the target of masked and gloved bullies intent on doing harm.

Today, conservatives and Republicans are the target.

I can't tell you how many e-mails I receive from other Democrats condemning me for not toeing the line, while others who write are genuinely curious. During the election, and after all the hatemongering and demonizing of Republicans, and the president specifically, the Authentic Democrats I hear from have retained enough of their individuality that they're not afraid to ask about what their feelings and thoughts mean.

My hope is to ease the fears of decent people who happen to be Democrats, and still want to do the right thing, regardless what the Democrat Gestapo tells them.

For you Democrats who support the president and yet struggle with what that means about you, there is a simple answer: It means you're a confident Classical Liberal, a thoughtful person who realizes that party loyalty takes a backseat to the safety of your family and this nation.

It also means you take the slogans of "choice" and "radical individualism" seriously. Isn't it ironic that there's nothing more radically individual these days than a liberal who doesn't conform?

For me, Authentic Feminism is rooted in making it possible for people to make the choices that best suit them.

The president and I hold dramatically divergent views on a number of important social issues. Yet for the three thousand people who died on September 11, abortion rights and same-sex civil unions mean absolutely nothing to them now.

These issues, while important to me and ones on which I will continue to speak out about, are luxuries in the face of a world war where the enemy is a stateless savage who hunts children and cuts off people's heads.

We all know, and must reflect on, the fact that the joy we have in our lives today is due to the sacrifice of hundreds of thousands of other Americans who died fighting for this country. Those soldiers did not die because they were promised seventy-two virgins in the afterlife; they fought not for themselves—they died in the most noble of American causes so future generations—us—could live in freedom.

I do not take that action for granted, and I have learned that generosity of spirit and commitment to freedom are inherent in each of us, and a duty we cannot shirk.

Those of you with children have a more immediate concern, which is the literal safety of the light of your life.

That little face stares at you in the morning, with a heart full of hope, limited only by her imagination because you confront, for her, the harsh realities of every day. And these days it's not just about making a living, it's about the Beslan school massacre, it's a new Al Qaeda tape threatening Americans at home, it's about war and mad savages who specifically target children.

While I know a Bush presidency makes my work as a feminist more complicated and demanding, I will love and be grateful for every day I have the luxury of working on those issues. And, frankly, it's not necessarily a bad thing to have a president who encourages social activism on issues.

Liberals make the mistake of thinking a Democrat president is indeed Daddy, who can be trusted in all things. Apathy soon follows that false comfort.

Bill Clinton showed us the decline of the Democrat party into a gang spouting slogans to make women, gays, and blacks feel Daddy was in the house, to our grave regret. What did we get? A sexual compulsive who put Monica Lewinsky on her knees instead of cutting bin Laden off at his.

Yes, there were plenty of Democrats, feminists, gays, and blacks in the World Trade Center, the Pentagon, and on those fateful flights.

I'm sure you would agree that in their last moments their literal lives were more important to them than party affiliation.

The Angry World, Part Deux

I know George Bush has made many in the world angry. I am dismayed at the hard feelings. A 2004 poll of Europeans revealed their general belief that Bush has made the world a more dangerous place.

Upon hearing that, I remind myself of the time President Reagan increased arms production and installed more Pershing missiles in Europe as we faced down the Soviet Union.

President Reagan grappled with European polls, anger, and resentment, all of which evaporated when the Soviet regime collapsed.

Yes, they hated Reagan, but he plodded on, never swayed by those polls or made doubtful by others' hatred. His resolve freed Europe from the shadow of a bear that had no mercy and the blood of tens of millions on its paws.

As a man of faith with a love of this country, Reagan stayed the course, and did what he knew had to be done. He was a leader and, I'm proud to say, one that only America could deliver.

The remarkable leadership of President Reagan, the decency of the man and his passion for this nation, shaped my political views as I grew up. Now, with the benefit of history and today's current challenges, I finally understand what makes George W. Bush similar to Ronald Reagan—they're both Radical Individuals.

With an acute understanding of what's important, they approach their work with a confidence and commitment that makes things happen. What makes them both great is that their individualistic spirit is not rooted in the depravity that afflicts so many on the Left. Instead, they're driven by the American passion for freedom and liberty, and the compassion that lights our fire to make the world a better place.

These qualities are not simply embraced by truly great men and women. On the contrary—the truly great, whether world-renowned or not, are made by these qualities. These traits are at the core of the American character, and are inherent not only in great American leaders, but in each of us as well.

Reagan is loved for not just leading us, but showing us how we were leaders of ourselves. His greatness is based in showing us our individual greatness. He led by not asking us to follow him, but by showing us what we were made of. He understood the greatness of the individual American, and that this nation was made continually great because of the capacity in all of us for personal greatness.

Yours and mine.

Today, President Bush faces the same polls, the same anger, and the same resentment as he, too, recognizes and engages a rabid enemy of civilization, Islamist Fascists.

He, too, understands himself and, immersed in the American spirit, is brilliantly sure of his mission. He can be sure because he understands at his core that freedom is a natural human right that can only be brought forth by democracy. As American individuals we live this dream: that no individual should be answerable to the false god of government, that our rights to freedom and liberty are God-given, not man-made, not man-given.

Europeans felt Reagan was leading them to Armageddon, as they now insist Bush is doing. We can't know what it's like for Europeans to see such a young nation doing so many things, but one thing Europe will find, again, is that while we may be wild, young, and even cowboys on occasion, we have a pretty good track record of making the world a safer and better place.

With George W. Bush at the helm, this time is no different.

Now, with freedom and democracy breaking out all over the Arab world, the European press is showing signs that they finally may be "getting it."

Since President Bush's policy, embodied by the American response to September 11, Afghanistan and Iraq have had free elections and are democracies where women vote and participate in the process. The people of Lebanon have risen up against their Syrian oppressors, the people of Kuwait and Saudi Arabia see the opening up of their political process, and Egyptians have reason to be hopeful with President Mubarak's announcement supporting a constitutional change to allow opposition candidates to run for the presidency.

The new Arab sentiment is best expressed by the leader of the Lebanese intifada, Walid Jumblatt. Jumblatt, a longtime denouncer of the United States and Israel, explained the change in the Middle East to the *Washington Post*'s David Ignatius:

> "It's strange for me to say it, but this process of change
> has started because of the American invasion of Iraq," ex-
> plains Jumblatt. "I was cynical about Iraq. But when I saw the
> Iraqi people voting three weeks ago, 8 million of them, it was
> the start of a new Arab world." Jumblatt says this spark of
> democratic revolt is spreading. "The Syrian people, the
> Egyptian people, all say that something is changing. The
> Berlin Wall has fallen. We can see it."[17]

After the January 30, 2005, Iraqi elections, the French newspaper *Le Monde* ran an editorial titled "Arab Spring" and acknowledged "the merit of George W. Bush." The cover of London's *The Independent* booms, "Was Bush Right After All?" A column in *Der Spiegel* asks: "Could George W. Bush Be Right?"

When the European press even begins to contemplate the fact that George W. Bush could be right, you know the consciousness of the world has changed. Some things are undeniable, once again proving truth will always prevail, regardless of Leftist naysayers.

Not Waiting for Europe

As a feminist, I thanked the president with my vote and vocal support, in solidarity with the millions of Afghan and Iraqi women who now, courtesy of the president and our astounding military, finally have hope, liberty, and freedom. I also stand with him because of the potential for all other Middle Eastern women to be free as a result of the New American Revolution and our facing up to our responsibility to the world.

Like all of our presidents, George W. Bush is quintessentially an American. He's a cowboy. A Texan. He will never be mistaken for a Frenchman. He's a Yalie. He's a man of faith, a husband and father. He's a man who has fought with and overcome addiction. He's a man of strength and character.

And while he is also wrong on some social issues, if I have to work harder on those issues, I want it to be against a man whom I can admire, who I know, despite our disagreements, honors me in his work to keep this nation free and great.

For those of you who are Democrats and liberals—and I know through my years as a leader in Left-wing causes, including feminist and gay activism—we all have gone through a sort of conditioning that makes dissent or difference a frightening prospect.

Republicans and conservatives have been decidedly demonized in your circle—perhaps by your own friends and family.

Let me tell you this—supporting and even liking the president does not change who you are or what you stand for. I stand for the Classical Liberal concepts of personal liberty and individualism, and have spent a great deal of my adult life working for those causes. I have found that "Choice" and "Individualism" are only slogans if you never act on them. Sometimes being yourself means straying from the expected, standing apart from your crowd.

From September 11, 2001, to November 2, 2004, and beyond, we are telling America's enemies, within and without, that the American spirit has returned. As a mosaic of the American individual, it now wears a cowboy hat, carries a gun, is not afraid of being called names, and has had enough of tyranny and oppression.

We are at a pinnacle of history, made possible because of the sacrifices of our forebears. Our greatness now relies on your enduring individual commitment to our responsibility to maintain freedom here at home, and to spread democracy and freedom to the world.

The New American Revolution is on the move, with liberty and freedom for everyone.

2

The New Radical Individual

*You gain strength, courage & confidence by every
experience in which you really stop to look fear in the
face. You must do the thing which you think you
cannot do.*

—ELEANOR ROOSEVELT

The unintended consequence of the Left Elite's undermining
our culture by redefining the acceptable cultural categories
(e.g., pro-choice, lesbian/gay, feminist, tree-hugging, vegetarian,
America-hating, socialist, tongue-pierced, "medical" marijuana–
advocating, rage-filled, useless, Howard Dean–supporting, PETA-
activist, or any combination of the above) is the creation of you, the
New Radical Individual.

I contend that the New Radical Individual is the straight, white
Christian man or woman who holds traditional values, worries
about the future of his or her children, and works hard for a living.
You, the New Radical Individual, don't believe the government
"owes" you anything. The only "entitlement" you expect is life, liberty, and the pursuit of happiness. You may or may not be a gun
owner, but at the very least you cherish the Second Amendment to
our Constitution.

You take the right to bear arms as seriously as all the amendments
and are disgusted by the abuse of it by the pond scum at the ACLU.

You know that people like you and me owning firearms helps to keep our nation free. You love animals, yet may enjoy the occasional hunt. You attend your church, despite the continued attacks on religion in general and Christianity in particular. You, most of all, do not let the malevolent affect your relationship with God.

You may relate to some or all of the above, representing your own special combination of individuality. The last thing I want to do is put you into a box! Essentially, you are the majority in this country and yet, paradoxically, you are the most ignored and the most obsessed about by the Left Elite in this nation, who find you troublesome, irritating, and ultimately dangerous to their agenda.

It's a sad state of affairs when the average American who holds these values and has the character that has made this nation great for over two hundred years is so at odds with popular culture and the direction of society. But this, too, has set you apart, as it has me.

Many of you, I've learned, are indeed like me—a minority, or someone who lives on the margin of society, who considers the politics of the Left to be rubbish. This, my friends, is even more astonishingly radical, because it removes us from the smaller community in which we live. For the average American who is the principal hero of our story, rejecting Leftist politics and culture does marginalize you in some ways, but usually it does not threaten your relationship with your immediate community—your church, your town, and, above all, your family. For gays, feminists, and blacks who dare to challenge the status quo—well, the price is even higher.

Why do they hate you? Because you represent what they will never be: decent, happy, and free people. It's much the same reason why Osama and his binLadentrons hate us. Islamist Fascists hate us primarily because we *are* beautiful—Americans have created the perfect blending of a free, secular society teeming with people of faith. We are free, have fun, make money, enjoy our toys, educate men *and* women, enjoy life, appreciate beauty in men, women, and art. And yet, we are also religious, are compassionate and tolerant, take care of those who cannot care for themselves, and are willing to risk dying to help set other people free. The Islamist Fascist is drowning in jealousy and envy. It is that simple, you infidel you!

It's fascinating to contemplate, and within all these turns of events, *you* are the New Radical Individual.

You worry about your children, even though the Cultural Elites tell you "it takes a village." They tell you your children are better off being told how to live their lives by strangers than by you with all that scary religion and morality you embrace.

You are radical because you love this nation even when you are bombarded by messages that tell you it should be hated. You still believe in the greatness of who we are even when told "the world" hates us.

And you pesky independent-minded person—you have actually dared to stray from the plantation by rejecting the socialism they try to ram down your throat.

In other words, you stick with your principles, your faith, and your sense of right and wrong, even though it would be easier, culturally, to abandon them. You "do not belong" to the elite set that tries to tell you that you would be a better person, more fair, less racist, less homophobic, and more accepted if you would just throw yourself onto the altar of groupthink.

You have refused. You remain yourself despite all you face. You, the stay-at-home mom, the working dad, the Christian family of four or more, despite your majority status in this nation, are now the marginalized fringe, and yet you do not back down.

In today's culture war, our fight is against a Left that has taken a seat at the table, has gorged itself on the food that we worked hard to produce, and yet still pounds its fists on the table demanding more, including that most priceless of things—our sense of self.

Even as the Leftists condemn you for your faith, accuse you of intolerance, use the media to scream invectives at you, and craft laws to make you distrustful of yourself and your intentions, you persevere. Today's Leftists work long and hard to destroy your inherent sense of American decency, morality, and freedom because they know it is the only thing remaining that can expose them in all their ugliness, inhumanity, and despair.

This is all about your greatness and the reality of what makes this nation tick, and about how we can save our nation from extremists.

I found my own true radical individuality when I dared to reject the stereotypical Leftist, gay, feminist positions—when I dared to be honest about my politics, views, and values. Oddly, I know that I am finally truly more myself because over the past few years I have increasingly found myself alone politically. The Left rejects me as—and this has become the favorite Thought Police label for Yours Truly—a "Puppet of the Right."

Many conservatives have their reservations about me and my politics, for obvious reasons. It just doesn't seem as if there are too many special-interest groups for openly gay, pro-choice, pro-death-penalty feminists with Ronald Reagan as their hero and a gun named Snuffy in the night table.

But while we disagree on some issues, the reality is that you and I are both New Radical Individuals. The tie that binds us together is our individuality as Americans, our fight against Thought Police conformity, and the belief that this nation is the greatest on earth in part because she embodies the freedom and liberty that gives rise to people like you and me.

Fighting the State of Mediocrity

In the past few years, I've done a great deal of work complaining about what's wrong with our politics and our culture. I have very directly identified the culprits responsible for our cultural meltdown. I haven't held back when it comes to describing the painful, the awful, and the unbelievable.

While writing my first two books, *The New Thought Police* and *The Death of Right and Wrong,* I learned a lot about myself. I also learned about you. I found that, while the problems we face culturally seem overwhelming, you and your greatness, your remarkable individuality, and the American character in each of you are strong enough to save your family's future, and ultimately our nation's. Even in the face of a Leftist culture war that is determined to take you and your family hostage, there is hope, and it rests in your singular commitment to the heart and soul of this nation and all that it has meant for over two hundred years.

In my earlier work, I exposed the problems we need to confront. I felt a responsibility to share my perspective because it comes from *inside* that unforgiving and malevolent Leftist machine. I knew I could at least give you the comfort of knowing you were not alone in your sense that something is going terribly wrong within our culture and perhaps even with ourselves. I've heard from so many of you that my insight was particularly helpful to you because it is based in real-life experience. It was born of my finally, somehow, being able to recognize the lie of the Leftist establishment and the importance of facing it down.

What that establishment would take from us is our very individuality: our values, our judgment, our singular role as thoughtful, critical, proud, and compassionate Americans. The Left, in its obsessive commitment to furthering its culture war, has in its sights the ultimate casualty: our very sense of self.

Because you're decent and thoughtful, you don't immediately understand why anyone would want you to become a Stepford American. But as I have explained in my previous work, there is a meaning to the madness. After all, the Leftist goal is one of a homogenized society, where sameness and literal "equality" rule. For the Left, the preferred state is mediocrity—a world where no one does better than anyone else, where no one must suffer the embarrassment of failure.

This explains why certain people are attracted to the Far Left. For those who are afraid to compete—who do not want to have to risk failure, let alone experience it—what an extraordinary solution this is: The creation of a society where competition, success, and the drive to become stronger, smarter, and better is the enemy.

That world is a dead world, filled with angry, cowardly people who hate you and this nation because you expect something of them. Democracy and capitalism require the individual spirit and reward it handsomely. For the incapable, the hate-filled, the self-loathing—the people I have described as Malignant Narcissists (or Mal Nars)—the idea of competing on any level for anything is terrifying and must be eliminated.

I contend that this fear of failure is at the heart of the socialism embraced by American Leftists. It is a political theory that naturally attracts those who believe that their lives will be made worthwhile only if the special, the unique individual is eradicated.

That is why the American spirit and, within it, your individual identity are under such vicious and violent attack by the Left. Only when you are emptied out like a pumpkin at Halloween will the mediocre, led by the Malignant Narcissists, be able to stop fearing you.

And that is why the drumbeat in the mass media, which is controlled by the Left, is for you to conform or disappear. Their agenda is to rip your sense of self to shreds, using depraved mainstream "entertainment" and public discourse, where profanity and personal destruction prevail.

You, your family, and your friends are berated one way or another every day in the formerly grand institutions of the American media. You are told that your values, your religion, your hopes mean nothing, because you, in your uniqueness, patriotism, and faith, are irrelevant.

I'm here to tell you differently. While I will continue to expose the Bad and the Ugly, it is now time to shine some light on the Good. The question I have been asked most by those who have read my first two books is, What can we do about this awful situation we face? The answer is simple—believing that the voice of the individual can make a difference. It always has and it always will.

The culture war bearing down on each one of us *is* personal. Your values are one element that define you as the person you are. Moral relativism, the handmaiden of Malignant Narcissism, is the first strike at the core of who you are. We see this new Standard of No Standard acted out every day. We know that it's often true, as the saying goes, that when bad things happen, it's because good men do nothing.

While I have unending faith in the ability and goodness of the American people, I've seen us grow more and more reticent about striking back. Perhaps we fear the price the Left has placed on dissent—name-calling and accusations, in all cases giving pain, and in the worst cases leading to loss of work, friends, and family.

Perhaps we think we're doing enough if we refuse to drink the Left's cultural Kool-Aid. Everything seems okay as long as we look away. And so we say nothing and hope that someone else does something. Perhaps the problem will fix itself.

But ignoring cancer has never been a solution. The price of doing nothing is much, much higher than the price of confronting the disintegration of our culture. Yes, sometimes it seems better just to look away, but no longer. The continuing internal attacks on this great nation of ours, ranging from the degradation of our popular culture to the twisting of our very value system and our ability to defend ourselves against external enemies, means that apathy guarantees your children an inheritance of hopelessness and enslavement.

Own Why You Think
What You Think

Of all the things of which I am ashamed, at the top of the list are certain actions or failures to act during my time as a feminist activist. Looking back now, I see that there were many situations I would have handled differently if I had not abdicated my individuality. Like someone involved in a mob action, I allowed personal responsibility to become foreign to me; responsibility belongs to "leaders" or "mentors" or someone higher in the food chain.

What I experienced while in the Left Elite is now being spread through our society as a whole. I chose to be in their midst, you did not, and yet the Leftist virus has spread to your home as well. The situation you face, the attempt to eradicate you as an individual, exists for a purpose: so you will not question, will not challenge, the goals of those in charge.

Simply put, today's Left is focused on lobotomizing each and every one of you because its leaders know their agenda is so repugnant, so opposed to what you hold dear, that you will not go willingly. But if your critical mind can be sufficiently anesthetized, perhaps you will simply look the other way as the cultural meltdown rolls on.

It has to be this way, you see, because it has always been the courage and uniqueness of the American Individual that have exposed the dead heart of the Left. Our society has been the manifestation of democracy, goodness, and freedom, which has been and remains the only true threat to the cancer of Leftist totalitarianism around the globe.

Indeed, the American Individual still stands as a monument to the strength of freedom. That, of all things, is what today's Leftists fear the most. And it is what we must reawaken in ourselves if we are to turn back their depraved success in our nation over the past thirty years.

It took me a long time to understand this, but the things of which I am most proud are the result of work that has been very personal and very independent. It is work that relies on my sense of self, and the concomitant requirement: ownership of what I am saying and doing.

You learn a great deal about yourself working where there is no one else to blame, no one else to look to for answers. I now *own* the success and the failure of my work and my personal behavior. I now understand the personal power of *owning why I think what I think*.

Asking the Hard Questions

One of the most important messages in all of my work is challenging people to think about *why* they believe what they do. In my case, during my time in the feminist establishment, it was because my mentors insisted I think and act a certain way. For students I encounter today in my lectures at universities, it's because a professor told them something that sounded good, something they liked or wanted to believe in order to support a point of view they were already committed to.

It might be: "The Iraq war is a war for oil." Really? How is that? What's the proof? How do you *know* this?

Or—and this one comes up all the time—"The media is run by conservatives." Really? Who are they? How do you know?

Frankly, I don't have a problem with people believing whatever they want. But it's frustrating to hear someone parroting a point of view without even trying to examine whether or not it's valid.

Owning *why* you think something does take a little work. It requires actually looking for proof of your foundational beliefs. Your original position may still hold up, but at least examining it allows you to know how honest you're being with yourself and how truthful your own position really is. It ultimately comes down to taking personal responsibility for your positions.

That's why people on the Left very rarely engage in assessing their own beliefs. Either they have no clue how to defend their position (because they don't know the details) or they *know* what they're asserting is simply not true. As a result, the Left has become the Thought Police to destroy or silence dissenters, because debating the details would expose the fallacy, and the downright absurdity, of most of their cultural, economic, and political positions.

Knowing why you hold your opinions, and holding them because you have found the evidence to back them up, separates you from the pack. Only with this kind of independence and individuality can any of us be confident about who we are and what's truly important to us. This is the benefit of the application of *reason*. Constant self-assessment brings confidence and understanding, and also compassion and tolerance of others—all the things missing from the American Leftist establishment, the things they are envious of and want to eradicate in you.

Mainstreaming the Marginal

Part of my romantic notion of myself through the years has been the idea of being different from everyone else. Let's be honest, we all want to be unique in one way or another. It's natural, and at the heart of what has always made Americans so ornery when it comes to authority.

Our nation's history is full of the success stories of wild, confident men and women who risked everything to further an astounding dream of liberty and freedom. Americans still have that rebellious, revolutionary spirit; it fills each individual, reminding us that we have something unique and special to offer the world.

And you know what? America has indeed shown the world what man, if left untrammeled, is capable of accomplishing, with all his talent, skill, and spirit, and under God's watchful eye.

Now our society is under the Left's watchful eye. Your choices are not yours to make, because you must be protected from yourself by the all-knowing and politically correct Left. They will determine what you can do, what you can think, what you can say (or more usually, not say, not think, not do).

You are expected to conform, to acquiesce to those who have sole possession of the truth. Your promise, your values are archaic, even dangerous, and must be suppressed. This New World, operated by a few Wizards of Oz, relies on your retreat, your disappearance. It relies on your believing that your time—as the average American, in all your boldness and greatness—is past.

In actuality, you, the embodiment of the dreams of your ancestors—mostly European Christian men and women, committed to family and freedom—are the light in a world that has begun to sink into darkness.

In my work over the past several years, as I've gotten to know more and more of the people who make up the heartland of this nation, an unexpected cultural fact has struck me: People like me, pro-choice, feminist lesbians who live on one coast or the other, are no longer the "Radical Individual." While that used to be the case, in the sixties and seventies, it is no longer. As the Left gained control of popular culture, through film and television especially, all the stereotypes were celebrated and elevated, and people like me became the cultural norm.

You can hardly turn on a television set, go to a movie, or listen to a political speech without the supposedly "marginal" person—all the marginal elements represented by Yours Truly as an example—being portrayed, catered to, lauded, romanticized, or analyzed.

Consider the television program *Will & Grace*, a sitcom based on the presumptively hilarious and endearing experiences of a gay lawyer (Will) when he and a straight interior designer (Grace) become roommates. Or even the Disney/Pixar movie *Finding Nemo*, an animated father-son fish tale featuring Nemo, a clownfish taken from the Barrier Reef to live in a dentist's office aquarium. This film is arguably the first to feature all three leads as handicapped in one way or another. Nemo is physically handicapped with a misshapened fin, his father is presented as obsessive-compulsive and generally neurotic, while Dory, a fish enlisted to help in the search for Nemo, clearly has a mental deficiency, demonstrated with short-term memory problems, which lead of course to the expected hilarity.

All of this without mentioning the sharks, which attend a 12-step program swearing to ward off their violence issues and killer instinct.

While many have enjoyed both productions (as I have), it's worth being conscious of the fact that both are exceptionally successful, and involve mainstreaming the marginal, in these instances, gays and the handicapped. But these productions are not unique. They follow a host of others attempting to do the same thing, to the point where the average American is now the one on the margin. Therefore, it is the average person—someone who doesn't identify as a handicapped person, doesn't identify as a gay person, doesn't identify as a minority—who is the new hero in this culture war.

I have confessed to you that I enjoy being different. I have appreciated not being part of the cultural norm. And yet I am now a best-selling author, I am a Fox News Channel contributor, I served on

Governor Arnold Schwarzenegger's transition team, and I have a nationally syndicated radio program.

One thing is obvious from this realization: The American commitment to equality and freedom has worked. People who had been marginalized and oppressed now have dynamic impacts on our popular culture. Minorities now not only are accepted but are very often calling the shots.

We now have *The L Word*, a program on Showtime, described as *Sex in the City* but with the city revolving around beautiful lesbians. This is supposed to be happening in Los Angeles. While there are some absolutely lovely women here, let's just say that this program is an idealized version of my town.

Ellen DeGeneres's talk show has been renewed for another season. What is this—the fourth chance she's had to have a show? Yes, dammit, Hollywood executives just *know* that our television tableau would be incomplete without the official lesbian being on the screen every day of the week. HBO's *Six Feet Under*, a program that moves an insidious and ugly nihilistic message into millions of homes, features a gay lead, and numerous broadcast programs now have gay characters—always in positive portrayals.

While these examples focus on the expanding opportunities for gays, I submit that the correlating message in these programs is one that marginalizes religious people, conservatives, and anyone else who doesn't think the Leftist status quo should be lauded and glamorized.

It is clear we will not, for the foreseeable future, see a broadcast or cable series that features a white, Christian, pro-life man in any positive way. Or a gay person who is conservative politically. Or a black man who rejects the politics of Jesse Jackson and Maxine Waters *and is vocal about it*. That man—perhaps a man you could relate to—has not recently been, and will not soon be, an American television hero.

If there is life on Mars and if Martian intelligence officers are forced to use today's television programming to make an assessment of life on earth, there would be a presumption that homosexuals account for at least 50 percent of the population, and they're *all* really good-looking and funny.

Obviously the goal isn't to control what Martians might think of Americans and American life—the target is you. The more out of touch, the more isolated, the more irrelevant you feel, the more distant you feel even from yourself, the better it is for the very few on either coast who are determined to squeeze your sense of self right out of you.

Coming to Terms with Our Greatness

I have described some of the qualities I have seen in the New Radical Individual, but the details are different for each one of us. However, the fundamental point is being answerable to ourselves *first* about what's important to us.

In the last few years, the individual in you has been unleashed. September 11 profoundly changed us all. That horrific assault on our nation suddenly made it clear to thoughtful Americans that tomorrow is not guaranteed, time is not to be taken for granted, and the future depends on the choices we make in the next ten years *as Americans first*.

I contend that our success on every front, here in the Homeland and on foreign soil, is dependent on our coming to terms with our greatness. I will be documenting, in the pages to come, the assaults on our pride and the maligning of our military. I will also be setting the record straight about the positive and even necessary impact of the values and culture of the United States on the rest of the world.

Put simply, the decent people in this nation are no longer willing to sit quietly and do nothing as the Huns of the Left rip through our beautiful cities, threatening the future of our children and the greatness of our nation. You, the average American, in all your freedom-loving, hardworking, family-devoted, perpetually optimistic, patriotic self, have indeed had enough and are now willing to do something about it.

I know this because you've told me. I also know it because I see it, and if you've forgotten or are not sure, by the time you finish this book, you will see it, too. I want you to remember who you are, embrace your greatness, and enjoy the pride you have in this nation.

The quality of your world is a result of your remaining unafraid in your opinions and actions. You spend your time acting on your beliefs that independence and freedom are linked to hard work, commitment to family, and personal achievement. You have an independent spirit that recognizes and revels in the joy of personal success. You see the rewards of taking personal responsibility. The idea of marching down a street laying blame on someone or something else for any misfortune you've had is anathema to you.

But not to Leftists. They have had great success screaming and crying like spoiled children and threatening their way to socializing America. They are, in macrocosm, the bully on the subway who "asks" for $5. You know what the penalty will be if you don't hand it over. You will be hurt, with words if not with a knife or gun.

The last few years have indeed been a wake-up call to all of you who had felt that no matter what social action to change this country the Left engaged in, you could keep your family safe and the future bright with your private hard work alone.

We now know that is, unfortunately, no longer the case. Your emerging willingness to be organized in order to make a difference, however, is not based on a desire to get some free handout. It is not an effort to improve your lot in life via temper tantrums. Instead, you are endeavoring to save America and the American Dream itself from the Malignant Narcissists of the Left.

You have become more willing to join with other individuals in combating the Left, because that's what it will take. Not forever, mind you, but as long as need be to make sure your children won't have to fight the same battles you and I have had to fight.

Well Worth the Price

Since the publication of my first two books I have heard from thousands of you, mostly by e-mail, but also by snail mail and as callers during the hundreds of talk-radio interviews I've given. Frankly, when I decided to put my e-mail address in my books, many friends asked if that was a wise thing to do. In fact, although I couldn't know this in advance, it turned out to be one of the best things I have ever done, as it has given me a window on the blossoming of the American character at a time when those who hate this nation would prefer that you simply go away.

It has been a deep, personal pleasure getting to know you.

In the pages that follow, I'll share with you many of the letters I've received. Your stories and lives have changed me. While I realize now and accept that my life is in constant transformation, I never thought the change could continue at the pace it has, and you are partly responsible.

Your e-mails also alerted me to the fact that some of you still struggle with what it means to embrace your individuality. Some of us, as I did for many years, push our individual critical minds and sense of self to the back because we want to belong. It's pretty difficult stuff, not belonging.

If you have wondered what kind of compromises young people especially feel they have to make to be accepted, consider this note from James, a young man who at the writing of this e-mail was attending an Ivy League institution:

Dear Ms. Bruce,

    I have never written to a celebrity before, but I felt I had your permission since you included your e-mail in your book. I think that is so cool! I'm writing because I wanted to let you know that I have read both of your books and have been very affected by them. I'm a junior at———, and wanted you to know that you have supporters and people who believe in

what you're doing. I think you are very brave and can't imag-
ine the kind of grief you're probably getting because of what
you have written. I have so much respect for you.

I also have been having some personal difficulty because
of how you make me think. I am politically conservative and
pro-life. None of my friends know this. I keep my politics to
myself, and sometimes even join in their discussions and pre-
tend I agree with them. I do so because I don't want to be
alone on campus. I am also a gay man, and most of my fam-
ily doesn't speak to me because of it.

What I'm trying to say is, I feel like a fraud, but if I was
honest about who I am I would lose that last family that I
know, I would be disowned by the gay community here, and
I'm afraid my friends would hate me.

I want to be myself, but the price is so high. Can you give
me advice about how to deal with this? I don't want to live my
life like this, and I admire you so much. I know how you were
able to deal with it would help me.

Thank you . . .

James

This letter, like so many others, moved me to tears. You see, I
knew when I was writing my earlier books that individual-thinking
people would be reading them, but I had not fully grasped what that
meant. I had a message I needed to impart, and so that's what I did.
Frankly, I did not consider the intensely personal impact. It was a
strategy I had subconsciously implemented from the beginning of my
activist days.

James's letter was one of the first I received after the publication
of *DRW*. James, I realized, was struggling with something that I, too,
had struggled with. And yet it ultimately is a phantom problem.
While I managed to avoid it for years, I had been essentially forced
by experience to realize that if we have to lie about ourselves—remain
silent about issues we care about or, even worse, pretend to hold po-

sitions we don't in order to "belong" to some special-interest group or social crowd—we're abandoning ourselves to a shadow existence, tossing our independence and individuality into the dustbin.

James had the courage and character to recognize the compromises he had been making and reach out for advice about how to change. I had to be publicly attacked by my colleagues in the National Organization for Women (NOW) in order to wake up from my self-imposed coma.

My response to James was as much counsel to me as it was to him. It also became the spark for this book.

I thanked James for his e-mail and made sure he knew how much his support meant to me. I was moved by his honesty and told him so.

I explained to him that I would be lying if I said there was an easy answer to his question. I spent the whole of my activist career compromising myself, my individuality, and my sense of right and wrong in order to belong. I not only harmed myself in the process, but other people as well. There was always a reason, always a way to excuse my behavior, but eventually the system itself turned on me, which was, I suppose, inevitable.

I explained when I became more honest with myself and the public about who I was (am!), yes, some people left my life. Many, in fact. Those people, though, never liked me, really. They couldn't, because they didn't know me. It was a false life filled with a false collection of pretend friends.

They were all I knew, however. I shared with him how I experienced and understood his fear of abandonment. I have lived with the same worry, and while I have accepted the fact that I will always be alone to some degree politically, the fear of what it means still lurks in the back of my mind.

While my old life fell away, including the pseudofriends, new and frankly better people entered my life. Interestingly, they were people with whom I disagree a lot when it comes to politics, but I have never had a better group of true, loyal friends.

I told James as I tell you, I am still finding the Individual in me.

In fact, I think that process is lifelong. I'm certainly not finished, but you must realize that being honest about yourself and taking responsibility for your beliefs and being proud of them will probably clear out a room or two in your life. All the better—because then genuine friends, who will really care about you, will have room to come in.

So there you have it. That was, in a nutshell, my response to James and his predicament. His situation illustrates how the struggle to fit in, to be liked, can come with a terrible price. I know it did for me.

In my case, the abandonment of self led to actions I now find deplorable. One event I even erased from my memory for several years because of the horrific consequences of the paradoxical combination of my selfishness and rejection of my critical, decent individuality.

During my time as a feminist activist, I had learned the fine art of self-preservation. The feminist establishment was such a psychologically unhealthy environment that the only way to continue in it was to condition myself in the belief that what I was doing and what was happening around me had nothing to do with me.

There are interviews on the public record in which I stake out this very claim. In 1995 Bettijane Levine, writing for the *Los Angeles Times*, was doing a story about me and the emotional reaction to my work on domestic violence during the O. J. Simpson murder trial. Levine discussed some passionate statements, especially from those who reviled my work, and then noted:

> "The interesting thing about Bruce's emotional response to all this was her lack of it. For a woman so passionate about issues, she is curiously dispassionate about those who insult her integrity and motives.
>
> " 'I don't worry whether people like me. If you're in the business of social change, you can't worry about that. I am a messenger, and my job is to move the message.' "[1]

In part, that's true. You don't go into the social-change business in order to make friends. But there is a way to keep matters in perspective without losing a sense of self. The reality is that a message doesn't exist in a vacuum—it's formulated and expressed by an individual. And yet, during my feminist activism, and even up until a few years ago, I did my best to constantly remove myself from the equation. I wanted to believe that I, as an individual, did not matter.

This protected me emotionally from the continuous attacks I was under not only from inside the feminist establishment, but also from the supposed enemies of women and feminists (the religious, pro-lifers, and, of course, men). Oddly, those external Bad Guys were never as harsh in their attacks as my feminist "sisters."

Even more important, however, the elimination of the idea of me as an individual allowed me to shirk personal responsibility for the impact I—yes, I—was having. I now believe this effort to depersonalize my work made it so much easier for me to ignore the hypocrisy and lies within the movement and the damage done by my work specifically. It was a disconnect that allowed me to look the other way while the most awful things were happening.

Looking the Other Way

It was less than a year ago that I remembered an action, or I should say a failure to take action, on an issue of life and death for women. The horror of a decision I had made, consciously and with that emotional disconnect I have just described for you, returned to me.

It involved an abortion doctor who endangered women through his negligence, eventually costing two women their lives.

Even now, as I write this, I have to fight the impulse to get up from my desk. Writing requires being honest on a deeply personal level. Many of you have that strength and pride of personal honesty, no matter what the cost. And yet it's still not easy for me. I have learned from you how to face reality and yet I still struggle to view my past for all it is.

In 1988, two years before I became president of the Los Angeles chapter of NOW, Dr. Leo F. Kenneally, an abortion provider in two poor areas of Los Angeles, was gaining quite the reputation. Kenneally operated clinics in South Central Los Angeles and Pacoima, predominantly minority areas. He was already under investigation by the state medical office and the district attorney for the deaths of three patients since 1986.[2]

In fact, since 1982 the California Medical Center—the hospital closest to Kenneally's Her Medical Clinic—had sent four letters of concern to medical authorities, "stating the circumstances of cases from Her Medical Clinic." You see, the California Medical Center is where Kenneally's injured patients landed after botched procedures. "There was enough concern that we felt it should be referred to the appropriate agency to conduct an investigation," a spokesperson for the hospital said.[3]

While my activism had its roots in the fight for abortion rights, this was a no-brainer. For crying out loud, our mission was to protect women, and women were being harmed, even dying, apparently at the hands of a specific person. This had nothing to do with abortion rights— it had to do with what seemed to me to be an incompetent doctor.

What are we speaking of? Kenneally, according to the *Los Angeles Times,* was accused of gross negligence and incompetence involving a twenty-two-year-old woman who had a seizure during an abortion. Kenneally continued with the abortion and did not take any measures to prevent another seizure. The woman died of a heart attack within an hour.

About a year later, an eighteen-year-old suffered a seizure in similar circumstances. Kenneally once again continued with the procedure. That young woman died fifty-eight days later.

When I learned about these women's deaths, I naïvely assumed that NOW would be out in front on the issue, demanding the prosecution of the doctor or, at the very least, the removal of his license.

In 1990 I was in my first year as president and approached my feminist mentors and other experienced leaders about how to proceed. I was also curious about why the feminist establishment hadn't spoken up years earlier, when it first became apparent this doctor was a problem.

The discussion that ensued was an education in compromise, abandonment, and destruction.

I was told by one feminist mentor of mine that it was important to say nothing because "the enemy"—pro-lifers, to be exact—would use the case for political gain. Besides, I was told, the poor women in these neighborhoods had no one else. If Dr. Kenneally were removed from the scene, they would have a harder time getting access to abortion.

And it wasn't only the Feminist Elite that took this view. Kenneally was praised by others in the liberal establishment, including many in the medical profession, for providing "affordable abortions in underserved areas." In other words, those supposedly promiscuous Latinas and black women have to put up with a butcher in their midst because they're poor. Welcome to the progressive Leftist mentality.

At first I was dumbfounded, but it was drilled into me, as it would be on a number of different issues in the years to come, that sometimes compromising was necessary, because the issue came first.

I was, in essence, being told these women would have to be sacrificed in order to save the issue. This was my first lesson about how the individual did not matter. Winning on the issue was the only thing I needed to be concerned about, the individual be damned.

I wish I could tell you that I rebelled and launched into a public attack on this doctor and supported the district attorney, but I did not. I accepted the arguments of my mentors and peers, and did nothing. I went along with this depraved approach and even, somewhere in my subconscious, agreed with it because I wanted the approval of the cadre of feminist leaders.

The moment I accepted allowing that doctor to apparently go on endangering individual, real women for the sake of keeping the upper hand on an issue, I willingly stepped into the Leftist abyss. I abandoned my own critical mind for the safety of groupthink. As I explored in my first two books, this is a fundamental part of the Leftist agenda: the annihilation of judgment and morality.

As I look back, I realize that I was able to accept doing nothing because I saw everything then as issues affecting groups of people. I had quite effectively removed myself as an individual from the scene. I was just, as I told Bettijane Levine, the "messenger." It was a subtle and insidious transaction. As I stopped valuing my own individuality (and all the responsibility that comes with it), it was inevitable that I would stop viewing other women as individuals. Instead, they became vehicles with which to move an issue.

So, ironically, I watched from the sidelines as "the enemy" began protesting about the quality of health care for women—in this instance, the lack of safety provisions for women—and the importance of removing an incompetent doctor from his practice.[4] I even accepted the argument that pro-lifers really didn't care about women—it was explained to me that their protests were cynically planned to make abortion look bad.

Funny, isn't it? I knew for a fact that the feminist and Leftist communities, the supposed protectors of women, had explicitly decided to do nothing because of politics, and our decision endangered women's lives. The pro-lifers, the supposed enemies of women, were using Kenneally to make political points about abortion, but they were also working to save women's lives.

This reality only slightly entered my consciousness, and I pushed it right back out. Here we were complaining about the pro-lifers, but at least their position allowed them to do the right thing. Ours did not.

In the years after I went along with my colleagues and said nothing, Kenneally was implicated in a number of cases in which women suffered from shock, hemorrhaging, and other significant injuries resulting from abortions.[5]

Eventually, Kenneally's license was revoked, but not until 1995, with who knows how many more thousands of women having found themselves on his table. I wish I could tell you that was the end of the story, but it's not. Through all of this, Kenneally never faced any criminal charges, and a superior court judge ultimately reversed the license revocation, allowing Kenneally to practice and perform abortions.[6]

I understand why I put this out of my mind. Even now, facing my failure of these women, my abandonment of myself and my conscience out of political expediency, is all but unbearable. The awfulness of my willingness to sacrifice the individual to the cause is something I will carry with me always. It will also serve as the reminder of what can happen if I am not vigilant about remaining independent in thought and deed.

I believe these events finally came back to me because of my continuing political and personal transformation, due in no small part to my relationship with all of you. James's struggle, as an example, and what it says about the price of honesty and individuality, struck a chord with me. His concerns and fears were my own. His letter, and the hundreds of others I have received from remarkable people, have provided the background to my own understanding of the importance and power of the individual in this culture war.

Americans First

I've heard from you about the most sensitive of subjects, including abortion and homosexuality. It has amazed me how Christians, in particular, have embraced me and my message despite our strong differences on those issues. It has become apparent that in my growing relationship with you, although we are each many things, we are all Americans first. This is our common bond, and it transcends the differences that we have the luxury of contemplating and debating.

Your comments about those issues especially have been passionate and intended to persuade me and explain to me why Christians and other conservatives hold the views they do on those issues. I have been so moved by the respect and thoughtfulness in each letter. Virtually all of you have approached me with an intelligent vigor I admire, and certainly appreciate.

While we will still have to agree to disagree on some issues, I must tell you that I have been forever changed by what I have learned about you—the New Radical Individual who remains committed to principles regardless of the social repercussions and backlash. Your foundation of personal principles, by its very existence, poses a tremendous threat to the Leftist agenda of remaking society.

In the pages that follow I will do my best to address the questions that have been asked of me in the years following the publication of *NTP* and *DRW*. The reactions I've received, from both the Left and the Right, will tell you much about the world in which we live.

Regarding the dire but necessary message of *DRW*, a common question in many letters I received was whether there was still hope for the future with all the damage being inflicted on our culture by the Left, and whether there is anything we can still do.

This e-mail from Ken, a Christian and Patriot, asks and then answers that very question. His message is especially honest and moving:

> Thank you so much for your book, *The Death of Right and Wrong*. . . .
> As a Christian I look at the gay lifestyle from a different view than yours. That being said I must also say a HUGE "THANK YOU" for your willingness to be daring enough to write this book. Not many of us are willing to expose ourselves, even to our closest friends, much less to a whole nation. Hopefully you will understand the following in the spirit in which it is intended, as a blessing. I thank God that He allowed you to go through the experiences you have had and for your willingness to use the gift of communication which is resident in your life to reveal this great evil which is threatening our nation, and especially our children. . . .
> While I am excited about your book, I must also confess that it is the hardest book I have ever read. Reading the many examples of perversion, including the perversion of justice,

makes one very angry. However, it is also very humiliating when we realize how we have been duped and brainwashed by those who wish to destroy the very moral fabric of our country. I hate realizing I have been a willing accomplice, especially as it relates to movies and TV.

The question is what can we do to make a difference? I for one will be telling many people about your book, so that others can see the depth of the problem and the challenge we face to try and save our nation and children. Hopefully you will reissue the book in a pocket version to make it more affordable for many, many more people. I will be looking for other ways to help open the eyes of my fellow citizens as well.

. . . Thank you, and God bless and may He continue to give you the strength for the battle ahead.

A fellow patriot who wants to see America continue to be the beacon of TRUTH on the hill for the rest of the world.

Kenneth M—Minneapolis

Now, Ken doesn't do this, but many people who have been generous enough to offer me the blessing of God have apologized first, or ask that I not be offended. They've done so because, as I mentioned, while I believe in God, I don't identify as a Christian. So let me make something very clear: Not only am I not offended by your wishes of God's grace, I am honored. I am always appreciative and touched by sentiments such as Ken's. This book is in part my answer to Ken and to many others of you.

A great part of what we must do is not abdicate our responsibility. The first step in making sure the Leftists do not win is maintaining our individuality, making judgments about what is happening around us, and deciding that the future is worth fighting for even if it means facing change in our lives because we place individual honesty before "fitting in."

There is hope, because you, like Ken—like me—care. There is hope, because while many of us disagree on issues, we are Americans first, and we know that the lives we lead are possible because of the greatness of this nation and our common past and future based in the courage, insight, and brilliance of the Founding Fathers. It's worth remembering that their dream was about freedom, democracy, and liberty.

There is hope, because as individuals we realize the future relies on our independence, our embracing our greatness, and our recognizing that we have weathered even more dangerous storms, and have come out stronger, more resilient, and, yes, better people.

The power is now in your hands. The following pages are for James, and Ken, and you and me. They will give you the weapons of information, encouragement, pride, and sense of self, so that the future will once again belong to the free, brave, and proud—American style!

3

Politics and the Individual

Whatever crushes individuality is despotism, by whatever name it may be called.

—JOHN STUART MILL

Despite what my critics (and even some supporters) claim, the last eight years of my life have been less of a political transition for me than they have been a time for personal honesty. As I noted to you earlier, I can't even claim that I truly believed in some of what I was doing as a feminist leader. I remained silent even when I knew something was terribly wrong.

Frankly, I wish I could claim I was misled, or have experienced some sort of dramatic theoretical epiphany, but I can't. All I can tell you is that it took attacks by my false friends on the Left to wake me up. I have to admit, I believe they saw the real me—my real politics—even before I was ready to acknowledge it.

The feminist establishment wanted people to be like stupid, submissive, noisy parrots. I was a parrot, but a reluctant one, and was seen by NOW leadership as a problem in the making. Patricia Ireland and the establishment cowards at Eleanor Smeal's Feminist Majority were right—I wasn't like them, even though I worked awfully hard to make it seem so.

Those were the days when all that mattered to me was what other people thought of me, especially those in the feminist and gay establishments. My identity, my self-worth, was based on their approval, their assessments, their reactions to me. Their definition of "self"— who a person is, what a person believes, what a person values—would be mine. It was like being part of a family where we children (or foot soldiers in the Left's instance) were to view adults (the leaders) as the people to emulate. We were to reproduce their example of how to think and act. Any deviation from their political norm, any questioning of tactics, position, or direction were capital offenses against the family.

Despite the ban on human cloning, the Left has quite the stranglehold on replicating themselves. Truly unique individuals, those who think for themselves and question authority, are not welcome, nor do they survive, in today's Leftist establishment.

Because I depended upon the Leftist leadership to tell me who I was, I also relied on labels to know myself: "Democrat," "Lesbian," and "Feminist." We all must rely on labels to some extent, but my problem—and what I believe is all our problem—is that I was dependent on the Leftist leadership's *definitions* of the labels.

I was a "Democrat," but never really thought about what it meant to be one. I was a "liberal" without thinking about the details. I was a "feminist" without worrying about what that meant either. What I knew was that those labels meant certain things to people I needed to please in order to feel accepted, in order to belong.

The Gay Ghetto

You may not realize this, but there's even no real discussion or understanding among the feminist and gay communities of what it means to carry the "gay" label. That, too, has become nothing more than a political code word, like a pass at the door of the Left in order to gain entrance to their special collective world. Being "gay" now is not even about homosexuality—it represents the nihilistic, personal irresponsibility of the narcissistic Left. It is meant to box people into victim-stereotypes, like all labels championed by the Left. It is meant to restrict certain people to their sexuality. It's a convenient euphemism with which to manipulate the rest of you.

So you're "gay"? Well, fine, now move on. Of course, those of us who are not victims do move on, but in order to eschew personal responsibility, those who are "victims" must be lost in a group.

Oh, I know there's one key element to the "gay" moniker, but that's called homosexuality. This is not the 1920s anymore, when one needed a code word in order to find romance (or easy sex). Now the label is completely politicized, so no one asks what else it means to be "gay." Consider this: Does a gay person wake up breathing different air than everyone else? I, for one, do not listen to Melissa Etheridge, or think the Ellen DeGeneres show is required watching. I don't go to gay film festivals to watch films about gay people. I do not breathe different air, see colors differently, or hear music differently from anyone else.

I don't feel compelled to wear flannel shirts (I will confess, however, to flannel jammies), only my earlobes are pierced (once for each). I do not own a motorcycle, I shave (I'll leave the hairy-armpit syndrome to the Europeans), and I am not tattooed.

Are these stereotypes? Sure. But it's no secret that group Identity Politics perpetuate, and rely on, these stereotypes. The dress-behavior-attitude code required of gay Identity Politics is in a full court press. To wit, there are now very few gay pride parades that are not led by the "Dykes on Bikes" contingent, women who embody the lesbian stereotype and make most parents understandably afraid if their daughter tells them she's "gay."

The gay political identity is not only unnecessary, it is insulting in its contribution to the destruction of the individual and its demands for conformity. It is an identity based in a stereotype that screams promiscuity and irresponsibility and sends messages of one-dimensional flighty creatures who, via an insidious Leftist message, owe their safety and very lives to the Left Elite.

Thanks to the narcissistic and power-hungry Gay Elite, being gay means leading a shallow, singular life of drinking, partying, and casual (now increasingly unprotected) sex. It is an identity based only in sexuality, because that really is the only thing that sets a gay person apart. Unless, as many people do, they adopt the behavior or dress code to indicate "gayness," whatever that is.

In all honesty, homosexuals who capitulate to the gay identity might as well throw their individuality down the drain. In fact, I challenge homosexuals who wake up in the morning believing that they've finally "found" themselves to reject completely a label that condemns them to a stereotype. I submit to every homosexual who folds nicely into their local "gay community" in the name of personal freedom that they are nothing but typical conformists.

Why do this? Because there's nothing like waking up in the morning and recognizing that you are the only one who will define you that day. I know what it's like finally to be completely in charge of my opinions, my actions, and the choices I make. I no longer worry about whether or not Eleanor Smeal will like what I'm thinking or doing, or what I can do to please the national leadership of NOW, or the Gay Pooh-Bahs in Los Angeles or New York. It is extraordinary to answer only to myself.

It is a freedom every one of us deserves.

With that freedom does come awesome responsibility—there is no one to blame if mistakes are made. But ultimately it is a small price to pay to wrest power from others over who you are and how you feel about yourself.

Being yourself for yourself—it is the ultimate personal political rebellion. This is true, obviously, for everyone, not just homosexuals. But it is especially pertinent for that group because of the control and manipulation of homosexuals by its cultural "leaders." And these days, when homosexuals abdicate their individuality to the "gay community," and the concomitant personal responsibility, it can cost us our health, our sense of well-being, and even our very lives.

After all, wouldn't the ultimate and free individual *refuse* to let someone else define her? Not so today. Absurdly, the self-proclaimed Radical Gay Individual looks and sounds and behaves just like all the rest of the radical gay individuals. If there was one book these people should read it would be George Orwell's *Animal Farm*. And one film? *Night of the Living Dead*. Perhaps it would shake some of the pseudoindividuals out of their collective nightmare.

A Conservative by Any Other Name

Ultimately, what I realized was that I had come to rely entirely on other people's opinions to feel accepted, to validate my existence—to define me! And when I ditched the leadership in the Leftist establishment—the very people I had looked to most for approval and acceptance—my very identity crumbled.

I finally understood that with all the labels attached to me, I had no real complex, deep understanding of what any of them meant to me. I knew what they meant to Leftists, to my feminist mentors. It became clear to me I was being controlled by labels, and I never took complete personal responsibility for my own identity.

I do take ownership now. And in the process of thinking about my individualism, I have found that, like Leftist name-calling, political labels and the Left's definition of them also wield considerable control over our own sense of ourselves.

None of us are immune from the brainwashing that comes with words and definitions. As an example, I think many people believe, due to Leftist conditioning through culture, that Republicans and conservatives are simply less compassionate than Democrats and liberals. And it's not just liberals who have bought that lie hook, line, and sinker.

I was privileged to be part of a panel at David Horowitz's Restoration Weekend, an annual event that brings together like-minded independent thinkers. After my presentation, two women approached me. They identified themselves as conservatives and confessed they had finally accepted that conservatives should acquiesce the moral high ground to liberals and focus on their strong points—economic freedom and limited government.

I was astounded. Here were two smart people, both business-women and quite successful, attending a conference that showed they were aware, educated, and in touch with the details and realities of our cultural and political civil war. And yet even they had been so brainwashed by the Left that they not only believed the Left was a moral force, they had lost touch with the power and morality of their own conservative foundation.

Here's what I told these women: It is the *conservative* who holds the moral high ground. The Left Elite, whether through lies or their own paralyzing groupthink, are the opposite of what they claim. Not only do they lack any sort of moral authority, but also they have des-ecrated the very idea of *decency* and *values* by using those ideals as slogans in their attempts to smash them into oblivion.

You must realize the Left's effort is *not* to gain the moral high ground, it is only to squat and defile that land once they have tricked you into leaving it. Make no mistake, their intention is not to act morally or enact decent policies or truly help the individual. It is to take that moral high ground from you so you will have no place to stand.

If Leftists can successfully make you feel as though they will take care of the moral needs of this nation (do you realize how absolutely absurd that sounds?), then you will stop daring to interfere, they hope. And when you stop interfering, when you retreat, the Left's own hypocritical inaction guarantees this nation will be condemned by their gods of nihilism, narcissism, and self-hate.

But they can only do it if they can manage to make you believe the sickening lie that they have morality and decency on their side, while you are sadly lacking. It is imperative for you to know that they are working feverishly to steal your identity. They want you to believe, as the women at the conference did, that you have been usurped by better, more thoughtful, more compassionate people.

The Morality of Conservative Politics

And let's be honest here—in reality there isn't any actual battle for the moral high ground. It has been securely in the hands of conservatives for quite some time, and still is. As I've already explained, there is nothing more important, more liberating, more moral, more decent than working to empower the individual. The efforts of conservatives to empower the individual with self-worth, true freedom, and the potential of the future comes with the values of this great nation—personal freedom guaranteed through capitalism, competition, and democracy.

The Left exists to destroy those values not just here, but globally. They seek to enslave the globe to socialism. Leftists self-righteously condemn everyone as they remake the world in their doomed collective self-images of hatred, hopelessness, and despair.

But their scheme will work only when that pesky United States—which dares to continue to liberate people—is eliminated. It is our hope, our understanding of freedom, that will free every individual on earth. By example, we remind the world's downtrodden that life *can* be better. That is why our internal enemy—the Left—remains obsessed with destroying us from the inside out.

Leftists reason that conservatives, especially, must be demonized and eliminated because they understand individual promise and responsibility. The women I spoke with at the conference walked away from our conversation with a renewed sense of who they are, and promised to face down the lies of the Left and hold on to the moral high ground that naturally belongs to them.

Were those women an anomaly, or have the Left Elite truly been successful at controlling the meaning of "conservative"? All we need to do is consider the approach George W. Bush made in an attempt to homogenize and rebrand the conservative label.

Think about it: Why would Bush, a compassionate man, like all Americans, need to adopt the "Compassionate Conservative" slogan if there wasn't a general acceptance that conservatives aren't as compassionate as liberals? This, my friends, indicates it's not just those conference women, but the president himself and his advisers who accept and believe the lying Leftist definition of conservatives.

President Bush and every mainstream conservative, instead of adapting to the Left's game, should retake what it means to be conservative and expose the hypocrisy, danger, and moral degeneracy of the Leftist agenda. We can begin to do so by retaking the conservative label and countering, without apology or fear, the lies, spin, and obscene definitions spewed by the Left Elite.

Leftist cultural and political leaders know if your individualism truly breaks free and you are no longer controlled by the Left's perspective, their control of culture, of politics, and of you collapses. My journey is the perfect example. They know authentic feminism, authentic freedom, and authentic individuality are rooted in and protected by Classical Liberal or conservative politics. It has taken me years to shake myself free from the Leftist grasp, but they know I am an example of what will happen if freedom-loving Americans are left to their own intellectual devices. We wake up.

Those same messages that keep Classical Liberals in check are meant to keep you in silence and force you to retreat. While the strategy has been successful in the past, Americans have had enough. Let's define ourselves for a change.

Classical Liberalism

As a conservative Democrat, I fit within the Classical Liberal framework. Make no mistake, there is a huge difference between Classical Liberalism and today's debased modern version of liberalism (which has become more and more socialist). I've discussed this term in television interviews, in speeches, and at dinner tables, and it usually elicits the same reaction: "What's that?" It also interests many people, especially those who left the Democrat party because of the pathetic ineptness of the Carter administration, which I contend is when the party began its long, slow devolution into socialism and hatred.

Classical Liberalism is not my term, though. It is rooted in eighteenth-century political thought, and was the basis of the founding of this nation. Its fathers are John Locke, Adam Smith, Thomas Paine, Thomas Jefferson, and James Madison. We owe Ayn Rand great credit for its twentieth-century renaissance.

The principles at the heart of Classical Liberalism are:

- The Importance of the Individual
- Freedom
- Private Property
- Reason
- Justice
- Toleration and Diversity
- Democracy
- *Conserving* these American Principles

Sounds like what we all ascribe to, doesn't it? But look again at that first principle: the importance of the individual. Oh, I know the Leftists mouth that a lot, but it's really just a meaningless slogan for them. After all, everything they advocate shoves people into collectives.

Their arguments are based on collective victimization. The Left's politics are Identity Politics. They demand redistribution of wealth, they condemn capitalism, industry, and Big Business—all the things that empower the individual.

How does Big Business empower the individual? Think jobs. Think opportunity. Think invention, creativity, products. Think profit and ingenuity. Big Business gives the individual the opportunity to live a good life with a job and money, and the chance to advance. It provides outlets for invention and products that improve all of our lives, despite what the rabble-rousers try to force you to think. All we hear is "Sweatshops!" and "Outsourcing!" while we thinking creatures realize that business—big and small—is what makes us the most desirous nation on earth.

Think IBM, Apple, Starbucks, Cisco, Microsoft. They have changed your life for the better, directly and indirectly. These companies and thousands more improve life around the globe with opportunity, progress, jobs, and even pleasure, to say nothing of glorious profit and the individual freedom that comes with financial independence.

The Left talks and talks and talks about the "worker," but even then it's a faceless, nameless, unknown person, because it's not a person they speak of, it's the collective idea of a worker.

At the heart of the American character are the rights of individuals, special awareness of the rights of minorities (and I don't mean in an ethnic sense), the right of property, limited government, and the free market and capitalism.

These are values—yes, values—that have made America great.

Sounds familiar, doesn't it? This is the heart and soul of our great nation. Notice the one thread that runs through each principle—the dominance of the individual. Not of the "group." Not of society. Not of the state, but the individual.

Authentic Democrats

Actually, because of all the dangerous nonsense now spewing forth from our Leftist friends, it is difficult to claim being a "liberal" these days, which is why I am more comfortable with the authentic description afforded by Classical Liberalism. It is one way to continue to embrace what we all care about, distancing ourselves from circus clowns like Jesse Jackson, Maxine Waters, and Hillary Clinton, while not abandoning the party or our great nation.

Thomas Paine, having published *Common Sense* anonymously in 1776, can be somewhat credited with introducing Classical Liberal thought to the New World. It is no secret this nation was founded as one that elevated the individual while rejecting the state. With his "Government even in its best state is a necessary evil; in its worst state an intolerable one . . ."[1] Paine exemplifies how American, how appropriate, and how Classically Liberal it is to be suspicious of government.

While we are a trusting people, we cannot afford to become gullible. We must be suspicious of government because the more powerful it becomes, the more individuals suffer. The bigger government grows, like any parasite, the more it will suck the life and freedom out of every man, woman, and child.

While this view is usually associated with modern conservative thought, the reality is it is rooted in the Classical Liberal framework that founded this nation. For example, as an Authentic Democrat, I believe the state has a certain, albeit limited, role in our lives. I believe that while those who cannot compete in our system deserve some limited governmental support, I also believe that communities should bear the biggest burden of caring for the poor or needy. I am not a religious woman, but I recognize the significant and important contributions Christianity and Judaism have made to the social realm and to community charity.

Ultimately, I want government to leave me alone, protect me from foreign invaders, represent and propagate freedom and democracy around the world, because that will protect us from the machinations of despots and ultimately make my life better by keeping me safe.

I agree that there should be limited social-service plans to assist those who cannot help themselves, but historically, community churches have done (and continue to do) a far better job than the government at improving people's lives.

I am a passionate supporter of our military. I love this nation completely and I believe the world is better off with the proliferation of American values such as freedom, democracy, universal suffrage, and complete equality for women. Of course, it is worth noting that freedom and democracy, while associated with the United States because we are the beacon for those values, are really universal human rights.

We, as a nation, are a vessel for ideas that are rooted in the truth and the beauty of what can be achieved when individuals are free to be themselves. Free to accomplish, free to become, free to govern, and free to grow as individuals. While it does seem these are "our" values, they are really everyone's.

But I also believe in the absolute privacy of the individual. Laws against homosexuality are archaic and absurd, and represent what happens when religion influences legislative decisions. I respect religious objection to homosexuality, but this is not a theocracy. Our history shows that our Great Experiment has worked—we have managed the brilliance of establishing a remarkable secular government for a nation of people of faith.

Spending money to spread democracy and ensuring our international safety is also fine with me, but I do not believe it is government's role to control or manage my life. It's that simple.

This is Classical Liberalism. It's not my definition, it's not the Left's definition, it's the definition handed down to us by the founders of liberalism, and it should be taken as an absolute.

Many Classical Liberals have turned to the Republican party and identify as conservative. Perhaps you are one of them. Many of us still identify as liberal in the classical term and have remained Democrats. The problem is, with Leftist control of the party and of the culture, the so-called liberal agenda that so many automatically support without question is destroying the values so important to all of us.

Conforming Nonconformists

This great nation of ours depends on how you react to what's happening around you. Our identities are undeniably based in how we describe ourselves. If you're reading this book, you are probably more politically minded than others. It also says that you're looking for answers about how to be released from the grasp that the Malignant Narcissists of the Left have on our very sense of self.

And the moment we seem to be breaking away, the moment individuals assert their critical, judgmental mind, is the time we get nailed with the Thought Police's favorite assault—name-calling. If you identify as a conservative, you have to defend yourself against accusations of racism, sexism, and homophobia. If you are a liberal and dare not to conform to the Leftist worldview, you are a "Puppet of the Right," a "fraud," or an "opportunist."

They make for easy sound bites, but remain hollow and meaningless, like the Leftist establishment itself.

The attacks are meant to punish you for straying from their control, for daring to be different. For daring to be yourself. Consider this e-mail I received after the premiere of my national radio show, in which I discussed being a Democrat and a Classical Liberal:

> *Do you think it gets you something to pretend to be a Democrat? Don't you understand that you're being used by the Right? . . . You're a conservative and you admit to voting for Republicans. What "Democrat" does that? Stop lying to us and to yourself.*
>
> *Jaime*
> *Portland, Oregon*

It is actually funny how quickly the self-righteous protectors of individualism and nonconformity (aka Democrats) get frustrated when faced with an individual who does not conform (aka you and me)!

Interestingly, labels do play an important role in defining who we are, and they shouldn't be avoided. For example, you are Christians, Democrats, conservatives, Republicans, feminists, and so on. It's not the label that's the problem, it's the standard we apply via that label, and the person or people who are defining that label. Are we living by our own understanding of the term, or someone else's?

I am a Democrat based on my understanding and commitment to a set of values that apparently have gone out of fashion in "Jaime's" world of politics. But I will not let him threaten and bully me from claiming for my own what was once a true beacon of freedom, individuality, and the American Dream.

I know from all-too-painful personal experience that as long as we continue to identify as something to please someone else, or by someone else's definition, we have completely given up our singular sense of self. We have indeed allowed strangers to tell us who we are.

That's what "Jaime" and his comrades hope to achieve. You see, he and people like him rely on group identity. For him, being a Democrat means being a Socialist, and everyone must be a good party member, or else.

Since the publication of my first two books, the "accusation" that I'm really a closet Republican is one I've heard quite often. It's why I chose to share "Jaime's" message with you, because it is so representative of the hair-pulling frustration that many liberals exhibit when someone steps out of line.

I have received numerous e-mails from Democrats condemning me for rejecting the idea of universal health care. Well, I do like the idea, I just don't think the government should pay for it! I have been called a bully because I think senior citizens should plan for their retirement, including being able to pay for their own health insurance and prescription drugs.

Let's think about this, at what point did it become government's business to take care of people who didn't plan properly for their retirement? In the "old days," which is not very long ago at all, seniors who were not independent, financially or otherwise, were their family's responsibility. Not the government's. In other words, not the taxpayers' responsibility.

Remember to stay conscious of labels here: I am a Democrat—a Classical Liberal—not a Socialist.

You see, my politics really haven't changed since my time in the National Organization for Women (NOW). Yes, I stayed silent many times instead of speaking out on certain issues in order to placate my colleagues and, of course, to gain their approval. Contradicting the Democrat party line in NOW was not tolerated. And even though I stayed silent, I still seemed somehow "different" to my feminist establishment colleagues.

In any socialist environment, there is no room whatsoever for individual thought or action, even when it's represented by merely a lack of homage. You see, where groupthink prevails, one must constantly reassert allegiance. To fail to do so by words and action infers that an individual, critical mind is at work. And individual thought will not be tolerated by the Left.

Home Invasion Robbery

I have been a registered Democrat all of my adult life. There is one brief exception when, for a moment, I registered as Libertarian while being overwhelmed with disgust at Bill Clinton during the Lewinsky charade. My politics, though, over the years have never changed. There have been times when, to my great regret, I remained silent, but the heart of my beliefs has remained the same.

While my social sensibilities have remained the same from my leadership in NOW to the present day, consider this e-mail from one of today's "Democrats":

> *Ms. Bruce, we, as Democrats, would appreciate it very much, if you would cease and desist calling yourself a Democrat. IT IS VERY SILLY for you to keep doing this. All you are at this point is a shill for FOX. Really, stop it, it is disgusting! I am sure there is not a Democrat alive that agrees with any of your talking points. Call yourself what you are: a true right wing Republican. You would be a real joke if you weren't so sad.*
> *Liz*

Classical Liberal attitudes are the basis for what has made this nation great—a foundation of opportunity that has allowed people to make choices that best suit them. Liz doesn't detail my "talking points," which she assails as "right wing Republican," so I'll try to guess at what she sees as disgusting. Could it be that I'm pro-choice? Nah, Democrats love that. How about the gay thing? No, even I know that's not Right-wing these days (but I do know of some Right-wing gay people!). How about my work with NOW? Hmm, I think that feminism stuff is still considered Left-wing, unless something weird has happened.

All kidding aside, the thing about me that irritates self-styled Democrats is the fact that I do represent what used to be. I am living, walking, talking proof that true liberals, Authentic Democrats, used to not be . . . Socialists! That's right—I represent Classical Liberal values that even today's Leftists cannot deny, and yet my very existence is a constant reminder that what is offered as "liberal" today via the Democrat party establishment and America's Left-wing is in fact Fascist and Totalitarian by comparison.

To give you some perspective, Liz's e-mail is fairly representative of the exhortations I receive from "Democrats" telling me I'm a conservative. What this rancor exposes is the fact that the Left has moved so far to the left that this pro-choice, lesbian feminist is now considered a Right-winger!

It is difficult to remain identified with a party that has sadly devolved into a part-fascist, part-socialist March of the Brownshirts. Don't get me wrong—I'm not saying every Democrat is a Fascist or a Socialist. Heck—I'm a Democrat and passionately reject Leftist fundamentalism. I'm also not saying every liberal has gone off the deep end. If what I describe here does not describe you, then you're not part of what I'm discussing. If it does, you know who you are, admit it. This is about self-selection and personal honesty, one way or the other.

This is what this book is all about—knowing in ourselves who we are, and *why* we are. If you're a Socialist, then admit it. If there's something that disturbs you about that possibility, look into it and decide if that's what you really want to advocate. The inherent problem with Leftists is, as I've noted, that logic and reason aren't their strong suits. But if you find yourself (as I did) diving into the Leftist void, you can pull yourself out by asking yourself some important questions about *why* you think *what* you think.

When it comes to my choice to continue identifying as a Democrat despite the horrific changes to the party in the last twenty-two years, here is the best analogy I can give you. This may be especially helpful for those of you who just don't get it, who insist, like Liz, that I am something other than I claim.

Imagine your political party being your childhood home—the place where you have lived since birth. In fact, your grandfather built the house and it is perfect for you. You're familiar with it, you understand it, and after all the years of living, and fine-tuning, its age has only made your home more comfortable, more familiar, and stronger in its history.

Your family has lived in this home for generations. The neighborhood knows you and the home, too. They've gotten to know you and your style by the way you've taken care of the home. Generations of neighbors have watched you grow up and have watched your home be loved, and cared for. The home itself and you have become an important part of the neighborhood community. You and your commitment to the home have been relied on for ages as a consistent, reliable part of the community.

That home, for me, is the Democrat party.

Now imagine one night there's a home invasion robbery. Mind you, the brutes that broke down the door and pried open windows have been watching you and your home for quite some time. These are people who have never been able to keep a home on their own; everything they touch they destroy. They fail because they expect everyone else to support them. Hard work, decency, and loyalty are foreign concepts to them. So, they travel, they look for a place to squat, a place they can take over parasitically and claim as their own.

They let someone else do all the hard work building a respectable, important home in the community, and then they invade. They know they will never be able to earn respect, so they plan, like vultures, to sit and watch, and then invade and take.

That is what has happened to the Democrat party in this nation. My home was invaded by thugs. They screamed and shouted and threatened those who own that home, hoping that the true owners would get too frightened or too disgusted to stay.

Think about it. John F. Kennedy once occupied this house. Now Hillary calls it "home." Harry Truman lived here, but Howard Dean now sleeps in his bed. I can't blame or begrudge those who left entirely, but while I have no desire to go back inside with the characters currently occupying it, I will not be chased out of the neighborhood.

I am determined not to abandon the party because a bunch of socialist squatters have managed to bully their way into power. And while the invaders continue to announce to the neighborhood (our great nation) that they are the true owners of my home, I will stand in front and tell the truth to everyone who passes. I will stand and remind everyone who will listen to whom that home really belongs.

Which is why I am an irritation to the Leftist parasites. It's because I remind the rest of the neighborhood who these squatters really are.

My Democrat party respects the office of the president. The squatters have made doormats, literally, of President Bush's face.

The life of my Democrat party does not rely on bad things happening to this nation in order for the party to succeed. The squatters talk and talk and talk of victimhood, failure, oppression, and hatred without offering any real solutions.

As of this writing, terrorist beast bin Laden has not been captured. And you know the squatters are hoping he isn't, because they believe his apprehension would benefit the Republican president.

My party does not pit one group of Americans against another. And yet that is all the squatters have ever done. They work tirelessly to make every neighbor suspicious of the other—paranoid, distrustful.

You see, Leftists understand through experience that their message of socialistic totalitarian control would never be embraced by the average American. So they must co-opt another entity and perfect the art of lying to you, and perhaps even to themselves.

Sure, they give lip service to democratic principles of freedom, individuality, and opportunity. They must do this, otherwise the contradictions would be too obvious. Then, slowly but surely, as you've seen in the past twenty-five to thirty years, the Democrat party is no longer representative of John F. Kennedy or Harry S Truman. No, it's the party of Hillary Clinton, Jimmy Carter, Al Sharpton, Maxine Waters, Gray Davis, and Howard Dean.

Pathetically revealing, isn't it?

Fascism: The Left's Mutant Offspring

The modern Left refuses to admit that Hitler, Mussolini, and nazism were all examples of what happens to Leftism when allowed to run amok. Yes, Stalin was an undeniable beast of the Left, but so was Hitler. Indeed, it was the Left that brought genocide, death, and destruction to the world in the twentieth century. It is time we recognize and admit that fact. If we don't, it will indeed be visited upon us again, all in the name of altruism and the Collective (or the Village if you're a Hillary Rodham Clinton devotee). This is especially noteworthy considering the fact that one of the Left's favorite Thought Police tactics is to slap the "Nazi" label on Republicans and conservatives. Nothing is further from the truth.

It's imperative to understand some key points at this stage. If you still don't believe that fascism is the natural outgrowths of Leftist theory, let me connect some dots for you.

First, let's agree on the definition of socialism: state control of the economy with the essential interest of redistribution of wealth to the poor and lower classes. Why? To create the ever-false (and destructive) notion of "equality." This forced homogeneity has nothing to do with bringing the downtrodden up, but focuses on the pulling down, the destruction, the demonizing of the special, the creative, the brilliant, the different, the successful.

Socialism, in the end, seeks to eliminate the individual, making the state the only independent creative body, allowing the failures and despots of society to wield power over the truly progressive and worthy individual.

How does this get us to the fascism that almost destroyed humanity sixty years ago? Let's consider its founder and origins.

The ideology was developed and the term was first used by Benito Mussolini and is representative of his dictatorship over Italy from 1922 through 1943. Hitler's National Socialist Germany and Franco's Spanish regime were also Fascist.

Mussolini was also a Socialist—he was editor of the socialist newspaper *Avanti* and believed in the absolutism of the state. Ultimately, he ascended to the leadership of his new political movement, which he termed "fascism." The word itself stems from *fasces*, the symbol of bound sticks used as a totem of power in ancient Rome.

Mussolini described fascism as an ideology that declares the state as the singularly important whole, the "total state" within which the individual must be absorbed, where the individual's reason to exist lies in supporting and helping others, to the exclusive benefit of the state.

Sound modernly familiar?

The only way fascism could even have been contemplated by Mussolini was through his dedication to socialism. You see, socialism and fascism are not mutually exclusive. Socialism demands the elimination of the individual for the good of the whole, effectively condemning individual thought and action. Government is the natural enemy of the individual, as proven by all Leftist ideology.

Today, the Right, on the other hand, is directly attacked by the Left for glorifying the individual because of the dreaded "inequality" that supposedly stems from it. Conservative politics, with its elevation of the individual, naturally demands small and limited government.

All we have to do is look at the results of the twentieth century to understand this dichotomy.

Here are some comments from Il Duce himself on the meaning of fascism and its relationship to that pesky individual:

". . . The Fascist State organizes the nation, but leaves a sufficient margin of liberty to the individual; the latter is deprived of all useless and possibly harmful freedom, but retains what is essential; the deciding power in this question cannot be the individual, but the State alone. . . ."[2]

Why does Mussolini tip his hat to a "sufficient margin of liberty"? He does what our own Leftists do to this day—while working feverishly to completely destroy individual life and freedom, they maintain power by *claiming* to be the champions and protectors of the individual. They throw a "liberty" bone to society, all the while hoping no one notices the arsenic poured on top.

In other words, it's a strategic trick, providing "sufficient liberty" to make them look like the good guys and further the lie, maintaining the manipulation while the parasite of fascism continues its deathly claim on society's body.

Fascism rejects reason and intellect. Emotion rules; logic is condemned. Why? If the individual were to really think about serious issues, which requires independent thought and value judgments, socialist and fascist rules would be rejected outright. Emotional response, as I think most of us know, is not about reason or contemplation. It is quite the opposite.

It was manipulation and emotional response that facilitated genocide. One must not think or judge when slaughtering millions. From 1930s Germany to 1990s Rwanda, we know the results of emotional, unthinking mob action. The destination of this desperate road is the elimination of personal responsibility, brought about primarily by the belief that the individual does not matter, does not exist. What the state requires is the only concern—what is best for the group, the only consideration.

Every genocidal event that has been and will come *requires* the emotional mindlessness of Leftist theory.

While the description I have given you here refers to fascism as applied by a state, it can also be applied to a movement. From what I have seen, and by the behavior of today's Leftists—their own comments, speeches, and statements—I believe the socialist foundation that drives many Leftist Elites has indeed slipped into a fascist framework.

At the heart of this is the constant attacks on the individual. As you will find throughout this book, the trouble we face today in this nation can be attributed to the relentless assault on the individual and the by-products of our retreat from politics and culture.

This is why your continued commitment to what you know is right and wrong is so important. Your loyalty to your family, values, and morality, and your faith, in a world where Leftists rule makes you the New Radical Individual.

Socialism

Do not think that our nation is immune from the disease of fascism. It has already manifested in American Leftists. Despite the destructive failure worldwide of socialism, American Leftists work to make America a socialist state (with fascist tendencies already revealing themselves). Never mind the spectacularly horrific reign of Stalin, or the pathetic economic failure of France's welfare state. Leftists in America continue their fruitless march toward Marxist nirvana.

If you think I'm overreacting, consider these sentiments:

"All our lives we fought against exalting the individual, against the elevation of the single person, and long ago we were over and done with the business of a hero, and here it comes up again: the glorification of one personality. This is not good at all."—Vladimir Lenin, quoted in *Not by Politics Alone*.

"Comrades, we must abolish the cult of the individual decisively, once and for all."—Nikita Khrushchev, February 25, 1956, 20th Congress of the Communist Party.

"We must stop thinking of the individual and start thinking about what is best for society."

"We can't be so fixated on our desire to preserve the rights of ordinary Americans . . ."

These comments are remarkable in their similarity and disdain for the individual. While the first two come from the ultimate socialist True Believers—Khrushchev and Lenin—the last two are not revelations from their Soviet comrades. They are quotes from the leaders of our very own "Democrat" party—Hillary and Bill Clinton, respectively. Rodham Clinton's remarks come from a speech in 1993, while Bill Clinton's come from a 1993 interview in *USA Today*. But it's not hard to imagine that they have expressed these sentiments on more than one occasion, as have a number of other Democrat leaders.

Hostility toward and desire for the elimination of the individual are hallmarks not of "liberals," but of malevolent Socialists and Fascists. The only difference between Khrushchev and the Clintons is at least the Communist leader didn't pretend to be something he wasn't. Khrushchev pounded his shoe for socialism. The Clintons, their foot soldiers and sycophants, as well as the rest of the Leftist leadership in this nation, will never own up to what they really are. Instead, they work tirelessly to prepare us for their dream of the annihilation of the individual—of you.

There is a very fine line today between "Democrat" and "Socialist." And as I've shown how fascism progresses naturally from socialism, the Democrat party is flirting with becoming fascist. I mean it, and I'm not kidding. This is not political rhetoric or hyperbole. I've never been more serious or more concerned. I do not do this lightly, or to shock people. If any lesson is to be drawn from history, fascist totalitarianism is indeed the natural endgame of Leftist politics.

As we've seen with the former Soviet Union, and currently in China, Cuba, and North Korea, socialism is nothing more than the smashing of the individual to guarantee total power and control of the few (or one) in government. The mechanism of socialism does not create "equality." It does not make life "fair." It, in fact, does the opposite. It crushes individual spirit, personal hope, dreams, and progress by eliminating the reward and excitement of rising above the crowd.

In the socialist world, being different, being better, being ingenious is treason.

While this sounds awful to the vast majority of Americans, the despots who have implemented this depraved system specifically intend to destroy the hearts and minds of the individual. You see, a free people, those who think and act for themselves, are by default a constant threat to the collectivist system. Individualism is the ultimate control mechanism that keeps government from becoming oppressive.

We are the natural antidote to totalitarianism in our freedom and individuality.

Speaking of Socialists, it is tragic that that the political arm determined to sink the individual in the swamp of collectivism—that is, the Democrat party—is doing so under a banner that traditionally protected individual rights.

Under socialism, the state is the living entity owning and controlling the results of the work of individuals, distributing product based on the government's assessment of who needs what, with "equality" the supposed standard. "Wealth" is not something that is to be accumulated by the individual—it is distributed by the state to control and guarantee "equality."

The Leftists who continue to advocate socialism despite the hell it has brought the unfortunate souls who have had it foisted upon them, revel in the idea of artificial "equality" because it is the only way these parasites know they can gain power. It is the only way the mediocre, depraved, and malignantly narcissistic can gain the position they crave to shape society into their image.

But isn't "equality" an American ideal? Does the Declaration of Independence contain socialistic undertones? Absolutely not. The Classical Liberal ideal that "All men are created equal" expressed the ultimate manifestation of a free world—freedom of opportunity. This was the revolutionary idea. American values eliminated the class system, destroyed slavery, and delivered voting rights to all citizens.

The Left in its socialism has mangled that beautiful child by twisting the ideal of "equal opportunity" to "equal outcome." No longer is it to be equality of opportunity, but equality of ability, equality of resources, equality of job interviews, equality of NFL coaches—the list goes on. Equality for the Left is nothing more than a mechanism to wipe out the differences and creativity that sustain society and life itself.

Let's be honest, not everyone is equal in ability—to borrow from Plato, a knife was created to be a knife, not a hammer or a fax machine. And under a free society, those who are more gifted than others or work harder than others should be allowed to reward themselves for their labors—via private property and profit. Socialism seeks to counteract differences in ability by eliminating private property and redistributing material possessions. In that system, there is no freedom.

Think about it: Who does forced "equality" destroy? The most creative, the most intelligent, and the most inventive. The best and brightest must be eliminated because their very existence contradicts the efforts to declare everyone the same. And even more significantly to the Socialist, extraordinary people naturally stand above the crowd. They obviously and continually pose a threat to the status quo, especially a status quo that is the enemy of individual achievement and singular accomplishment.

The despots of every socialist regime have systematically hunted down and murdered their nation's educated: the doctors, the artists, the engineers, the academics—anyone and everyone who reminds the populace of the beauty of individual accomplishment. Stalin, Castro, Kim Jong Il, Hussein, and Pol Pot all murdered or imprisoned the educated, the creative who threatened the "social order" by being individual thinkers.

Conservatism

Now let me address the label with which many of you probably identify: conservative. These days it's funny, bordering on the absurd, to read dictionaries or reference books' definition of "liberal" and "conservative." "Liberal" is defined, with several paragraphs expounding on the wonderfulness of the philosophy, as "fighting for individual rights and working for progressive change in society." Sounds lovely, doesn't it? "Conservative," on the other hand, is afforded one sentence—"opposed to change" or "favoring the status quo."

My favorite, however, is the *Oxford American Writer's Thesaurus*. As a writer and a rhetorician, I like words. A thesaurus is a writer's best friend, helping find alternative words, new words, and different ways of saying things. A thesaurus is supposed to provide us with synonyms, antonyms, slang words, all the things we need to make our ideas more clear, to be more precise with what we mean.

With that in mind, consider how the word "liberal" is defined by the Oxford thesaurus. Here is a tiny sample of the, well, extraordinary meaning of "liberal" with italics and capitalization exactly as in the thesaurus:

1. *The values of a liberal society* TOLERANT, unprejudiced, unbigoted, broad-minded . . . enlightened . . .
2. *a liberal social agenda* PROGRESSIVE, advanced, modern, forward-looking . . . enlightened. ANTONYMS: reactionary, conservative.

Ah, there you have it—the antonym of "liberal" is "conservative," which means being the opposite of all that is liberal, so conservatives are prejudiced, bigoted, closed-minded, and unenlightened, among other things.

That's not the best part, however. What they've done with the word "conservative" itself is even more revealing. Here again is just a small sample of what you need to know about "conservative":

1. *the conservative wing of the party* RIGHT-WING, reactionary, traditionalist; Republican. *Informal*: redneck.
2. *our more conservative neighbors may object to the modern*

architecture being proposed TRADITIONALIST . . . conventional, orthodox, old-fashioned . . . unadventurous . . . *Informal*: stick-in-the-mud.

No wonder some people are resistant to being called conservative! Every writer who has read the *Oxford American Writer's Thesaurus* has been told that appropriate informal synonyms for conservatives include "redneck" and "stick-in-the-mud." To say nothing of being backward and made nervous by things modern. No judgment there. With this sort of conditioning of communicators in society, it's no wonder conservatives continue to be portrayed as, well, rednecks.

The editors, by the way, do not even provide the "informal" definition of liberal, so I suggest they do so by including equitable "informal" synonyms for liberal in their next edition. I have a couple of suggestions. Since "conservatives" can be referred to informally as "rednecks," how about the very informal and familiar "fag" for liberals? And if a conservative is a "stick-in-the-mud" how about the informal "sexual compulsive" for liberals? After all, if the shoe fits Bill Clinton, it must fit other liberals.

I hear the outrage right now! What? I'm "generalizing" and tainting all liberals with the same insulting brush? The Oxford editors set that standard, not I.

Here I'll dare to inject some Real World facts—it has become clear that it is the Liberal Elite, not conservatives, who are enamored with the status quo. Their politics and cultural message for the past twenty-five years have been to institute a fascist cultural framework, punishing anyone who dares to dissent, or question, or, heaven forbid, come to a different conclusion than theirs about a serious social issue.

If one looks at history clearly, it has been conservatives who have been out on the front line in the last two decades (with Ronald Reagan leading the way), creating change and expanding freedom, not only for Americans but for the world.

Kind of throws that silly notion of the Left being the purveyors of freedom out the window, doesn't it? Just think Jimmy Carter and Michael Moore if you're unsure about what philosophy is expansive, frees people, and makes the world a better place. Last time I checked, the famous feminist-tolerant-expansive-freedom-loving-progressive Left here and around the world were still tearing their hair out over the idea of the people in the Middle East being free.

And purveyors of change? There is a no more progressive change than the destruction of communism, which proves that the power of individualism and freedom can overtake the darkest of the dark.

Reagan and England's prime minister, Margaret Thatcher, through "conservative" politics, were committed to creating an environment where the individual could flourish. Where individual achievement, ideas, dreams, creativity, reason, logic, and the intellect were the ultimate sovereign.

If that's the Modern Redneck, sign me right up.

You can guess I would argue that Reagan and Thatcher are and were indeed Classical Liberals.

You Bigoted Redneck You

The Left has indeed been surprisingly successful with demonizing the word "conservative." In fact, as a public figure if the media attach that label to you it is meant to cross a line through your name.

It is, in reality, meant to keep *you* in check. The Left's efforts to demonize the conservative identity are an attempt to make true conservatives feel out of step and question the morality of their positions. At the same time, this dance is also to keep Classical Liberals from daring to stray from the Modern Liberal plantation, out of fear of what it would mean to be considered a dreaded conservative.

In fact, a new term has even been developed by a Socialist in an effort to smear Classical Liberals—"neoconservative." It was the Socialist Michael Harrington who coined the term "neoconservative," meant as an insult to Leftists who had dared to act on their Classical Liberal ideals.

You see, neoconservatives can't be called "neoliberal" because then the label becomes problematic for the squatter Leftists who claim to be "liberals." For example, liberals can't think we should close our borders. Liberals can't support the war on terror. Liberals can't believe that personal responsibility and independence help people more than the pathetic and disastrous welfare state. That, you see, would upset the Left's control of the political ghettos.

So, in order to keep the stranglehold on the word "liberal," while also effectively demonizing Classical Liberals, the term "neocon" was coined, and meant as an insult to people who came from the Left and who challenged, dissented, or critiqued the Leftist spectrum.

David Horowitz, in the introduction for his book *The Politics of Bad Faith*, explains more fully the genesis of the neoconservative label:

> To acquire even more protective coloration from the po-
> litical center, socialist radicals coined the term "neoconserva-
> tive" to describe those adversaries who were genuine liberals
> opposed to an alliance with the Left. Norman Podhoretz, Irv-
> ing Kristol and other neoconservative spokesmen have writ-
> ten at length of their efforts to retain the term "liberal" for
> themselves and preserve the integrity of the political lan-
> guage. But, despite the indisputable logic of their position,
> they were unable to withstand the dominant influence of the
> Left in the culture, and the "neoconservative" label stuck.

It is a shame, but is an invaluable lesson when it comes to who is making the rules about how we identify ourselves, how others view us, and how we view ourselves.

Our freedom as individuals relies on your being conscious about yourself and understanding the importance of *how* you identify and *why* you identify the way you do. It is also fundamental that you make the choice, and not be swayed by other people's definitions. The moment you allow your identity to be determined by someone or some group, you have completely lost yourself. You have given up all your power, and are surrendering to what fascism wants most from you—your individualism.

This is at the heart of why I will not let today's Socialists determine how I will identify myself. I am a Democrat, whether they like it or not (and they don't).

While today's labels and political machinations demand that I identify as a conservative, simply so my politics will be understood, it is fundamentally important not to abandon Classical Liberal thought in deed or concept, otherwise Marx, Lenin, and Stalin will all have the last laugh.

4

The Sleeping Beauty
of America

*Any power must be an enemy of mankind which
enslaves the individual by terror and force, whether it
arises under the Fascist or the Communist flag. All that
is valuable in human society depends upon the
opportunity for development accorded to the individual.*

—ALBERT EINSTEIN

There has been only one event in our history that represents the seminal moment of our awakening from a multicultural coma: September 11, 2001. Before this date, in a sort of bizarre malaise, we had accepted being banished to political, sexual, and racial ghettos. Designed by the Left and couched as a benefit of "the all" or "society" or "the common good," these ghettos were designed to shun, demonize, and smear the individual.

None of us could have imagined that it would take a devastating attack on our own soil and the murder of three thousand people to shed light on this festering internal cancer, i.e., Identity Politics and the slick manipulation of each of us under the guise of "multiculturalism."

The tragedy on that horrific day didn't change us, it woke us up from the interminable cultural coma the Left had beaten us into. Some years before 9/11, it was politically incorrect to be patriotic, lest one risk having another Thought Police label lobbed one's way: "jingoistic," "Nazi," "imperialist." Whatever it took to have the average

American retreat from enlightening patriotic national appreciation was the order of the day from the Left.

The attacks on our great nation have been deconstructed ad nauseam in the few years that have passed. Most thinkers and writers have analyzed the madness behind the assault, the political ramifications, the responsibilities, and the general meaning and impact.

No one, however, has touched on what I contend is the most remarkable by-product of the mass murder on that day—the exposure of the importance and power of the American Individual, and how Leftist policies and neosocialism in this country were doing great damage to our ability (and willingness) to defend and declare the greatness of this nation.

I see America in the three decades prior to 9/11 as Sleeping Beauty—still full of all the hope, dreams, and potential this great nation has always embodied, but slumbering under the influence of the drugs of the Thought Police, the Misery Merchants, and the Far Left Cultural Elite who want to tear down the nation we all know and love.

Keep in mind, the generations of Americans that preceded us were really no different than you or me. They embodied living examples of how democracy, freedom, capitalism, and the free market empower and set people free to pursue their dreams. The difference is what the generations of the first half of the twentieth century were faced with.

From 1914 to 1918, and then again in the 1930s culminating in World War II, Americans were reminded what made this nation different from the rest of the world. These were not cultural differences as much as they were revelations of the disease that can spring from centuries of monarchical, despotic, and tyrannical rule. Europe and Asia reminded America of what she had fled, and what happens when individuals are sacrificed to the state. Monsters arise and, like a cancer, inevitably move to swallow the world.

This is Europe's history, and Americans came face-to-face with it again and were compelled to fight against a return to the Old World, old ideas, and old death. Americans saved the world from itself, gaining a renewed sense of how important America was and the courage Americans have in fighting for individual rights and democratic freedom. Rightly, patriotism sprang from this experience.

People around the world, especially those in Eastern Europe who are only now experiencing the flowering results of freedom and democracy, appreciate American patriotism. But here at home, Leftists have worked diligently to make patriotism unfashionable and even dangerous. It will be snuffed out and with it all hope not only for this nation, but for liberty worldwide, if we do nothing.

In the Left's contrived, conformist, and godless world, gone is the individual, wiped out is singular success. Disappeared are the entrepreneur, the inventor, the writer, the actor, the painter, the doctor, the intellectual—gone, maligned, imprisoned, or in exile. In every country where socialism has prevailed, individuals simply and completely disappear.

The Rewards of Competition

What is quickly being ignored or forgotten, of course, is how we came to be the richest and freest and most hopeful nation on earth. It's because in our society, individuals are free to profit from their own work and succeed on their own efforts. Competition makes people push themselves to be better. Reward and profit fire imaginations. Knowing we are limited only by ourselves gives people hope, and with hope comes happiness.

The American Dream was built on the character of the American Individual. It was a future that existed on hope and could be achieved through hard work, not through a group telling you whom to be and how to act, and certainly not by the group handing you life on a cold, steel plate.

Ideas, innovation, creativity, and invention would give the individual the critical edge in our competitive society. Nothing fuels creative genius like reward. The efforts to be the best, the fastest, the most innovative, the most daring, the most useful, the most intriguing, the most creative shaped the United States. Our competitive edge and rewarding the individual spirit gave the world the lightbulb, the telephone, and the airplane, the sewing machine, the artificial heart, and the computer.

Keep in mind, the desperate failure of the Soviet Union, of Cuba, of North Korea is due to the most simple of realities—why should a "worker" work more, when there is no reward? Whether he works hard or doesn't work at all, he will still get paid (the least amount possible) in a socialist society. So where is the need to be creative, inventive, and entrepreneurial?

Human beings require a whole host of rewards and recognition. But the difference between us and the Left in this country is that we think rewards and recognition should result from our own hard work and creativity. The Left believes rewards should be given to everyone equally.

Medical research thrives and continues when geniuses, inventors, and researchers realize their own personal dreams and are rewarded based on what they're worth. In the Soviet Union, doctors got an apartment and maybe heat for the winter.

Here, the sky is the limit.

And yet unions and the thugs that run them have managed magnificently to convince entire generations of "workers" that their lives will be run one way and one way only. No advancement, no change, no progress, no improvement. That is the union worker's life. Being cemented into a hopeless, futureless mire is not the America I know—but it is to what unions across this country have condemned countless Americans.

Artists want to influence and create, but also want to live a life that is full and free. Who in the American schema doesn't want at least to know they can try for more? More skills, more money, more prestige, more success. Many don't try, many become comfortable within a certain level and that's fine. But that only works if they're the ones choosing. Not the union, not the union boss, not the government, not the "party."

Americans Divided

What was wrong with society on September 10? Some had lazily accepted a world where it was workers versus management, rich versus poor, black versus white, men versus women, gay versus straight, cats versus dogs versus ferrets. You name it, our culture then and now still aches under the burden of the unnatural efforts of Socialists to separate, categorize, and package individuals into cultural sardine cans.

Our accepting this is due to our greatest strength and greatest weakness as Americans. We are a nation of people who, in our hearts, want everything for everyone. Yes, of course, we're competitive in our efforts to succeed personally, but an optimistic individualism has always complemented our revolutionary spirit. In true American spirit, we expect everyone to reach for what they want, and as we hope for the success of our neighbor, we also recognize that some will be better than others in a competitive environment.

We root for our neighbors, our friends, our fellow Americans because every success story gives us all hope that we, too, can achieve our dreams if we try hard enough. Each win further confirms the truth of the beautiful ideals at our nation's heart. While you may not think this way consciously every day, I think you, like me, feel a special sort of pride in what Americans have accomplished and what our success represents to the world.

Some would consider me a romantic optimist. I suppose I am, and that too is a rather common American characteristic. I dare say we are a nation of romantic optimists. In fact, it's the kind of optimism we saw and loved in Ronald Reagan. He didn't invent the feeling, but he reminded us that it was okay to recognize and embrace our greatness, nationally and individually.

The French may mistake our optimism for foolhardiness. But, as they know, it is a kind of hope that gives us the courage and ability to save nations where cynical pessimism wrapped in arrogance masquerades as "European sensibility."

We are a nation of individual hopeful dreamers, in a place where dreams actually come true. We are not a nation of "classes," where one is doomed from birth to fester for life in a conscripted station and no amount of work or success creates upward mobility.

We are a nation of people who fled these feudal classes in Europe, Asia, and the Middle East. We came from a stock of people who were determined to build a home where the future was limited only by each person's imagination and ability. We knew each time we saw the American Dream realized, it reinforced the reality of it, and the fact that it could happen for us, too.

The effect of the socialist influence in our country has been to brainwash generations of Americans into believing that compassion means that it is somehow immoral for an individual to be successful, and downright obscene for that person to benefit from his own success. Socialists have wailed about this "unfairness" for decades. Some people doing better than others epitomizes inequality, they say. While the initial rhetoric was crafted by Marx and finessed by Stalin, their agenda, their warped worldview now sadly dominates the American cultural scene.

This socialist mentality (that your efforts, your work, your success, your uniqueness, even your children, belong not to you but to "society") thrives in two extreme environments: the dark, depressed state and the bright, vibrant, fertile state. The first is exemplified by 1930s Germany—a country on the brink of collapse, drowning in a swamp of nihilistic state-based Malignant Narcissism. A society suffering from no money, no food, and no hope provides the perfect breeding ground for socialism. After all, what better snake oil than socialism to declare that all that exists belongs to everyone.

On the other hand, socialism also yearns to sink its teeth into the neck of the successful society and feed off its rich lifeblood. The lifeblood of this society—our society—is based on compassion and hope. Attracted by the opportunity to subvert this success and gain power, socialism and its bedmate, fascism, will slip in.

The Tyranny of the Short Poppies

Our success, coupled with great compassion and commitment to fair play, has been manipulated with arguments that personal success is incompatible with equality. Fascists tell us individual achievement is the hallmark of inequality. We face now the epitome of the Tall Poppy Syndrome—where the drive by the mediocre to level the field can only be achieved by lopping off the heads of the poppies that have grown stronger, better, or simply different from the rest. To Socialists, those who are different, those whose existence reminds people that everyone is not the same, are dangerous.

Why is this so? In America we have always embraced the rene-gade, the one who is different, the one who challenges the status quo. It is our nature to romanticize the Radical Individual, because all (or most) of us aspire to have some bit of that in our own lives. It is your appreciation of that, your desire to grow into your own, that must be snuffed out if American Leftists are to have their way.

Childhood trauma, the resulting Malignant Narcissism and its concomitant paranoia are necessary ingredients to embracing social-ist and, ultimately, fascist politics. For the American Left, this has manifested in the socialist nightmare that individuals and personal dreams and success must be banished for the "common good." This is a nightmare people throughout the world have suffered for nearly a century. And now it is beginning to haunt our nation.

If you think I'm being an alarmist, think again.

Consider Hillary Clinton's comments to a group of Democrat party supporters during the 2004 election season. Clinton was head-lining a Democrat fund-raiser where, in addition to vowing to defeat the Republicans' "extraordinary ruthless machine," she said the most honest thing I have ever heard her utter.

Clinton proclaimed that if the Democrats win the White House and Congress in 2004, they should expect to lose the tax cuts passed by President Bush. To a crowd that had paid as much as $10,000 per person to attend the event, she declared,

Many of you are well off enough that . . . the tax cuts may have helped you. We're saying that for America to get back on track, we're probably going to cut that short and not give it to you. We're going to take things away from you on behalf of the common good.[1]

The last time I checked, the beauty of democracy and freedom was that we kept the fruits of our labor. The fact that Clinton felt comfortable vocalizing this blatant socialism in public is disturbing.

Of course, in all the press coverage of this event, no one brought up the absurd conflict in Clinton's comments. Here she was speaking about getting America "back on track" to a room full of people who have enough expendable income to pay $10,000 merely to stand in the same room with a woman who sold her soul to marry a politician with no pants. If that's not a testament to the success of George W. Bush's economic policies, I don't know what is.

The underlying message of the generally deluded Leftist establishment, Clintons and all, is that your specialness, your particular values, your principles, your drive, your ambition, and even your hope for the future are wrong.

And while it is contrary to human nature to condemn ourselves, we do it each time we feel guilty about being successful, financially secure, physically healthy, or, in other words, ourselves. For many, these feelings of guilt arise when we do something for ourselves, or think of ourselves first. You are not important, they tell you. The group is everything.

You, sir and madam, as the New Radical Individuals, the Tall Poppies of America, are the Left's obstacle to ruining this nation. Their success or failure relies on something extraordinarily simple: *your own frame of mind*. There is no secret, complex political structure that will stop this Leftist rot from progressing—all that matters is how you think and feel about what's happening, and your not being afraid to act on it.

The truth of my assertion is evident in how obsessed the Left is with keeping you silent. You must ask yourself, why are most of the Left's efforts focused on destroying the individual? It's because you, in your singular independence, are the living antidote to the cancer of their plan.

Leftists know the real power of your individualism. It's time you did, too.

The New Thought Police have been successful in keeping you quiet during the past two decades. The Misery Merchants have made it dangerous for you to question the scourge of groupthink.

The Feminist, Multiculturalist, and Gay Elites, through legislation and control of media, have made it nearly impossible, and even dangerous, to counter any of their socialist plans for this nation.

The Ultimate Paranoid Conspiracy

Eleanor Smeal, considered the default leader of the feminist establishment, first became president of the National Organization for Women (NOW) in 1977 and is mostly known for leading the drive to ratify the Equal Rights Amendment. In 1987, Smeal founded a new organization she named the "Feminist Majority." I met Smeal in 1987 when I was completely (and blissfully) unaware of the bizarre Leftist foundation under the American feminist establishment.

Prior to my involvement in NOW, I had naïvely presumed that corrupt political ideologies plagued the rest of the world, but certainly not the U.S. While I appreciate my optimism, it has led me blindly down a path or two. Fascism, I believed, could only erupt in a place where there was no hope, where people were desperate.

One of my biggest mistakes in this thinking was applying a political ideology to a collective *place* or environment (as a good Leftist does), ignoring the fact that it is the choices of the human *individual* at the heart of social change, good and bad.

As a young leader in NOW, I had always heard about mysterious late-night "strategy" sessions with Smeal. Being asked to attend one of these "meetings" was the ultimate sign of acceptance within the feminist establishment's small leadership clique.

It was also an indoctrination into the reasoning behind how everyone who was not a feminist—every Republican, virtually every man, and certainly every Christian—was out to get us, as I was to find out. It is the best example of how Leftists convince their own to accept the notion that the world is so evil, so corrupt, so oppressive that only Leftist extremism will save us.

When I had first started my abortion rights activism, I was invited to join Smeal for my first "strategy session." The evening began innocently enough with dinner and political discussion, the kind you can imagine when people of like minds get together. But as the night went on, the discussion became stranger and stranger. As everyone settled into the living room with Smeal at the table, "instruction" and revelation began.

Feminist leaders and some up-and-comers sat in a semicircle around Smeal, creating a devotional environment. Smeal sat at a main table at the home of Toni Carabillo in Los Angeles and began a dissertation about the Straight-White-Religious-Right-Conservative-Republican-Male-Conspiracy against women, against feminists, and against anyone who wasn't like them. In other words, she pitted the average American against minorities, and white men against everyone else.

Smeal's quiet but methodical focus made it clear that she believed we were facing a battle that transcended differences of opinion. It was a direct and calculated conspiracy to throw women back into the Stone Age.

America was a world of unrelenting racism, sexism, and homophobia, according to Smeal. It was the American system itself that was part of the problem. The "tyranny of the majority" that democracy allowed had to be smashed and changed.

Smeal's insistence that it was a deliberate calculated conspiracy by Them against Us wasn't limited to just rhetoric—Smeal drew pictures. Literally. Her diagrams of the conspiracy became a highlight of the evening. Steeped in paranoia describing the elaborate conspiratorial schemes against us, for hours Smeal filled countless pieces of paper with names, arrows, and circles, all connecting the various Evil Victimizers to the Grand Scheme of Oppression.

These papers filled the table and overflowed onto the floor, passed along from feminist to feminist as proof positive that everything that was happening in conservative politics was designed to destroy us.

The genesis of this sort of behavior could not be more clear to me now. It is the root of Malignant Narcissism unleashed. Smeal and everyone else in the room believed (and probably do so today) that everything that happens is indeed happening because of them. The malignancy of this severe narcissism is manifested in Smeal working to defeat this supposed conspiracy by destroying its foundation—the American system itself.

The Contingent of the Bobbing Heads

During these sessions, which would last until three or four in the morning, I, like everyone else around me, became the human equivalent of the head-bobbing doggy usually reserved for the car rear window. My head went up and down, up and down, amazed that the Great Smeal entrusted me with her remarkable, insightful view of the world.

We saw the conspiracy with the names, arrows, and circles. This was war, and America was the enemy. Capitalism, "the American Dream," and religion were the opium of the masses and were to be rejected, as Stalin noted and Smeal inferred.

This was where my mental reconditioning began, and where Leftist politics naturally eclipsed American values and principles because they were, well, evil. Democracy, you see, allowed the Great Unwashed Masses to dare to believe their racist, sexist, and homophobic voices mattered. And, most frighteningly to the feminist establishment, their values and their votes mattered.

I quickly realized that this evening was not for questions and answers. No one, not even the more famous people in the room, ever interjected, ever questioned, ever contradicted what Smeal dictated. What are so obviously Smeal's paranoid conspiracies were simply accepted as the truth—to be listened to, absorbed, and "understood." I was told I should be grateful I was included, and not waste the importance of what I was being told.

This, in a nutshell, is the absurdity of what we have faced during the past forty years from the socialist Left-wing special-interest groups attempting to divide and conquer America. We individual freethinkers have been tranquilized with threats and fabricated guilt into accepting a monumental lie.

We have been force-fed the argument that because the American ideals of capitalism and individualism have made us the greatest nation on earth, we must now reject those evil values and embrace a system of entitlements, handouts, and humiliation. This has taken form in many ways, from outrageous demands from the Black Elite for slavery reparations to an insistence that the United Nations is better suited to dictate American foreign policy than we are.

This is why the American way of life is now under attack, not only by Islamist Fascists abroad, but by our own homegrown Leftists. Let us admit that there is an enemy here at home. This has moved beyond differences of opinion about how to make democracy and capitalism work better. The battle has now exposed the ultimate desire of Socialists everywhere to destroy the benchmark of the success of democracy and capitalism. In addition to freeing people at the most personal of levels, individualism brings with it personal accountability and responsibility, and consequently, higher expectations of ourselves and others.

All of these values will be nothing more than footnoted anomalies in the fall of Western civilization if we do not act now. First and foremost, this rejection of the Left's Identity Politics, special-interest groups, and its multiculturalism must happen at an individual level. You must see it for what it is—not as an ideology that frees and liberates people, but as one that sows distrust, isolation, and dehumanizes individuals.

Then came September 11.

Sleeping Beauty Awakes

Dear Ms. Bruce,

I have just finished your book The New Thought Police, *and I was very impressed. To be honest with you, I was surprised by the fact that I was reading it. You represented everything to me that was wrong as a feminist and Democrat, I saw you as a turncoat. I remember you from your work at NOW during the O. J. Simpson case, and I was really impressed with that. It seemed like no one else was dealing with domestic violence and we all knew racism had nothing to do with it. But when I heard about this book, I felt you had simply sold out. I presumed you were like Madonna—reinventing yourself as a way to make a buck.*

Then I saw you on some Fox show about the book and it had been only a month or so after 9/11. I had been feeling lost and afraid in general. Don't get me wrong, I'm a grown woman, and very political, but that's what started to change. All the things I cared about politically suddenly didn't seem to matter. I think a lot of us began to look at each other in a different way.

I suppose this is what war does. I found it interesting because as I listened to you I felt less angry about you and was curious about what you had to say. Not that I would agree or anything, but it was surprising to me that I felt happy people like you and even Sean Hannity (God help me for saying this) are on our side.

I guess what I'm saying is I finally saw you first as an American. I'm seeing a lot of people that way now, and I'm

feeling less angry at people who I disagree with. It's weird,
but September 11th, with all its horribleness, made me want
to read your book, and in a weird way, made me a better per-
son. I'm glad, too, because I agree with most of what you
write in your book. I never would have known had we not
had our tragedy.

Thanks for doing it and being there and staying the
course. . . .

Bernadine
New Jersey

Dear Bernadine,

I can't tell you how moved I was by your e-mail. I, too,
have been changed by September 11th. When I wrote The
New Thought Police *it was an exposé of a point in time of my*
life, with a narrow agenda. Yes, I was exposing the problems
of the Left but I was still quite limited in my own personal
perception of the world.

September 11th has helped me to be more open, too. I
feel I am moving beyond special-interest-group issues and,
yes, trying to understand what it means to be an American
first.

This great tragedy has shown us we're all in this together.
And, frankly, I'm thrilled that you're happy we're all on the
same side. And while we may indeed disagree on some issues,
I'm quite honored that someone as thoughtful as you is on my
side. Together we can win this, abroad and at home.

Best
Tammy

This was one of many exchanges in the aftermath of 9/11 that
made me realize something was happening to our sensibilities as
Americans. *NTP* was released just a few weeks after the attacks, and
there was some discussion about whether or not the release should be

delayed. But I argued for it to come out as scheduled. I knew something as horrific as 9/11 would have an unimaginable impact on generations of Americans who had grown up comfortably in a nation not faced with an enemy that threatened our very existence.

I was only eight or nine years old when I watched the evening news accounts of the Vietnam war dead. In those days (the late sixties) our local newscast was only fifteen minutes long. There was no twenty-four-hour cable news, no hourlong news, just a short segment of local and perhaps a longer segment of national news. That was it. This was the extent of my generation's relationship with war and death.

Now, over thirty years later, I truly had no idea how I or the nation would respond to the carnage of 9/11. It didn't take long to find out.

I had already begun to openly question the value of Identity Politics long before 9/11, but as I watched the attacks unfold on my television, the cataclysm seared into me something I had never experienced before. As the twin towers and the Pentagon crumbled, so, too, did my view of myself as a woman, a feminist, a gay, a prochoicer, an activist—all the labels that had for so long defined me.

At that moment I realized I was an American, first and foremost. I can thankfully say I was on my way in that direction, but it may have taken much more time to reverse the conditioning of the Left, with their condemnation of Authentic Individualism, to say nothing of nationalistic pride in America. That was the absolutely forbidden feeling.

Americans First and Always

Todd Beamer, one of the more celebrated heroes of Flight 93, when his flight was hijacked tried using his cell phone to contact his wife. He was unable to get through. He then used the Airfone in his seat and spoke to an operator. In the event something happened to him he asked her to tell his wife that he loved her. Todd then asked the operator to pray the Lord's Prayer with him. She did.

After that prayer, the operator heard Todd yell, "Let's roll!" to the other passengers. Moments later United Flight 93 crashed into a field in Shanksville, Pennsylvania. Todd and his fellow passengers took things into their own hands. They had been ordered by the hijackers to be quiet and remain calm—but the forty heroic individuals on that flight, all different and all American, decided to do otherwise.

Passenger Tom Burnett called his wife and told her that he and others "are going to do something." Flight attendant Sandy Bradshaw told her husband, Phil, that she was boiling water to use in the attack. The call ended when she declared, "Phil, everyone's running to First Class. I've got to go. Bye."[2]

We began to see the faces of the dead, the stories of those lost and missing. We heard famous names and names we did not know. Men, women, children, black, white, Christian, Jewish, Muslim, gay, straight, old, young, pro-choice, pro-life, rich, poor, Republican, Democrat, all were suddenly the same.

My point here is that a hero is a hero. An American is an American. When Sandy told her husband that "everyone" was running to First Class, her thoughts transcended the superficiality of their skin color, sexual preference, or gender.

They will live on in our memory as "everyone." We became, beautifully, Americans first. We found in tragedy that the false and destructive boxes the Left had constructed for us were actually made of cards. They fell when the crisis brought home the finality of death and a reminder of our mortality.

Death does that. It is the ultimate equalizer. It wipes away the political games of man, the arbitrary political "identities," the groupings meant to give or take away power from one group or another, the cynical efforts to divide Americans for power, or money, or prestige, or fame. Death banishes those differences and brings forth the commonality in each of us. For Americans that commonality is courage and a willingness to die for what is right.

There was no black or white, gay or straight, man or woman on that plane. In those last moments they were Americans all the same. They were going to die fighting, and nothing the NAACP, or NOW, or GLAAD ever said mattered. It was all useless and stupid in the face of mortality.

In the end, their heroism and self-sacrifice is a thousand times more American than the NAACP, the ACLU, NOW, GLAAD, and the Misery Merchants who run those elitist groups could ever be. The phone calls to loved ones, whether they were from the doomed people on hijacked airplanes or flame-filled offices, were sent from unique individuals to those who were about to suffer unbearable personal loss.

Contemplating impending death opens the door to the epiphany of self-realization. I think it's safe to say the influences we allow in our daily lives have their impact for a variety of reasons. Either we don't think it matters, or are too tired to fight, or too busy to notice what's happening. The brainwashing we have all been subjected to has been applied slowly over a long period of time.

Socialism has plodded along with all the patience in the world, content to incrementally destroy the heart and soul of this nation. What is the heart and soul of America? The free and singular American. You, without labels, with a sharp, critical, and, yes, judgmental mind. Full of opinions, self-confidence, and character.

For too long we have been asleep in the cultural coma the Left works so hard to cast us into. But this Big Lie that your individualism is wrong, your patriotism is evil, your critical mind dangerous is a fragile delusion. There are some things that can wake us up, and the Left knows this.

Cocker-Spaniel-Americans

No one could have known, but the tragedy of 9/11 is one of those things that woke us from our slumber. Shedding the labels and co-

coons created by the Left, we emerged to understand the exquisitely heroic meaning of being an individual. The American Individual regained consciousness.

We woke up from something we really didn't know had enveloped us, just as we sleep at night, blissfully ignorant of the state we are in. It's only when awakened that we understand, by counterpoint, what happened to us. A crystallization of this societal awakening after 9/11 was in, of all things, a public service announcement from the Advertising Council.[3]

The campaign was titled "I Am an American," and it featured men and women, young and old, black and white, each saying the simple line "I am an American." The Ad Council described the intent of the campaign this way:

> ". . . [D]iversity unites America, and that in the wake of this national tragedy, now is the time to embrace and celebrate that diversity instead of letting it divide us. By showing people of many ages, races and religions saying the simple yet powerful line 'I am an American,' the advertising communicates the idea that our differences equal the very foundation and spirit of this nation."

And that's what was so fascinating and yet exemplified what was going wrong in this nation. I was struck not necessarily by what the people in the ads were saying, it was what they *weren't* saying. The hyphenated identities given to us by the Left in this nation were gone. *That* was the point of the ads.

It's a fairly well-known fact that the Ad Council tends to tackle more progressive issues, so it's safe to say that they are a fairly liberal group. The point of their "I am an American" campaign was initially seen as an effort to prevent violence against Muslims in the wake of the attacks. That is not an exclusively liberal cause, because no sane person from the Left or Right condoned violence against innocent Muslims.

The ad campaign, however, also had an ironic effect—those four words "I am an American" reawakened a latent American Nationalism among many. And you can bet that the liberals on Madison Avenue never intended for that to happen. A bright light, if you will, shone on the beautiful thing that the Left has told us for far too long we are supposed to ignore, and even revile—the power and completeness of being an American, first and always.

This reveals what conservatives had been arguing for ages—that the little cultures proffered by the Left, multiculturalism and hyphenated identities, were *bad* for unity. It's not our diversity that has divided us, as the Ad Council's press release notes, it's the manipulation and exploitation by the Left Elite jamming us all into little boxes.

African-American, Asian-American, Mexican-American, Gay-American, Disabled-American, Cocker-Spaniel-American (ooh, that's a good one! It has two hyphens!). It's all a word game, meant to separate you from your mind, and yourself. It's meant for you to surrender to the fascists in our midst.

I argue against the cancer of multiculturalism on the very basis that it is designed to divide us. It is designed to erase our very history as Americans.

American Values

Clearly, a nation's unity and progress require the simplest of nationalist understandings—including a common language, common culture, and pride in what that American culture truly means.

Now, you may hear arguments (as I have) that advocating for pride and nationalistic sensibility itself eradicates the individualist principle, that we all become mindless drones as soon as we pledge our allegiance to the flag. Nothing could be further from the truth, because it is *American* values that unite us: human rights, freedom, and liberty, not concepts of ethnicity or race or even party affiliation.

Much to the Leftists' chagrin (who see this nation as evil), America is viewed as the purveyor of these values. This fact speaks loudly to what is missing in much of the world. It also reminds us that it is indeed our great responsibility to advocate, promote, and export American culture and values to the rest of the world, without fear, and without apology. We must have a complete understanding that it has been left to us to open the door to freedom for those who continue to suffer under the unforgiving hammers of socialism and its brother-in-arms, fascism.

The Left argues that this is imperialism, that our reason for being in Iraq is to claim Iraqi oil and let McDonald's colonize the Middle East. I say if a democratic society chooses to pursue importing McDonald's (it's the locals who would be employed), then more power to them.

It is worth noting here that individualism is **not** about being singularly and incomprehensively different from everyone else. It is **not** about being contrary for the sake of being contrary, or odd for the sake of being odd. Instead, it represents the American value of people being free to make the choices that best suit them. We live in the only nation where the *idea* of what's possible, the *idea* of the future, the *idea* of happiness, the act of the individual mind being free to fantasize, free to imagine, and free to create are at the foundation of who we are.

And while the end result of the ideas, our personal hopes and dreams and accomplishments, will be different from person to person, it is the foundation that allows us to *pursue* that happiness, that personal future that makes us uniquely American.

We have seen the world struggle and partly collapse under the diseased fruit of monarchies, empires, kings, dictators, fuehrers, and "comrades." Our adventure into secular government for a people of faith has found the perfect blend of personal freedom tempered by moral expectations as defined by Christianity, especially.

This has been a good thing, and singularly responsible for the greatness of this nation. Christian values, applied through the social arena, allow the value of freedom and liberty to be truly understood and appreciated by demanding respect for the individual while at the same time expecting decency in our interactions.

As I have noted earlier, even a quick glance at history reveals the horrific results of the unchecked Left. We not only have proof that democracy and capitalism work beautifully together, they are the only human schema that makes people's lives better.

Embracing American Nationalism

It's time to swing back the curtains and invite the light in. And that light is American Nationalism, perennially shunned by the Left, condemned by Socialists, and without any special-interest group fighting for its rebirth. It has no legitimate advocates. And yet it is the very idea that will save not only our nation, but the rest of the world as well.

There is so much surrounding nationalism, and appropriately so, considering the context in which the world has been subjected to it. Nationalism as propagated by Hitler's Germany and Mussolini's Italy brought the world to the edge of destruction.

But let's take a closer look, as I ask you a specific question: Was it *nationalism* itself that consumed those nations and propelled them to consume the world, or was it the nature of those cultures?

I contend that nationalism is like any tool—implemented by good people, it will create good. Implemented by bad people, it will be an instrument for destruction.

Nationalistic feeling bubbling over in fascist countries can come to no good. Let's be honest here—the United States is the only nation that was founded and exists on the idea of liberty. Europe and Asia, on the other hand, have thousands of years of history based on conquest, expansion, colonialism, oppression, socialism, and fascism. Or, to use Bill Clinton's personal excuse for using and abusing people, European nations did horrible things to each other "because they could."

Our boys and girls died in World War I because of the shallow and narcissistic nationalism of Europe. We entered that war to free people who seemed intent on destroying themselves.

Our boys and girls died in World War II because of the shallow and narcissistic nationalism of Europe and Asia. We entered that war to free people who seemed intent on destroying themselves.

Our boys and girls died in Korea and Vietnam against our communist enemies during the Cold War. We fought those wars because of the shallow and narcissistic nationalism of the Soviet Union and China.

In fact, it has been *American Nationalism* that has given us the wherewithal to defeat countries mired in the hell of socialism and determined to take everyone with them. Make no mistake, no matter what you call it, our devotion to American values and willingness to die for them moves beyond patriotism. It is the only nationalism—American Nationalism—that has saved the world three times over since our inception and has liberated hundreds of millions of people worldwide.

It's time we admit that American Nationalism has been and remains the antidote to the scourges of socialism, fascism, and extremist Identity Politics around the world, including Radical Islam.

Why is American Nationalism different? Put plainly, it is because our nationalism is based in the power of the individual, and the ideas of freedom and liberty. It is not based in ethnicity, race, or geography.

Your realizing and embracing the enlightened reality of the importance and power of American Nationalism is the last thing Socialists and the American Left want. Why? Because American Nationalism reinforces the power of the individual. It historically has destroyed communism and exposes the lie of Leftist politics worldwide.

As American values spread throughout the world, tyrants and despots have no hope. Those who wish to make you a drop in the collectivist bucket fear the power of American Nationalism because *it sets people free*. And with freedom comes natural individualism, which rings the death knell for collectivist socialist policies wherever they lurk, whether it be in Iraq, Korea, New Zealand, or even in our own backyard.

Leftists condemn American Nationalism specifically because they know it not only will set you free, but enlightens the rest of the world. It reminds people everywhere that there is hope, a better way of life.

As an example, as of this writing, American troops are still in Iraq, but the country is being run as a sovereign nation under its own ruling body. Political parties are forming, elections are being arranged. Women will be a part of this new government; girls can go to school; and women can vote, work, and play politics.

Democracy has yet to be fully implemented, and yet even the idea of its existence in Iraq is causing change in the region. The Lebanese kicked Syrian occupiers out of their country. Kuwait has announced that they are "considering" giving women the vote, and a woman now serves in their parliament—how twentieth century of them! Saudi Arabia has announced they "may" lift the ban on women owning businesses—how nineteenth century of them!

Of course, bin Laden and his followers are still stuck in the fifth century, so I suppose this is progress. At this rate, even the Middle Ages look good to those systematically oppressed by the Islamic equivalent of a sociopathic Fred Flintstone.

I realize the musings of Islamist leaders in Saudi Arabia and Kuwait do not even remotely begin to solve the problem of the misogynistic Arab and Islamist policies toward women. My point is, freedom spreads by American Nationalism. The moment people realize that things can be better, the crack on totalitarian systems splits wide open.

Unless, of course, Jacques Chirac is your daddy.

That Bad, Bad, Scary Oppressive Democracy

During the 2004 Group of Eight summit in Georgia, French President Jacques Chirac criticized the Middle East initiative, sarcastically noting that the countries in the region "have no need for missionaries of democracy." I bet the one million Iraqis found in mass graves would disagree with that sentiment. And I bet the political prisoners in Iran would disagree, too. As would the women in Saudi Arabia who are not allowed to leave their homes without a male escort.

But then the view is so much nicer from the Champs Elysées, with a glass of red wine in hand and a baguette in mouth. Yes, much nicer than the Radical Islamist pastime of cutting off people's heads. But what do I know?

What was the basis for Chirac's derision of the plan? The initiative would include greater NATO involvement in Iraq, plans to bring Western-style democracy and economic reform to the Middle East and North Africa, and a resolution to the Israeli-Palestinian conflict—you know, those pesky ideas that set people free. How dare we!

Instead, Chirac revealingly chided the plan by stating, "There is no ready-made formula for democracy readily transposable from one country to another. Democracy is not a method, it is a culture. For democracy to take root solidly and durably in the Arab world, it must be an Arab democracy above all else."[4]

What are these reforms that Chirac feels are culturally repugnant to those pesky Arabs? What "Arab" culture impugning American-style reforms are the arrogant and imperialistic Americans planning? Free elections, independent media, improved legal systems, training for lawyers and judges, loans to small businesses, and campaigns to reduce illiteracy for twenty million people. It also sets a target for training 100,000 teachers.[5]

Yeah, I can see why Chirac would think those backward, freakish Arabs would be culturally shocked and repulsed by these sorts of suggestions. But then again, let's remember the sort of Arab that Chirac has been close to—his buddy Saddam Hussein.

Maybe if we paid for free French classes for everyone and encouraged the eating of garden pests as the preferred dietary change of the Free Iraq, France would be more helpful.

And make a careful note here about Chirac's choice of words. He describes democracy—also known as liberty and freedom—as "cultural." This is serious in that the cultural argument has been used for the past century to excuse doing nothing about genocidal maniacs in our midst.

More troubling, however, is President Bush's response to this French betrayal of democratic ideas and insult to Arabs. At the same G8 summit, Bush had this to say about Europe's "concerns" regarding the dreaded spread of democracy: "There were certainly concerns that we want the world to look like America. This will not happen."[6]

Is Bush suddenly possessed by the ghost of Jimmy Carter? This came from the same guy who told the terrorists in Iraq to "bring it on." So, you can imagine his response to the French is stunning. It does, however, seem to indicate how severely even he has been affected by the toxic, manipulative rhetoric of European and American Leftists.

It is imperative to realize that we *want* the world to be free, primarily because it will make the United States safer.

Let's be honest here—despite what Leftists will lead you to believe, there is *no* true freedom under Castro, Hussein, Arafat, Kim Jong Il—the list goes on and on.

Even in the countries of our democratic so-called allies—Canada, Germany, France, Italy—there is much less freedom than here in America. For President Bush to capitulate to Leftists and abandon the idea that every human being deserves to be free allows the disease of extremism and totalitarianism to flourish. And it gives good men an excuse to do nothing, to be bystanders as terror reigns, all in the name of being culturally sensitive.

What Bush should have said is: "If liberating people from the scourge of oppression under any totalitarian regime, no matter how it cloaks itself, makes the world 'look like America,' then so be it."

The Germans know American Nationalism. So do the Japanese. When we vanquished those enemies, we did not colonize them—we set their people free. We gave them the extraordinary gift of democracy and freedom, American style. France and Germany, the two malcontents wringing their hands over the—God forbid—proliferation of that dastardly freedom thing—owe their freedom to that pesky

American Nationalism. It is mind-boggling that "looking like America" is good enough for the nations we have liberated in Europe, but it is simply too complicated a concept, according to Chirac, for those silly and backward Arabs.

Yes, I want the world to look like America, for the sake of women and children everywhere. For our own sake. So should you because people, including the president of the United States, need to hear and bend to *your* opinion, not to Monsieur Chirac's.

By Jingo!

In order to be heard, you must recognize, embrace, and advocate American Nationalism with no hesitation, no guilt, and no fear. You must realize that it is your understanding of the condition of the world, and the determined role America must accept, that are the last bastions of Classical Liberal values and the last hopes for people everywhere who yearn for freedom.

What would be the difference if we retreated and let the French and Germans make decisions for the world? We tried that twice in the last century. Isolationism, refusing to accept our role in the world, and delaying our response to evildoers ultimately *cost* fifty-three million lives in World War II alone. The preemption policy of the Bush administration, taking the war to the enemy and exporting democracy and freedom, has *liberated* fifty million lives.

Don't fall for the Leftists' Big Lie, propagated by "statesmen," Hollywood-types, and terrorists alike, that some people simply can't handle freedom or don't want it. That is the mantra you will hear from self-obsessed narcissists in Europe and rotting Leftists everywhere. And don't believe that American freedom means nothing more than commercialism invading untapped markets. Starbucks will come and go, but freedom will stand forever.

Of course, espousing American Nationalism will get you called names.

Because you are a critical, thinking individual, coming to judgment and cultivating opinions, you have or will face being called a "racist," "imperialist," or "warmonger" because you dare to contradict the Left's worldview. Now you can add the word "jingoistic," which you will hear as you advocate American Nationalism. "Jingo," by the way, is a Basque word meaning "God."

We've all heard the term used as a pejorative against those with nationalistic pride, so it's worth knowing a bit of its history.

Russia and the Ottoman Empire were in conflict in the 1870s. British Prime Minister Benjamin Disraeli advocated for neutrality in the conflict, contrary to the popular sentiment in Britain. The following pub song about the conflict gave rise to the term:

> We don't want to fight
> But, by jingo, if we do,
> We've got the ships,
> We've got the money, too.

The world will always be filled with more people who prefer to do nothing when faced with questions of searing morality. Questions of responsibility have always divided the Left and the Right in this nation. It's no different when it comes to our national responsibility to the rest of the world.

As a reminder of what Albert Einstein said on the issue:

> Any power must be an enemy of mankind which enslaves the individual by terror and force, whether it arises under the Fascist or the Communist flag. All that is valuable in human society depends upon the opportunity for development accorded to the individual.

The Radical Islamist "flag" of terrorism is indeed a fascist one. Islamist states, with their bigotry, misogyny, and brutality, should also be considered an enemy of mankind. It is this extremism, manifest in virtually all Middle Eastern governments, with the exception of Israel and now Iraq, that must be seen for what it is—a destroyer of individuals, the crusher of hopes, dreams, and the very future.

What makes the United States safer automatically improves the lives of others. It is important to become comfortable with the reality that, within our individualist framework, there is absolutely nothing wrong with being comfortable with making decisions based on what's best for America, what's best for you and your family.

In the words of one of the Madrid train bombers, "we will win because we love death and you love life." Only the American Individual, with the strength and conviction of American Nationalism, will prove them wrong and banish that mindless savagery, once and for all, from this planet.

This is your remarkable duty as an American. It can be daunting, but we have proven ourselves in the past, and we are proving ourselves now. It continues to be our charge, as Americans, to provide and defend liberty and freedom into the future.

5

Individualism in
the Palm of Your Hand

*A strong body makes the mind strong. As to the species
of exercises, I advise the gun. While this gives moderate
exercise to the body, it gives boldness, enterprise and
independence to the mind. Games played with the ball,
and others of that nature, are too violent for the body
and stamp no character on the mind. Let your gun,
therefore, be the constant companion of your walks.*

—THOMAS JEFFERSON

So far, I've discussed the elements of the Radical American Individual and how we have been lulled to sleep by a nefarious Left—a Left that, were it left to its own devices, would probably ring in a new era of wonderful totalitarian socialism on this great nation of ours. And now that we understand that the Radical Individual has been awakened from his slumber, it's time to pick up the tools and the weapons we need to make sure this country is not usurped by that Left. Most of these weapons are harmless—economic measures, activist measures that have been used by the Left for decades and can now be put to good use against the Left, and so forth.

There is one serious weapon, however, that we must also take up, and that is the firearm. And this is a weapon we do not embrace lightly. We are not going to storm NOW or GLAAD headquarters with guns drawn. In fact, the most useful thing we can do as Radical Individuals is to put a gun safely in our dresser drawers, or in our closets. For it is not staring down the barrel of a pistol that scares the dickens out of the Left as much as it is the mere knowledge that the American citizenry is armed.

My argument goes far beyond the application of an esoteric and debated "right" to bear arms. While Leftists would like to limit our debate to small discussions about "sporting rights," let's not take that bait. This real discussion is about us being armed, to the teeth if you wish, for the sake of ourselves, your sense of individualism, and for the United States as a whole.

Both individualism and patriotism, while ideas first, rely on determination and action in order to truly exist, to come to life. While there are many avenues to develop your own individual responsibility, owning a firearm is an important element. For many of you, this may sound surprising, but hear me out.

I own a gun. Her name is Snuffy and she's a .38 Smith & Wesson snub nose. I love Snuffy. She's very quiet, requires no feeding (unless, of course, we're at the firing range), and lives to protect me. Yes, Snuffy is an inanimate object, but owning Snuffy, possessing that weapon, reminds me that I am an individual with serious personal responsibilities. Having a firearm in my home also reinforces the fact that I live in a free nation where my choice and ability to defend myself and my nation are real, vibrant issues.

The responsibility I embrace by owning Snuffy includes my deciding never to use her in anger, only in self-defense. And while, thank goodness, I have never had to brandish Snuffy, I will not hesitate to use her in order to defend myself, someone I love, or this great nation of ours. When you own a gun you have to think seriously why you use it, how, and under what circumstances.

I've asked myself these questions, and have come to conclusions that make me more than comfortable, even safe and happy, to have a weapon I know will be my ultimate equalizer in a situation of life and death.

When the power to kill is in your hands, your individual power becomes undeniable. I'm not speaking here of a base sense of oppressive power. Just like every other manifestation of your personal power I have already discussed, it is worth reminding you not to put a negative connotation on expressions of the potential of your individual power.

Power takes many forms, some esoteric and some much more tangible. It's about your social relationships, influence, and persuasion. How you affect the world, locally and globally. This is your esoteric power. Owning a firearm is a manifestation of your tangible power.

Think about it—most of us have been so brainwashed that we immediately question our own intentions, our own goodness when contemplating our complete potential. Whether it be American Nationalism or personal power, we tend to retreat automatically. I am here to tell you to stop stepping back. Trusting yourself, and your own intentions, is the absolute first step in becoming your own individual.

When it comes to who we are as decent, good Americans, when I speak of personal power and even the power to kill, it is within the framework of the integrity and responsibility we attach to that reality.

For example, as a woman, I know that a firearm is the only thing that truly equalizes me if I'm faced with someone determined to do me harm. Yes, physical defense courses are good, but if a man who wishes me harm is close enough to touch me, he's already too close. Anyone who enters my home with malevolent intentions will not leave standing up. It's that simple.

My willingness to defend myself to the death stems from my own self-esteem. I know I am worthy of being saved, and I am willing to act on that worthiness. It reminds me of my uniqueness and the power of my decision making, and the fact that I can act on what I deem to be important.

At the same time, I have parameters. I will kill to defend myself, but I am not capable of malicious murder. In making these determinations, and thinking about the differences, I learn a great deal about myself. My individuality, like yours, is further shaped and guided by such issues as life and death. This is the key ingredient to what makes us American Individuals.

Ultimately, the personal responsibility of owning a firearm, knowing how to use it, and learning about the power, principles, and parameters of gun ownership are part of the psychological moral foundation of individualism.

Of course, there is a physical reality to Snuffy as well. Our commitment to defend ourselves personally extends to our duty to defend our nation. All of us hold in great esteem our courageous military, but here at home the fact that Americans are armed is a significant reason why this great nation remains a free nation. It's not the government that makes us free. It's not our laws that make us free. It is the expression of our individuality that makes us free.

Government Is Not God

Government, by its nature, does not want to have to deal with a well-armed citizenry. When people like you and I are armed, we present an unknown factor to the machinery of the system. This is a good thing. When armed, we are a constant reminder to the beast of government that the citizenry is the sovereign, that we are in charge, at least in America. We remind the government, regardless of what party is in charge, of its ultimate powerlessness when it comes to the people.

Without a tool to exercise that power, like firearms, our sovereignty would mean nothing. Ask the people of China, where gun control rules. Ask the people of North Korea—if you can find them, because so many have been herded off into concentration camps—defenseless because guns are banned. Ask the people of Cuba about personal property—which simply doesn't exist in that country—Castro, er, the government, owns everything. Of course, guns are banned there, too. Just as they were in every other sick communist and fascist regime in the world.

In fact, if there is a singular necessary element to a socialist or fascist takeover of a nation, it is the disarming of the citizen. Leftists in their inevitable fascist track actually understand in some way that their "design" of rule can only survive if the individual is crushed and made unable to fight back, to fight for himself, for his identity.

Our nation is not the freest and greatest on earth "just because." It's not due to happenstance, or luck, or coincidence. Our freedoms are not just embodied in the idea of our individual rights, but in the deliberate, thoughtful, and decent *exercise* of those rights. The Founding Fathers knew exactly what they were doing with the Constitution and the Bill of Rights.

In fact, let's make sure we're all on the same page here when it comes to the Bill of Rights. Many people think the Constitution and the Bill of Rights confer rights to the people. Nothing could be further from the truth. Our government exists to serve us—it does not have the power to give us rights; if it did, that would mean it is the sovereign, with the power to give or take away life and liberty. It does not have that power—we do.

Remember, government represents us, its power given to it by *us*, not the reverse.

The Bill of Rights does not bestow rights on the people—it safeguards the citizenry against federal interference with rights *naturally* assigned to us.

Many of you will interpret "nature" as "God." The Founding Fathers certainly did. But even the agnostics or atheists among you would agree that natural rights flow from the nature of humanity itself. Both perspectives must recognize it is simply and utterly contradictory to argue that an artificial body—government—designed and run by human beings emerges as somehow superior to the body that created it. That is an impossibility, philosophically, and as we've seen historically, in actual political application as well.

It may survive for a period of time, but the socialist and fascist states are doomed to failure because they violate nature. Communist regimes did their best to ban God, knowing that as long as God exists the state can never be omnipotent. In the socialist/fascist worlds, the state is God.

Banning God is as effective as banning love—you can make all the declarations you want, but it won't make it so. God, like love, will always be present and inexplicable. Manifest and invisible. It can be avoided, I suppose, and even denied, ignored, or condemned, but in the end both love and God are ideas that are not at the mercy of human decisions. Our nation is the manifestation of both ideas, and our eager, joyous embrace of both.

Whether it be freedom of expression, the right to own and bear arms, or the right not to be subjected to unlawful searches and seizures, our rights are not given to us by any document. The Bill of Rights, in fact, is a *proscription for the federal government*. It is a message to the Feds about what *not* to touch, about what *not* to toy with, and serves as a reminder to us of what the government is prohibited from doing, not what we are "allowed" to do.

Put simply, it is a warning to government never to think it is God.

The very first case in which the U.S. Supreme Court addressed the Second Amendment in this context was *United States v. Cruikshank*, 92 U.S. 542 (1876). The Court recognized that the right of the people to keep and bear arms was a right that existed *prior to* the Constitution when it stated that such a right "is not a right granted by the Constitution . . . [n]either is it in any manner dependent upon that instrument for its existence."[1]

One of the indications of how powerful the Left has been in this nation is the fact that many Americans, perhaps you, have always believed that the Bill of Rights *granted* us rights. It is imperative that you be disabused of that notion right now. Make no mistake, the Leftists who control our universities and popular culture are loath to have you understand fully how all rights rest with you and not the government.

Why? Because if you were to realize and embrace the truth about how your rights as individuals existed prior to the Constitution, it would be the biggest reminder of your individual importance, your personal power, and your personal dominance over government.

It also broaches the concept that there is a higher authority than the ruling construct of man. Think about it, and consider these few lines from the Declaration of Independence:

> "We hold these truths to be self-evident, that all men are created equal, that they are endowed by their Creator with certain unalienable Rights, that among these are Life, Liberty and the pursuit of Happiness.—That to secure these rights, Governments are instituted among Men. . . ."

With that background and information, there really is only one way to interpret the Bill of Rights and the intentions of Jefferson and the other founders of our nation. At the very heart of their philosophy is the fact that government, regardless of type, should never be considered the supreme ruler, with absolute power. From this concept sprang the tyranny that the colonists wanted to escape.

Naturally, a people of faith recognized that man stood above government, and enjoyed those "certain unalienable rights" granted by our Creator, not by a monarch, or a president, or anyone else. That, yes, our rights exist naturally and not at the whim or generosity of government.

When you think about it, the Court judgment in *Cruikshank* makes perfect sense, considering the intent of the Founding Fathers and their understanding of the totalitarian nature of all government.

The brilliance and beauty of the Constitution and the work of Jefferson and Madison celebrate and elevate the individual person above the machinery of government; above the whims of the elites, which would love to be looked to for governance, advice, and "rights" on a day-to day basis.

A Healthy Distrust of Government

I hear from listeners of my radio program all the time via both e-mail and snail mail. My discussions with them on the air reinforce my faith in the American character and that the revolutionary heart of the founding Americans lives on today in each one of us. Here's a message from a young man who, even being afraid of guns, gets it regarding the vital importance of gun ownership:

Dear Tammy,

I've never owned a gun. I've never even held a real gun in my hand. Once, when I was with someone who had a gun and was examining it, he teased me because I moved as far away from the weapon as possible even though the gun wasn't loaded. Yes, I'm afraid of guns, even ones that are unloaded because I've heard the horror stories about people who were shot dead by guns that were said to be unloaded. I'm also not fond of the idea of hunting.

Nonetheless, I am a fervent supporter of the Second Amendment. If I ever thought the government were to attempt to ban firearms, I would move as quickly as possible to buy a gun. I don't think I'm paranoid, but I don't trust the government. I believe the government may one day provide me with the need for a gun to protect myself. It happened in Nazi Germany, and it could happen here. Like they say, guns don't kill, people kill. Of course, guns can make it easier for people to kill, but it's still the person that commits the act. Liberals, of course, blame only the object—the gun—and forgive the person who pulled the trigger, assuming they ever feel inclined to blame him at all. . . .

Brian

Brian's a regular guy. His support of the Second Amendment is vital. While I recognize the relationship of gun ownership to your sense of self, there is another even more tangible reason to protect the right to bear arms: the nature of government.

Distrust of government is a healthy and normal feeling and assessment. I know it is usually cast as the favorite paranoid obsession of militia members who live somewhere in Idaho. But make no mistake—it's presented that way to marginalize not only those who dare to acknowledge the issue, but the idea itself. Looking askance at government is one of the more important things that helps to keep this nation free.

You can also be suspicious of government while also recognizing the obviously important role it plays in our lives. The constant effort on our part is to trust, then verify, as Ronald Reagan put it when commenting about dealing with the Soviet Union. The same admonition goes for our government.

Certainly, an open society with democratically elected representatives is much more trustworthy than the Evil Empire during Reagan's leadership. I'm certainly not equating our great system with that of the depraved communist system, but government is government, and any type will, if left unchecked and allowed do so, run roughshod over the citizenry. It is its nature to do so.

The American citizen and patriot, in my humble opinion, is one of the best people on earth. I had to ask myself, as you may, how a government made up of Americans could be at risk of slipping into totalitarianism. The simple answer is that politics is the game of seeking power.

A certain type of person is attracted to that game. I noted earlier that our political scene is primarily populated by elites, those who had access to money and power that helped facilitate their political ascent. It also doesn't help that the majority of U.S. senators are lawyers. That alone explains the eventual disconnect between politicians and their constituencies, the lack of principles and malingering moral relativism among many of our own officeholders.

It is the nihilism and moral relativism drilled into students at law school that ultimately provide this nation with politicians who have apparent difficulty discerning right from wrong, or even caring to make the assessment at all. Put people pursuing power in an environment where right and wrong are nothing more than bothersome side issues, and you get the march toward totalitarianism, regardless of the nation, the democratic system, or the goodness of the average citizen.

It should be clearer now that gun ownership not only reminds you of your personal worth and power, politicians in your home capital and in Washington, D.C., are reminded of your power as well. While we've been mostly discussing the concrete realities of guns, this is where the esoteric idea of an armed citizenry makes all the difference—in the back of your mind, Mr. Bad Guy, Politician, or Foreign Power who may wish to do us harm, know that we are armed and capable of protecting ourselves.

Facing Down the Night Stalker

In addition to reinforcing your individualism, owning a firearm has some important and serious concrete benefits. The thing you hear all the time from gun advocates is how difficult it is to prove a negative—that is, how many times a gun has stopped a crime or saved a life.

On the other hand, when a dastardly deed happens with a gun, as when a freak decides to shoot randomly at innocent civilians in the Beltway, we hear about it and all the ensuing drama. With that unbalanced view of reality, it's no wonder Americans (and the rest of the world, for that matter) view firearms with such fear and disdain.

Here's a story to give you just a sense of the sort of event that happens that you would normally never hear about. It is the kind of confrontation every woman fears. And while I can hear the men out there howling now that they, too, have fears, the reality is a man's relationship with the outside world is simply different from a woman's when it comes to issues of safety.

In physical confrontations with menacing men, women usually don't have an ace in the hole against their attacker—we are almost always smaller than any man who might choose to attack us. For a woman, having a gun is indeed the ultimate equalizer, and makes its possessor larger than any beast who might decide he wants something that is not his.

With that in mind, here's a story that is both frightening and enlightening. Knowing I'm a gun enthusiast and feminist, a listener, I'll call her "Julie," wrote to me about an experience she had when facing a beast in front of her own home:

Dear Tammy,

In 1985 I was living in a suburb of San Francisco. I worked evening shift, and arrived home every night around 11:00 P.M. My partner, a Deputy Sheriff, would arrive home later, around midnight.

I have always felt comfortable with guns, but my experience has always been at a shooting range. I am too tender-hearted to hunt, and until this incident, had never pointed a gun at another human being. . . . As I came around the corner into my quiet, well-lit neighborhood, my view extended 2–3 blocks, and at a glance I could see that there was no one out on the sidewalk. As I drove up to, and into my driveway, I noticed no one in any vehicle. The houses were dark, the middle class neighborhood was mostly asleep.

I parked in the driveway, and was outside the car, leaning back into the car across the driver's seat to gather up some clothing and my briefcase from the other seat. While in this position, I noticed a fleeting shadow move across the garage door in my peripheral vision. At that same moment I instantly experienced a shudder, an immediate sense of extreme danger. My heart skipped a beat, the hair on my neck bristled, and prior to standing upright I reached under the front seat to grasp the .38 caliber handgun hidden there.

As I stood upright, and turned in the direction of the street, I brought the handgun up straight in front of me in one smooth motion. There, as close as my rear bumper, stood a man who had appeared literally out of nowhere. I knew he had not been on the sidewalk only a minute or two before. I knew he had to have been hiding in the bushes along the driveway in my yard.

I stood there facing him, just a few feet away, with the

handgun pointed directly at his chest. He seemed tall to me (I was 5'1" and weighed 105 lbs), he had a dark complexion, appeared Hispanic or Asian. He wore a dark knit stocking cap pulled down to near his eyebrows, and wore an oversized Army style parka with lots of pockets. He kept his arms folded across his chest, with his hands tucked inside the jacket as though concealing something in both hands. He said nothing to me. Instead, he just stood there silently grinning at me, as if almost taunting me to pull the trigger.

Nothing. We said nothing. We stood there silently for what seemed like a very long time. He just grinned at me. Although I was too frightened to talk, my head was still thinking, and I was watching his every twitch. He was very menacing in his presence, and seemed extremely dangerous, but I knew I couldn't, wouldn't shoot him for just being here at the rear of my car. I also knew in my heart that if he made any forward movement in my direction, or pulled his hands out from under his jacket, and had anything clasped in them, that I would fire the gun at him.

After staring at my gun and face for some time, I think he sensed that too. He continued with his silent broad smile until he suddenly stepped backwards, turned, and bolted down the street. He ran several blocks in the direction of a nearby park & lake.

I immediately phoned the police regarding the incident sans my having a gun pointed at the man. I knew that due to my having a gun readily available "to point," would most likely make me the center of the police attention, not the man who had run away.

It was the next morning we awoke and learned the "Night Stalker" [Richard Ramirez, the Los Angeles area serial killer] *had made his way to the Bay Area. He attacked a sleeping couple in their bedroom who lived bordering the lake where the man had gone after running from my house. One of the*

victims died. The Night Stalker left distinctive markings at
crime scenes, and was rapidly identified as the killer. . . .

Because of my partner's status as a Deputy, there was al-
ways a loaded handgun under the driver's seat. Although I'm
sure having the gun there was illegal, I'm here to tell you that
if it had not been readily available that August night, I would
not be writing to you now. I would just have been another of
Richard Ramirez's victims.

Julie

Julie's is not the kind of story you will normally hear, primarily
because "nothing happened" in the conventional sense. As you
know now, something extraordinary and important did happen that
night, but it is not the sort of event that our politically correct and
disabled society embraces or appreciates. Certainly the Leftist
media are loath to report stories where even just the presence of a
gun saved a life.

Julie notes the handgun was never fired, yet it saved her life. In
her e-mail she reminded me of what she learned about Richard
Ramirez's twisted psychological profile: He believed he was a soldier
in Satan's Army, and had been given the task of killing "weak" and
"vulnerable" people.

Open windows with curtains blowing were especially inviting to
him, and unarmed women, people asleep in their beds, or anyone
who would not fight him were marked for death. He believed that
anyone who offered resistance or displayed strength was also a soldier, and was to be spared harm. Ultimately, he was charged with
nineteen counts of murder. Because of her gun, Julie wasn't among
them.

We have been told most of our lives that it is the availability of
guns that causes crime. Guns are dangerous. Guns are the problem.
Guns kill. If you take one thing away with you from this chapter, I
want it to be your understanding of something which, while a cliché,
is also true: Guns do not cause crime or murder, people do.

Washington, D.C. (District of Chaos)

When some are faced with the proposition that individuals are responsible for events, not inanimate objects, their usual retort is: "Well, ah gosh, it couldn't hurt to get rid of guns anyway—nothing good comes from them, so what's the harm?"

That is not only a false premise, it is dangerous. Guns in fact do save lives.

In her book *Guns and Violence*,[2] Professor Joyce Lee Malcolm provides evidence that firearms actually reduce violence:

- National polls of defensive gun use by private citizens indicate that as many as 3.6 million crimes annually are prevented by armed individuals.

- As many as 400,000 people each year believe they saved a life by being armed. Contrary to Handgun Control's propaganda, in fewer than 1 percent of confrontations do criminals succeed in taking the gun from the intended victim.

- Thirty-four percent of felons said they were scared off, wounded, or captured by victims who turned out to be armed.

Even more telling, the seventeen states (and the District of Columbia) without concealed-carry permits suffer an 81 percent higher rate of violent crime. In fact, restrictive gun laws produced 1,400 more murders, 4,200 more rapes, 12,000 more robberies, and 60,000 more aggravated assaults.[3]

How is this possible? Let's agree for a moment with the premise that guns do not have minds of their own—like a kitchen knife, or an automobile, or a hammer—a gun's use for good or evil is dependent on the person in charge of it. Only when a gun gets up and makes you breakfast can you claim it thinks for itself. Now consider the fact that only law-abiding citizens respect and follow the law; ergo, laws only affect the law-abiding.

This explains why a community like the District of Columbia, with some of the most restrictive gun laws in the nation, was again declared the Murder Capital of the nation for 2003, according to a study released by SafeStreetsDC.com. They compared the annual number of murders per 100,000 residents in American cities with populations greater than 500,000. This was the same standard used to determine D.C.'s previous year's rank as Murder Capital.

For the past thirty years it has been illegal to own a handgun in D.C., giving criminals and savages carte blanche. As the national crime rate has declined, D.C.'s has gone up. Finally, in 2003, the D.C. chief of police declared a "crime emergency." That's an awfully ironic position to be in considering the banning of guns was supposed to make everyone safer.

Think about it—criminals *know* that the citizens of D.C. are unarmed. Those who would rob, rape, or kill you know the odds are automatically in favor of them having their way and getting away with their crime. They know there will be no "Julies" there to stare them down with a .38 pointed at their chests.

While it is hell for the residents of D.C., that town has unwittingly proven the absurdity of the antigun crusaders' favorite claim that banning guns makes people safer. If that were truly the case, Washington, D.C., would be heaven on earth—a bastion of safety and love. Instead, its homicide rate and violent crime statistics make it more violent and unsafe than Baghdad.

If you think the D.C. example is a fluke, consider Modoc County in California. What's different about Modoc? Forget about simply owning a gun—according to the state's Department of Justice, one in twenty-nine citizens has a concealed-weapons permit. Compare that to one in eight hundred for the rest of the state, and equal to the number of permits issued in Los Angeles County, which has fifty times the population.

Bruce Mix, the sheriff of Modoc County and the person responsible for issuing concealed-weapons permits, said, in addition to his not having enough deputies to patrol the vastness of his county, he believes everyone who lives in the country has a constitutional right to self-protection.[4]

If you consider the primary argument of gun-control fanatics, that access to and availability of firearms cause people to kill each other, will result in epidemics of violence, the sky will fall, and cats and dogs will begin sleeping with each other, Modoc County must be the most dangerous, violent place in California, and perhaps the whole nation.

Of course, the opposite is true. The truth of the matter is, as reported by the *Los Angeles Times,* "Records kept by the state attorney general's office indicate that violent crimes occur here at less than one-third the rate in Los Angeles County. According to FBI statistics, there was only one homicide in Modoc County from 1993 through 2002. Sheriff Mix says the county averages about one 'questionable death a year, including suicide.' "5

The facts of this situation are this: In cities and counties where firearms can be legally owned, crime is lower than in cities where draconian gun-control laws prevail. And in counties where concealed-weapons permits are liberally granted, crime plummets.

The reasons are obvious and worth repeating: Laws only affect the law-abiding. Criminals and those who wish to do us harm, like terrorists, will always have access to and get the weapons of their choice.

Shouldn't We Ban Airplanes Instead?

Those bent on banning guns in this country have no shame, and have even invoked the war on terrorism in their efforts to brainwash you into believing that you will only be safe if Big Daddy Government confiscates your firearms.

When discussing the sun setting in September 2004 of the so-called assault weapons ban, Senator Charles Schumer, a Democrat from New York, bizarrely claimed the ban is one of "the most effective measures against terrorism we have."6

What planet is that man on! Here is one of the senators from New

York, one of the targets of the terrorism of Radical Islamist savages. Last time I checked, the preferred weapons of choice of those freaks of nature were automobiles and trucks with bombs and passenger jets to commit mass murder.

It would be worth noting to the senator that it is also illegal to slit the throats of flight attendants and fly jumbo jets into buildings to kill thousands of people, but the terrorists did it anyway.

Why? *Because terrorists do not follow the law.* The only thing banning weapons does is make law-abiding, decent Americans more vulnerable to any type of attack, including that of the terrorist variety. Even the Homeland Security bureaucracy seems to get this point, allowing pilots to arm themselves and placing armed air marshals on flights.

Of course, guns in the hands of the law abiding is a good thing in the fight against terrorism. Terrorists and others meaning to do this nation harm must know that anyone who dares to come to this nation to murder Americans, or even dare to invade our shores, will indeed be met with a populace armed like no other.

Hollywood provides one of the more entertaining (and realistic) examples of what an armed enemy would find with an armed American citizenry. In 1984, with a Soviet threat still looming large, the film *Red Dawn* was released, depicting a group of armed teenagers taking on the Soviet army in the mountains of Colorado and defeating the enemy to liberate their town.

In this instance, art imitates life.

When you compare D.C. and Modoc, it seems quite obvious that guns aren't "evil" any more than box cutters or airplanes are "evil."

If you think I'm being an alarmist when it comes to the intent of our government to disarm the American public, and their willingness to cynically use the scourge of terrorism to do it, consider this comment:

> When anyone uses a firearm, whether it's the kind of terrorism that we are trying to combat with al Qaeda and these

non-state terrorists, or as a former district attorney involved in the conviction of an individual who used firearms against innocent citizens—regardless of how we define terrorism. . . . Brandishing a firearm in front of anybody under any set of circumstances is a terrorist act and needs to be dealt with.

Now, we all agree that a crime, committed with a gun or not, should be prosecuted to the fullest extent of the law. What this person is suggesting, however, is extraordinarily ominous and reveals a much larger agenda of labeling any use of a firearm, by anyone under any circumstance, as a *terrorist* act.

You may try to find solace thinking something this alarming was uttered by some staffer or someone on the lunatic fringe. Well, think again, and worry. *It's a quote from then–Homeland Security Secretary Tom Ridge* in January 2003, testifying to the Senate Government Affairs Committee.[7]

Gun Owners as Terrorists

Consider very carefully what Ridge is suggesting—that the use of a firearm by a citizen is the equivalent of a terrorist act committed by Al Qaeda. The key is this phrase, ". . . regardless of how we define terrorism." This should be an immediate red flag for all of us. Ridge is implying that the definition of "terrorism" will be expanded beyond the Radical Islamist savages who have declared war on this nation.

Note also the last line of Ridge's quote—his declaration that "brandishing a firearm in front of anybody under any set of circumstances is a terrorist act and needs to be dealt with."

Really? Should we label Julie a "terrorist"? And what about anyone else who "brandishes" a gun in the name of self-defense? Are they "terrorists," too? From the *American Rifleman Magazine*,[8] consider these self-defense actions of other law-abiding, decent Americans who, in Tom Ridge's world, should be labeled terrorists:

- From the *Fresno Bee:* A 20-year-old man on an alleged crime spree eventually picked the wrong house where he allegedly attempted to stab resident Lonnie Dugger. The armed citizen then put a stop to the rampage by shooting the deranged man once in the arm and detaining him until sheriff's deputies could arrive.

- From the *Oakland Tribune:* An 82-year-old retired Air Force pilot and his wife of 59 years were awakened early one morning to the sounds of someone rummaging through their Oakland, California, area home. When an intruder turned on the homeowner, he was met with a single, fatal shot from the same pistol that had seen the veteran through World War II, Korea, and Vietnam.

- From *The Bee,* in Modesto, California: Lillian Hazard wasn't kidding when she told an intruder in her Riverside, California, home he should "lay down or I'll shoot you." Obviously thinking the 85-year-old grandmother wouldn't shoot, the man tried to stand. Hazard shot him in the shoulder. "I wasn't scared, because I had my gun," said Hazard.

- From the *San Diego Union-Tribune:* An El Cajon, California, woman was relaxing with her two-year-old child when she heard a noise in a bedroom and decided to investigate. Upon finding an unknown male intruder there, she picked up a handgun and yelled, "Go away!" but the man advanced. A second warning from the woman went unheeded so she shot the housebreaker once in the chest. The man left the house and fell unconscious in the street where police arrested him.

I've said on my radio program repeatedly that during time of war, small retreats on "civil rights" are indeed necessary, when they address finding, arresting, or killing our enemy. In fact, each time our nation has been at war, we have given law enforcement the tools to root out the enemy here and abroad. The important historical note to remember, though, is that this nation has always come back stronger after war on civil rights issues, primarily because the people have demanded it.

We should applaud and approve actions that help us find and defeat the enemy, but we should also be wary of and reject efforts used under the guise of Homeland Security that impinge on the rights of decent, law-abiding Americans.

Of course, groups like the ACLU, with their malignant hatred for this country, argue that all tools given to law enforcement are oppressive, even if they are designed to keep us safer. The ACLU's view is as absurd as security agents at airports strip-searching eighty-year-old grandmothers from Des Moines.

Be aware, however, that if what Ridge said became policy, it would not exist in a vacuum. Remember Senator Schumer's bizarre statement that banning assault weapons is one of the best tools we have to combat terrorism? These are the footfalls of the quiet attempt to demonize gun owners and shift American sentiment toward the complete ban on all firearms, especially handguns.

Death by Incrementalism

There is a method to the madness of equating gun owners with terrorists. In fact, it is a cynical manipulation that should not surprise us. Those who are antigun have found the American public understands and embraces the brilliance of the Constitution and the intentions of the Founding Fathers. Those who are antigun have been unable to overcome clearly articulated arguments about the importance of the Second Amendment and the facts about how gun ownership actually prevents violence.

So, if you're opposed to guns, what do you do if reality, facts, and deep-rooted American values are against you? You co-opt the emotional reaction Americans have about another Bad Guy—terrorists—and paint the issues as one and the same. And presto! You have instant strong public support for something that might only capture a small minority of the public otherwise.

There is also a realization among those who prefer a totalitarian government that laws that restrict our natural rights cannot be implemented overnight. The citizenry needs to be snuck up on. You would notice a rock being smashed to bits right in front of you, but you may indeed pass by a stone slowly eroded by drops of water. So, too, with our right to bear arms.

Still not convinced? Take it from a 1993 editorial in the Left's Paper of Record, the *New York Times*:

> Gun violence won't be cured by one set of laws. It will require years of partial measures that will gradually tighten the requirements for gun ownership, and incrementally change expectations about the firepower that should be available to ordinary citizens.[9]

What other extraordinary insight did the *Times* offer with this editorial? The same stunningly absurd premise all antigun advocates promulgate—banning guns will keep people safe from Bad Guys. The *Times* declared:

> The gunman who shot 23 passengers on a Long Island railroad commuter train two weeks ago allegedly emptied two chambers of 15 cartridges each and was reloading . . . cutting that chamber capacity from 15 to 10 would increase the survival odds for the law-abiding public.

It is astounding to see so exposed such blind, ignorant stubbornness on an issue. Look closely: Here the *Times* lauds the idea of making illegal 15-shot cartridges as they are writing about a man who had no regard for the law in the first place and set out to murder innocent people. It's safe to say that he would feel comfortable breaking the law, including the size of his cartridge.

But even more important, they then have the shocking gall to declare that this type of law would increase the law-abiding public's *survival odds* against a maniac. This in and of itself acknowledges that not only do gun laws not keep the innocent safe, they do not keep guns out of the hands of criminals.

Let's get real here—the only thing that would increase the survival odds for the law-abiding public is if they were able to shoot back at any maniac shooting at them.

This type of fantasy social engineering and brainwashing will only work if we let it. When you hear individual statements like Schumer's or Ridge's, they're easy to reject as oddly extremist and nonsensical. These guys didn't have a bad day, they have an agenda. Taken together, I contend they represent the new approach to prepare Americans for the confiscation of all firearms—ironically, in the name of ending terrorism and crime.

I say "ironically" because if that were to happen there are two things that will immediately destroy America—violent crime and terrorism. Just ask the people of Washington, D.C.

From the Horses' . . . Mouths

Still not convinced that the ultimate goal of the Left and its government operatives is to ban all guns? Consider these statements:

"I don't know why people carry guns. Guns kill people."—NYC Mayor Michael Bloomberg, July 2003.

Tammy Bruce: "I don't know why people fly on airplanes. Airplanes kill people."

"We can't be so fixated on our desire to preserve the rights of ordinary Americans to own firearms . . . that we are unable to think about reality."—President Bill Clinton, March 1, 1993.

Tammy Bruce: "Reality demands that we eliminate those pesky rights of 'ordinary' Americans. But 'extraordinary' Americans can keep their rights, including the right to have gun-wielding bodyguards."

"Banning guns addresses a fundamental right of all Americans to feel safe."—U.S. Senator Dianne Feinstein, Associated Press, November 18, 1993.

Tammy Bruce: "Hmm. Perhaps Senator Feinstein should venture beyond the Hart Senate Office Building in Washington, D.C., without her bodyguards or driver, and hang out where senators dare not venture: into the heart of the Murder Capital of the United States. Perhaps then she'd find out how 'safe' people feel in a gun-free zone. But then again, *feeling* safe can be entirely contrary to actually *being* safe, especially when you've been lied to about the impact of gun laws."

"If it were up to me, we'd ban them all."—Representative Mel Reynolds, CNN *Crossfire*, December 9, 1993.

Tammy Bruce: "I trust you, Mel Reynolds, especially after you received a commutation from Bill Clinton of your six-and-a-half-year federal sentence for fifteen convictions of wire fraud, bank fraud, and lies to the Federal Election Commission. And I really trust you after you were sentenced to five years for sleeping with an underage campaign volunteer. I'm so glad Jesse Jackson's Rainbow/Pu$h Coalition took you in as a 'Youth Counselor' after you left public office."[10]

And these are the people who so distrust the people of the United States that they want to take away your right to own a firearm. Hmmm, I wonder why.

Charles Krauthammer, *Washington Post* columnist, states:

Ultimately, a civilized society must disarm its citizenry if it is to have a modicum of domestic tranquility of the kind enjoyed by sister democracies such as Canada and Britain. Given the frontier history and individualist ideology of the United States, however, this will not come easily. . . . Passing a law like the assault weapons ban is a symbolic—purely symbolic—move in that direction. Its only real justification is not to reduce crime but to desensitize the public to the regulation of weapons in preparation for their ultimate confiscation.[11]

At least Krauthammer's comments reveal that some are concertedly lying to the population about their actual agenda—not gun "control" but gun confiscation. For those of you who consider Krauthammer to be conservative, you may be surprised by his sentiment. Wrongheadedness isn't confined just to the Left, and for a man who worked for the Carter administration and wrote speeches for Walter Mondale during his run for the presidency, it's even less surprising.

What's actually laughable about Krauthammer's comments is the absurdity of his referring to Canada and England as having a "modicum of domestic tranquility" due to gun laws. That's like saying people will never go hungry again because the moon is made of cheese.

Don't be fooled. Here's the truth about both England and Canada.

In 1996, after the murder of sixteen children and a teacher in Dunblane, Scotland, by a deranged man, the British decided that banning all handguns would reduce violent crime. Handgun owners complied and turned in all their guns by the February 1998 deadline.

The theory, of course, was that the United Kingdom was supposed to become a safer place. Just the opposite has happened.

According to an article in the *Edmonton Journal*, in the four years since the U.K. gun ban, "the incidence of gun crime in England and Wales nearly doubled from 13,874 in 1998 to 24,070 in 2003. And the incidence of firearms murder, while thankfully still very small, has risen 65 per cent."[12]

The article details statistics from another report issued in 2003 by Britain's Home Office, which reveal that there has also been a dramatic increase in robberies in recent years. They report that robberies "rose by 28 per cent in 2002 alone and, since 1998, there has been an increase in the annual average of muggings of more than 100,000. England alone has nearly 400,000 robberies each year, a rate nearly one-quarter higher per capita than that of the United States."[13]

And Canada—Krauthammer's other gun-free nirvana? Our northern neighbor has reported a dramatic increase in the percentage of handguns used in all homicides during a period in which handguns were most strictly regulated.[14]

Domestic tranquillity? Please. It's clear some prefer delusion to accepting the facts that they're wrong about gun control.

Snipers and Politicians

Perhaps one of the best-known examples of both the failure of gun control and how swamped in groupthink antigun fanatics are come to us via the awful Beltway snipers who left ten people dead in the metropolitan Washington, D.C., area, during three weeks of October 2002.

As a defender of the Second Amendment, I knew it was only a matter of time before opponents of our right to bear arms couldn't stand it anymore and started to exploit the tragedy brought to us by cowardly freaks Lee Boyd Malvo and John Allen Muhammad. Prior to the capture of the murderers, antigun political candidates used it to make hay with their self-defense-supporting opponents; professional haters of firearms shouted from hill and dale that the sky was falling.

After all, they argued, look at what happens when people get guns! Look at the tragedy brought to us by firearms, was the call of Chicken Littles everywhere. Ginni Wolf, executive director of Marylanders Against Handgun Abuse, declared that the Beltway snipers have proved her group's argument that there are "too many guns out there, and it's very easy for these types of people to obtain guns."[15]

On the contrary. What the snipers have proved is that there aren't enough firearms in the hands of law-abiding citizens! Here's a newsflash for Ms. Wolf—the Beltway is a *gun-free zone*. There, law-abiding citizens do not carry weapons, leaving them unarmed and defenseless to face a maniac killer who does not care about rules.

Smack-dab in the middle of the sniper shootings, then–Lieutenant

Governor of Maryland Kathleen Kennedy Townsend took out a thirty-second ad criticizing her opponent in Maryland's gubernatorial race. A voice in the ad says Bob Ehrlich voted "against banning assault weapons and cheap handguns" while the viewer is shown a row of high-powered rifles and a man pulling a handgun from his pocket.[16]

Politicizing that event was unseemly, but it did illustrate once again how willing politicians are to exploit events that cause fear and trepidation within us. Let that be your first clue, however, that facts and reason are on our side, when opponents can do nothing but use emotion and exploitation to further their agenda.

The snipers weren't cowed, nor are terrorists, by gun laws or the firearms-are-evil rhetoric from Kathleen Kennedy Townsend. Gun laws wouldn't have saved her father, Robert Kennedy, just as they didn't save the innocent people who were murdered by a deranged sniper and his accomplice. The savage and the criminal will always get their guns, just as those who wanted a drink during Prohibition got their booze.

Clearly, Ms. Kennedy Townsend is missing a lesson she could have learned from her own grandfather's legacy—someone with the determination and the right connections can easily make a mockery of the law, and themselves quite rich.

Those who argue that Americans should be disarmed are naïve, irresponsible, and promoting arguments that are ultimately fatally dangerous, not only for human life but also for liberty itself.

It is law-abiding citizens like myself and so many others who own firearms who not only are personally safer, but also keep this country free. If the antigun zealots insist on cynically politicizing the situations with the snipers, terrorism, and crime, those of us who support the Second Amendment have a duty to stand up and remind people that gun ownership is an issue of civil rights and self-defense.

Those who argue to disarm us simply do not trust Americans and perhaps even despise what has made this country great—traits like the individualism fostered by rights like the Second Amendment.

It is time to reject the Left's vacuous arguments that we Americans need to be protected from ourselves and cannot be trusted to implement self-defense. Europe's history has shown us that a defenseless citizenry invites nothing less than criminal anarchy and tyrannical dictatorships.

While the Left wants you to believe that you need to be protected from yourself, it took terrorism and two serial killers to show us who the real enemies are, and they're not you and me—they're those who salivate at the idea that only government, the military, law enforcement, and savages will be armed. You can ask the people of China, Cuba, North Korea, and Washington, D.C., what that's like.

Action Steps for the New Radical Individual

1. Realize and truly understand that gun ownership is not only a fundamental personal right, but a key to exercising and developing your personal sense of individualism.

2. Join and support organizations that defend the Second Amendment and the right to gun ownership, as well as counter the lies of antigun operatives. There are many excellent groups out there that educate, inform, and train. Learn about them and choose and support the one that best suits your interests and concerns. Among them are:

The National Rifle Association
Widely recognized today as a major political force and as America's foremost defender of Second Amendment rights, the NRA has, since its inception, been also the premier firearms education organization in the world.
www.nra.org

Gun Owners of America
"The only no compromise gun lobby in Washington."
www.gunowners.org 703-321-8585

Liberty Belles

"Putting the Second Amendment First."

A national membership organization with a focus on women gun owners.

http://www.liberty-belles.org/

3. **Become a gun owner,** if you're not one already. Of course, only people who are comfortable with owning a firearm and will train to use it properly should take this step. If you are at all unsure, then don't do it, but in the meantime, commit to Action Step 2 and support organizations that support the right itself.

4. **Be vocal** about your support of the Second Amendment. This is especially important in our increasingly toxic politically correct society in which the Left would prefer that you not speak up about issues like gun ownership. When people hear others speaking confidently about any issue, it gives them permission to consider the idea.

5. **Stay informed and get active.** Antigun operatives, both in government and Leftist special-interest groups, are obsessed with comprehensively banning firearms. As they chip away at the Second Amendment, they count on you not noticing, not caring, or being brainwashed by their fear-based spin. Prove them wrong—all of the organizations I noted above have plenty of things you can do to make a difference and counter those who would leave you disarmed and defenseless.

6

Tearing Down the Institutions

Every revolution was first a thought in one man's mind.

—RALPH WALDO EMERSON

Think about Dan Rather and CBS News being so obsessed with destroying President Bush that they smear him with fake documents just prior to the 2004 presidential election. Remember the mini-series *The Reagans*, which paints both President and Mrs. Reagan as homophobic miscreants? Think about VH1's *Music Behind Bars*, which morphs child killers, murderers, and rapists into "rock stars." Think about paying $3.5 million to stop fifty separate indecency investigations by the FCC, including a radio show that prompted people to have sex at St. Patrick's Cathedral.

These examples are just the tip of the iceberg, and while they contribute to cultural nihilism, they also have something else in common: They spring from the loins of Sumner Redstone's Viacom, Incorporated. There's a thing called "corporate culture." It's the environmental dynamic fostered within a corporation to reflect the desires of its leadership, primarily its CEO. When it comes to Viacom's culture, we're dealing with Redstone's view of the world, and it's not a pretty sight.

Simply put, when it comes to Redstone, you have a Malignant Narcissist in control of one of America's largest media conglomerates, with a nihilistic view of life and an obsessed effort at making your world look like his.

And the *New York Times*—so much needs to be said. The *Times* has sunk from respected newspaper into birdcage litter paper. Blatantly partisan, its Leftist agenda has completely eclipsed even a modicum of effort by its editorial staff to even *appear* fair.

Attacks on conservatives, a continuing jihad against Christians, coordination with Redstone's CBS to smear the president with a dismal 2004 October Surprise (explosives are missing in Iraq, that bastion of peace and safety before we barbarians entered the gates!), opinion slopped on as "news," morose editorials, and commentary about how the end of the world is near because Republicans win elections.

In the world of the *New York Times,* all is hopeless, America is evil, and George W. Bush drinks the blood of your children. No wonder Leftists and Kerry supporters are depressed! At the rate the *Times* doles out Doom and Gloom you'd think they make a commission on every Zoloft pill sold.

With their All-Victims-All-the-Time agenda, the *Times* feeds the anger, isolationism, and hate that now consumes the Left and even well-intentioned liberals who have been conditioned to believe that the *Times* is on their side. Furthermore, the *Times* is looked to, essentially, as the Desk Sergeant for mainstream media. It sets the tone and the direction, the agenda, and gives permission for others to move biased, Leftist-based coverage to the nation.

I consider the *New York Times* and Viacom the media companies at the heart of what's damaging our culture. These entities are important, as they are the most aggressive and most determined to have their way with our culture; they set the standard (or substandard) for other news outlets; and they have determined that they will do whatever they can to perpetuate their morose, victimized, and valueless worldview in our society.

Just because an entity has been around for a long time doesn't mean it is entitled to exist. I think it's clear to all of us that a world without the Internal Revenue Service, the *New York Times*, Viacom, and the ACLU would be a better place.

So let's get started.

I know that the cultural cesspool we face is not the result of these two media companies alone. And the idea itself of changing, eliminating, or even "tearing down" entities that seem to deserve to exist is in itself rather revolutionary.

My work, while it addresses politics and popular culture, is really about the quality of our own lives—are we in charge of our lives, or is a removed, disconnected, sordid elite running a media conglomerate going to be? The Media Elite further the agenda of the Leftist Thought Police and the perpetuation of the moral relativism that continues to eat away at our culture.

Not surprisingly, the disconnected, malevolent Media Elite have only gotten worse in the last few years, but one thing has changed—our attitude about what's acceptable. And even more important than that—our realization that we can indeed make a difference.

It's both ironic and sad. The sources we've traditionally been able to rely on—a historic newspaper, the *Times*, and a company supposedly committed to a variety of entertainment, Viacom—end up being the Anticulture or, to adapt a phrase, the Cultural Axis of Evil. And now it is their day of reckoning.

Before we launch into this revolutionary action plan for the Radical Individual, I do want to address what may be popping into some of your minds right now as you read this: "How can I make a difference? I'm only one person . . . there's no way what I do will matter." Let me assure you, what you do *does* matter. It matters in so many ways. Let me explain.

One Bite at a Time

First of all, when we think of the handmaidens of cultural rot, it can get a little overwhelming. There just seem to be too many forces trying to tear down our culture, and the problem of Leftist media is only one insidious, albeit massive, part of the problem.

And, really, forget about calling it "liberal" media; that infers some sort of value-based programming. No, what we're dealing with now, just as with the Democrat party, is no longer liberals, but nihilistic Leftists who have indeed grown to hate this nation so much they work, both consciously and subconsciously, to destroy America as we know it.

When it comes to the mainstream, about 85 percent of media is controlled by Leftists, with 15 percent considered "conservative." Of course, anything not acting as a propaganda arm for the Democrats or the Leftist agenda is considered conservative these days.

But for argument's sake alone, those kinds of numbers can be pretty daunting when contemplating whether or not the individual can actually have an impact.

Whenever I felt overwhelmed with my work as president of Los Angeles NOW, I was encouraged with a well-known metaphor: When the task at hand seemed insurmountable or even perhaps impossible, I was told to "eat the elephant one bite at a time."

This is my first request of you—when looking at how you can make a difference, don't focus on the whole problem all at once. Take on the monster one bite at a time.

Actually, there are several fronts where your taking action can make a world of difference. The first, and possibly even most important, attack is on your own frame of mind. One of the most disturbing trends among individuals in our culture is the feeling that things—media, politics, culture—are so big, so controlled, so beyond us, that we're simply along for the ride.

That's simply not so. Taking a stand, however small or large, reinforces in your own mind the fact that you are a player, you matter, you have free will and will be heard.

Interestingly, Left-wing activists are schooled in the belief that a collective can and does make a difference. It is a wing of politics that relies on group pressure and even threats to change the cultural or political scheme.

On the other hand, I have found that individuals who identify as conservative tend to doubt their influence or eschew collective action because they have seen the damage wrought by groupthink and Identity Politics.

In other words, and to borrow one of the more amusing comparisons, organizing conservatives into grassroots action is a bit like herding cats.

Of course, we cannot dismiss the impact of the New Thought Police on your sense of comfort confronting this nation's cultural enemies. After all, you have been conditioned to believe that stepping up to the plate to face down the Leftists who are trashing our nation may get you called a racist, a sexist, or a homophobe. And make no mistake, the Cultural Axis of Evil we will begin to confront has played a major role in conditioning you into that discomfort.

And remember—getting called these names and actually being those things are two very different things.

One of my main complaints about the Left is the fact that it is there where racism, sexism, and homophobia truly thrive. It's an interesting experience of mass projection by the Left—accusing conservatives and the religious when the ugliness of all those isms is refined and honed within the very special-interest groups that claim to fight against them.

I have to admit, although I've written about the problems at the *New York Times* or Viacom before, and felt both entities were completely lost in a sort of Leftist tar pit, I have always had a little bit of hope that somehow, someway, they would change.

Perhaps it's the optimist in me, but I always felt that the marketplace would not continue to stand for Leftist propaganda presented as "news" by one of the nation's most important newspapers. I felt Americans, collectively, would finally recognize the damage Viacom's programming was doing to mainstream culture.

It's time both machines find out who's boss. It's not a publisher, managing editors, CEOs, or producers. It's you and me. It's our culture and our politics, and it's time we not only remind ourselves of this fact, but it's also time these cultural bullies get a major dose of reality about who is in charge of the marketplace. They must realize by our actions that we have not only had enough, but we're ready and willing to take action.

It's a Pillbug!

Your choosing to take a stand, big or small, against a corporate entity that moves the Left's nihilist agenda, first reminds you that you are in charge, you matter, you can make a difference. The Left has worked very hard to make you feel as though there's nothing you can do (or should do) about American "institutions" such as the large newspaper or huge mega-media corporations determined to drown you in their cultural nihilistic cesspool.

When I became president of Los Angeles NOW, I really looked at it as a hobby. Frankly, I had no clue what the job would entail; I was politically clueless. I act on what is right, I don't compromise well, and I have a firm grip on right and wrong. I want to make a difference and improve the quality of people's lives. That's all I knew when I was elected president in 1989.

How I was going to make a difference really hadn't occurred to me. I had no idea how the system worked, nor had I thought far beyond winning that local election. While I have made clear my critique of NOW as an entity, I must tell you that being a Leftist grassroots activist taught me about the power of the individual. I saw firsthand the impact one determined and focused person can have.

How? Being a feminist activist allowed me to see culture in a very special way. The Leftists who control our culture have created a brilliant external façade—very much like the Wizard of Oz, they present their special-interest groups and corporate foot soldiers as huge, impenetrable megaliths that are bigger than you and beyond your reach.

But the image the Left presents of these institutions of giant, scary creatures is just that—an *image*. To my surprise, I saw the underbelly of that creature, and it's really much more like a pillbug—all scaly, uniform, and resilient on the outside, but with a shallow and vulnerable underside. The only way to keep you from poking around and discovering that vulnerability is (a) to make you feel it is personally dangerous to do so (accomplished by brainwashing you), and (b) to make themselves appear all-powerful and too important—too established, too permanent—to disturb.

How do I know what's under that apparently armored exterior of the Left? I know because I was one of those armor plates, meant to frighten Americans into acquiescing to the Leftist agenda. I was able to accomplish my mission of seeming huge, powerful, and morally righteous with the help of the press. I was only one person leading only a few other radicals, but once I made a decision about a lobbying agenda, boycott, or other action, my success relied on the media facilitating the lie of great power.

You see, power only exists if the target acknowledges it. It is a dynamic that relies on a give-and-take—as a Leftist activist, my power relied on others responding as though I had power. It's like if you throw a party and no one comes—then it's not a party at all, is it? As a Leftist, I had to convince the general populace that I had power and was in control of whatever I was promoting. If I wasn't believed, or was ignored, then it meant nothing.

But with the help of the press, I was believed because the media paid attention. On purpose. That is how the alternate Leftist/media reality is created, and for far too long you've played a role in that false front by accepting what you hear and responding as though it were true.

I must ask you to forgive some of my past actions, but I can tell you now that those experiences are what gives me the information with which I can now show you what has been happening. I wasn't the first to implement this—I was trained to do so. And it continues today. Courtesy of the *New York Times* newspapers, and CBS News, among others.

Potatoes and Abortion

I recall quite distinctly when I first began to realize that mainstream media were my political partners, for lack of a better phrase, in feminist activism.

In 1990, the abortion war was in full swing. There were a variety of states that were looking to pass laws that could be used to challenge *Roe v. Wade* at the U.S. Supreme Court level. Idaho was one of those states.

The statehouse of Idaho was sending one of the most restrictive antiabortion measures in the nation to then-governor Cecil Andrus. We all knew if he signed that legislation, the next natural step was to appeal to the U.S. Supreme Court, which is exactly what abortion opponents were hoping for.

Although only in my first year as president of Los Angeles NOW, I learned quickly that the media was my friend. With no strong feminist establishment in Idaho, I knew I could use media based in Los Angeles to put national pressure on Andrus. I contacted the various heads of Leftist organizations in Los Angeles, including the ACLU, NARAL, and the Feminist Majority. I called a press conference and invited everyone to participate. I decided we would announce a boycott of Idaho potatoes if Andrus signed the abortion bill.

While I realize many of you are pro-life, I share this story with you to illustrate the power of one person. You must consider the fact that the idea was mine alone, and other Leftist leaders thought it a good idea (it was obviously a rather standard approach to consumer-based activism). It was only made possible, however, with the complicity of the media.

I put out a call one day, and the next day we had our press conference with over two dozen cameras. Press included local, national, and even international media. I was very new to the activist scene, but even the Leftist veterans there were amazed at the turnout.

Ultimately, our Idaho press conference was major news that day. My statement, despite my being an uppity twenty-eight-year-old in Los Angeles and new to activism, received the most attention. Representing a local NOW chapter with just a few thousand members, I arrogantly and without any clue how it could actually be implemented, declared, "If the state of Idaho declares war on the women of this nation, the women of this nation will declare war on the state of Idaho."

Make no mistake, I meant it. But it only became reality because the media gave it cachet. The statement itself became the organizing tool. Without the media, my activism would have been hopeless and useless. I knew, however, that the media were on my side, and I made much use of them during my entire career at NOW.

In addition to immediately reaching millions of people, the media save the Left extraordinary amounts of money and time organizing. I contend the complicity of the mainstream media (MSM) is the only reason why today's Leftist organizations have any impact, or even survive. A "story," like my Idaho potato boycott whim, becomes immediately legitimate because of the coverage itself.

I'm sharing this story with you to remind you that the media only have power if you allow it. The battle is for your *mind*—but your mind cannot be taken, it has to be willingly given. In the past you have allowed the MSM a certain power over you because you have trusted it. Over the years, I have enjoyed seeing that trust eroded enough to where the media and Leftist organizations no longer control your view of the world.

You see, I, along with the other women at the press conference, made up the outside armor, made to look extraordinary only with the complicity of the media. Ultimately, we didn't need to do anything—

the news coverage of the threat itself was enough for Andrus eventually to veto the bill that would have been used to challenge *Roe v. Wade*.

Normal, by Default

I have to tell you, it's a pretty heady thing to have the media on your side. This is a little difficult to explain—when I was in NOW and worked hand in hand with the media, I never saw our relationship as "biased" or unfair in any way. You see, we all have our opinions, our points of view. Those positions are deemed as *normal* for us. So, being on the Left, and working with media that think just like you, is not perceived as "bias," it's seen as normal.

Of course, when you don't associate with anyone who thinks differently from you, it does begin to seem as though everyone thinks like you. Eventually, those who dissent or have different ideas are marginal and odd. They are not like you and certainly not part of the real world.

It is in this environment where groupthink festers and prevails. This is why, when a Leftist or a water carrier for the media insists there is no liberal bias, they're serious, they really mean and truly believe that to be the case.

While groupthink can also infect the Right or conservative individuals, here's one reason why it is simply less prevalent: Liberal media are the vast majority of all mainstream media. It is unavoidable for most of us. Conservatives, as a result, not only see liberal media, but then they make a point of specifically choosing to consume other media. You may, as an example, watch NBC's *Today* show (which you should stop watching, by the way), and then glance at the ABC Evening News, and then go specifically to the Fox News Channel.

Or perhaps you read the *Los Angeles Times,* and have the *Weekly Standard* delivered to your home as well. Conservatives, in their effort to go to nonmainstream news sources for views more like their own, also see, simply because of their insidiousness, the MSM Conservatives do get, with other coverage, via the Internet and other outlets.

Liberals simply do not. It is easy for anyone to be saturated with liberally biased news coverage, as it represents the majority of mainstream news outlets. It's safe to say that Leftists or even the average liberal avoid the *Weekly Standard*, or the *Washington Times*, or *Human Events* like the plague.

Without being exposed to alternative points of view, they are consumed by groupthink. It's inevitable, and it's what we face today as we see an increasingly violent and hostile Left. The Leftists are responding to a world they do not understand and couldn't imagine, primarily because they shut reality out of their lives. They didn't have to choose liberal news outlets to watch, the culture thrusts those outlets upon them and the rest of us. The mistake they make is avoiding other opinions or worldviews.

The Power of Perspective

Sometimes even the simplest action makes the biggest difference down the road. Unfortunately, our society has fostered a desire for immediate gratification—we want to see results right away. While sometimes there is an immediate impact with personal activism, the reality is the best and most lasting change is achieved over time.

For perspective, I will now focus on the two media corporations that I mentioned earlier as keystones to our cultural meltdown—Viacom and the *New York Times*. Yes, there are certainly more than two problem companies out there, but remember—one bite at a time.

There will always be issues popping up that will raise your hackles, actions that you know demand your involvement. As an example, I'm writing these particular words on Veterans' Day 2004. Today, in what many considered a new salvo in the culture war, a handful of

ABC affiliates announced they were refusing to air the network's presentation of the Oscar-winning film *Saving Private Ryan*.

Perhaps one of the most moving depictions of the impact on humanity of World War II, the dynamically realistic film includes a graphically violent depiction of the D-Day invasion of Normandy, as well as profanity.

Fueling speculation that some station owners were "punishing" Americans for having the gall to demand an end to television programming's race to the cultural bottom (in a post–Janet Jackson Super Bowl world), Raymond Cole, the vice president of ABC's affiliate in Des Moines, Iowa, bleated, "We regret that we are not able to broadcast a patriotic, artistic tribute to our fighting forces like 'Saving Private Ryan,' "[1] He noted that he had concerns that the film violated the Federal Communications Commission's decency standards.

That statement itself is clearly facetious. For those of you who think someone like Cole may just be a supercautious guy, he also cited President Bush's reelection as a reason to pull the film: "We're just coming off an election where moral issues were cited as a reason by people voting one way or another and, in my opinion, the commissioners [of the FCC] are fearful of the new Congress."

Oh, I see—the scary and freakish Republican-controlled Congress will pressure the FCC to punish a network for airing a film depicting American heroism in war. Yes, and next week Congress will once again institute witch hunts in Salem. And I'm Zsa Zsa Gabor.

The Last Straw

Clearly, Cole's attitude is unmistakably giving Americans the bird, verbally. Cole and everyone else knows that context is everything. FCC regulations say specifically the context in which such material is presented is of critical importance.

Americans know the difference between gratuitous violence and a story about war where violence is in context and central to the story line. Cole and others like him are suggesting, like good moral relativists, that there can be no line of judgment because everything is relative. They salivate at the idea of pushing the notion that something like Janet Jackson's and Justin Timberlake's insult of a basic standard of Americans during the Super Bowl is the moral equivalent of a story about the human condition during World War II.

There are obvious differences. We thought we knew what to expect with the Super Bowl halftime show until someone decided to make it an MTV sex romp. We do know what *Saving Private Ryan* is all about. The issue is adults expect to have enough information so they can make informed choices about what they want their family to see.

When I noted on my radio show that a few ABC stations were refusing to air the film, many listeners had an immediate reaction, made their anger known, and chimed in with the local affiliate if it was one that was joining in the refusal to air.

That's a legitimate "in the moment" action. An event worthy of your involvement materializes, and you may have just one day to make your voice heard. I can't stress enough the importance of the automatic urge to make a phone call, send an e-mail, or mail a letter. It means you're in the right frame of mind. In an instance where time is of the essence, calling the local affiliate was what untold numbers of Americans did when they heard their local station was indeed playing political games.

In addition to the personal empowerment of remembering you have every right to be heard, station owners find out directly that moves like this resonate in local communities. They're reminded that you are not a knee-jerk reactionary, and you know the difference between gratuitous violence and contextual storytelling.

This sort of little game is insulting to you, and meant to shut you up. The message is if you get too uppity there will be a price to pay. To some, a handful of stations choosing not to air this sort of film, while citing our demand that standards be upheld, is significant.

I believe it is an opening salvo in the Leftist argument that "standards," "expectations," and "responsibility" are concepts that are simply too complicated to enforce.

To their credit, the ABC network issued a statement saying they were "proud to once again broadcast" *Saving Private Ryan,* which "depicts the harrowing and devastating realities of the men who fought" in World War II.

Like you, Cole and others in the media know what the cultural fight is about. Calling these little spoiled brats on a slight like this helps to bring them back down to earth to face the owners of the airwaves—you. These cultural gatekeepers are the last people on earth to punish you, but only you can remind them of who's in charge.

Perpetual Problems

Let's now consider the impact you can have on Viacom. Yes, it is one of the world's largest global media empires. You may think, "What can I do about the scourge this corporate creature is exacting on my culture?" Plenty.

Your first project is to change the way you think about corporations. The reality is they're not machines devoid of the human touch. Our tendency is to see them as monolithic monsters beyond our control, beyond our influence because we don't recognize that very few people are at the helm. The truth is, there is no "Viacom," but a company controlled by a few individuals with names and agendas.

As noted earlier, Sumner Redstone is Viacom's chairman of the board and chief executive officer. Co-presidents and co-chief operating officers are Tom Freston and Leslie Moonves.

As an example of Freston's background, just so you know who you're dealing with, he was one of the founding members of the team that launched MTV. Prior to his elevation at Viacom, Moonves was chairman and chief executive officer at CBS.

While there are fourteen members of the Viacom board of directors, make no mistake, Redstone controls that entity. At Viacom, these Big Three, as I term them—Redstone, Freston, and Moonves—direct and control the corporate culture. While they may not be involved in the day-to-day decision making, these individuals set the internal standard regarding programming content, news agenda, and cultural spin.

I've introduced these three men to you specifically to individuate what seems to be the nameless and faceless monstrosity of Viacom. It is indeed a monster, but it certainly has names and faces.

Individuals at every level of an entity like Viacom can see, hear, and feel action you take. It is imperative you do not view big companies as impervious. In many ways, the people who run a company like Viacom are like the Wizard of Oz—very small men and women who manipulate smoke and mirrors, hoping to keep you and your judgment at bay.

As the 2004 election results have reminded us, we're the ones in charge. Let's pull back that curtain on Viacom.

Why Viacom? Over the years, Viacom has not just stayed the same when it comes to the acid they've thrown on our culture, they've gotten worse. This shouldn't surprise us. Any virus left unchecked will indeed gain strength, grow, and consume even more. This is what the people at Viacom have done.

There is no doubt that Viacom's subunits have contributed to the decline of our culture. Ranging from cable channel VH1's elevation of murderers and other depraved prisoners to "rock star" status with its *Music Behind Bars* series, to Viacom literally rewriting history to suit its worldview by electronically replacing boos and catcalls with cheers and applause for Hillary Clinton at a televised 9/11 memorial event in New York.

In late 2003, Viacom, through its broadcast unit CBS, offered to this nation a smear of President Ronald Reagan and Mrs. Reagan. *The Reagans* made-for-television movie depicts Nancy Reagan as a pill-popping control freak and the president as homophobic and uncaring about the AIDS crisis.

Such a film, made by some of Hollywood's most well-known and activist liberal Democrats, could be nothing but a smear. Its producers, then–CBS chief Les Moonves, as well as the film's star, James Brolin, and his wife, Barbra Streisand, are Democrat activists. It's safe to say their agenda was not to present a true historical account of one of this nation's most dynamic presidents.

As an example of this agenda, one of the more controversial lines in *The Reagans* casts the president as hateful and careless about AIDS victims. He is shown telling Mrs. Reagan about sufferers, "They that live in sin shall die in sin." In a *New York Times* story, the movie's writer admitted to making up that horrible line portraying the president as someone who thought gays deserved to get AIDS, but explained, "We know he ducked the issue over and over again."

Do we really know that?

Truth to Power

My good friend Marc Christian was Rock Hudson's last partner. Marc, like most other Americans, was appalled at the reported portrayal of the former president, not because he *believes* it to be an untrue portrait, but because he *knows* it is.

Marc wrote a letter to CBS entertainment head Moonves, making clear his disgust at the portrayal of the president, especially the assertion that Reagan was a cruel homophobe. While Marc did not write his letter for public consumption, I found it important and asked if I could share it with you. He graciously agreed.

Here is the education Marc Christian gave Les Moonves:

> *The notion that President Reagan was a homophobe strikes me as silly beyond belief. Not only did he have several gay men on his staff when he was Governor of California, he called my lover, Rock Hudson, when he was on his deathbed*

just weeks before he died of AIDS and wished him well and voiced his and Nancy's concern and prayers.

. . . The Reagans had known Rock for years and knew he was gay (as did most in Hollywood). The point is Reagan could have ignored Rock's illness and didn't. He could have just issued a public statement concerning his "official sorrow"' but made a personal phone call instead.

CBS used to be the network of class, now it's the official arm of the Democrat party and its sources for information regarding truth below that of The National Enquirer. I bet President Reagan's phone call to Rock Hudson isn't in the screenplay or should I say smearplay, is it?

Marc Christian
Hollywood, California

This note from Marc to Moonves is important for several reasons, mostly for injecting truth into a world ruled by vacant, malevolent Leftists. Their elite actively work to destroy any idea, or any individual, who challenges the dead, cold heart of their glorious Leftist establishment. The CBS depiction of the Reagans, as one string of the Redstone Viacom agenda, epitomizes this callous agenda.

Consider a comment to the *New York Times* by Judy Davis, the Australian actress who portrayed Mrs. Reagan. Revealing an attitude that must have won her many fans at Viacom and in the Streisand household, she declared:

> With the climate that has been in America since Sept. 11, it appears, from the outside anyway, to not be quite as open a society as it used to be. By open, I mean as free in terms of a critical atmosphere, and that sort of ugly specter of patriotism.

American patriotism as "ugly." This is what the mega-corporate liberal media design for us. In all honesty, what sort of telefilm did Viacom think it was getting when people who hate the Reagans are the ones making a film about . . . the Reagans?

Follow the Money

Of course, Viacom accepts this tripe because it perfectly suits Viacom's worldview. The vast majority of individuals on the board of this publicly held company are Democrats. Sumner Redstone is one of the Democrat party's largest donors. Recipients of his largess include Ted Kennedy, Tom Daschle, John Kerry, Hand Gun Control, Inc., and the Democratic Congressional Campaign Committee. You personally can learn the details of political contributions at www.opensecrets.org.

Leslie Moonves, because of his support of the Democrat party as one of its bigger donors, sat next to Hillary Clinton at the 2000 party convention. He also enjoyed what is known as "Clinton Sleepovers" at the White House when Clinton and Gore were ensconced.

In 2001, both Freston and Moonves indulged in a four-day junket to Cuba, where they got chummy with Fidel Castro, one of the world's longest standing Marxist dictators. Moonves was apparently so taken with Castro he returned with the dictator's autograph on a cigar box.

This is the same Leslie Moonves who greenlighted *The Reagans*. Lowell Ponte, a columnist with Frontpagemagazine.com, opined:

> Moonves returned from Havana clutching a cigar box signed by Fidel with the same hand that has murdered tens of thousands of people. Moonves seemed both comfortable and proud to have shared intimacies with a Marxist dictator who not only violates all other human rights but is also notorious for systematically imprisoning, torturing and executing gays just because he dislikes homosexuality.[2]

Of course, Redstone, Freston, and Moonves can be Democrats or Marxists and be completely oblivious to their own absurd hypocrisy when it comes to getting chummy with a murderous dictator, responsible for the suffering of untold thousands. Our concern is the fact that these same individuals are in astoundingly powerful positions with which to project their own sick worldview onto our culture.

As an example, another Moonves project at CBS was *Hitler: The Rise of Evil,* which created a stir when it drew comparisons between the rise of Hitler and the Bush administration *and* American society as a whole after 9/11. "It basically boils down to an entire nation gripped by fear, who [sic] ultimately chose to give up their civil rights and plunged the whole nation into war. I can't think of a better time to examine this history than now," bleated the producer to *TV Guide.*[3]

The insidious nihilism that infects virtually all Leftists is clearly having its way with the Viacom board. This is no longer about "entertainment." We are now faced with material that is nothing less than propaganda, suited with an agenda to rewrite history into a version that casts this nation, her greatest leaders, and people as sick, mean, and depraved.

Once *The Reagans* script was revealed, the outrage was undeniable; pressure on CBS mounted as advertisers threatened boycotts and other actions. Ultimately, Viacom moved *The Reagans* from CBS to its cable network, Showtime.

I believe, however, that it may never have been Viacom's intention to air the movie on CBS. It is quite possible that the announcement to air on CBS was a test to see if they could begin to move the more salacious material, better suited for a network like Showtime, to its broadcast outlet.

You see, broadcast networks have been losing young male viewers to cable, which affects advertising rates. It's inevitable that the liberal corporate gatekeepers would become fixated on moving that material—and the audience that comes with it—out of cable and into the broadcast network.

One need only consider the biggest media story of 2004 for another sign that Viacom chief Redstone wants to remake the CBS network—the same network that once aired *Touched by an Angel*—into his marginal Showtime/MTV rot.

Breaking the Camel's Back

In what will forever serve as the straw that broke the camel's back, CBS aired the 2004 Super Bowl and farmed out the halftime show to Viacom unit MTV. The rest is, well, history. Some pundits mused that Americans had suddenly somehow lost their collective mind when Justin Timberlake ripped off part of Janet Jackson's costume, revealing her breast to a nation full of seven-year-olds watching with their families.

After all, we were told, a breast is a beautiful thing, and considering that porn is one of the largest industries in the United States, it was suggested Americans were being weirdly hypocritical.

Nothing could be further from the truth.

We didn't suddenly become prudes. I contend the Jackson debacle was simply the last straw for Americans who had remained generally silent as they watched their culture being shredded. We remained quiet because we do believe in freedom of expression and are tolerant, and embrace and support art.

As a preview to Leftist complaints about the results of the 2004 election, some in the Media Elite argue that it was a bunch of frenzied Right-wing Christian fundamentalists who led the charge. This argument, of course, exposes two things. It illustrates how truly out of touch Leftists are with the average American, Christian or not. They simply cannot conceive of the fact that regular Americans have had enough on plain, old commonsense grounds.

Feminists had issues with the nature of the entire Jackson "act"—highlighting sexually aggressive males in an act of stripping a woman, culminating in nothing less than female sexual subjectivity.

The other effect of trying to cast the public's reaction as limited to one group allows that group to be painted as extremist—another oft-used tactic of the Thought Police. After all, if that weird, isolated, ignorant group over there thinks this way, you certainly don't want to go there!

But this was different, and it was a slap in the face to everyone, everywhere. Average Americans who are Democrats, Republicans, conservatives, and liberals are usually parents first when they're sitting in front of the television with their children.

Since its inception, the Super Bowl has been an event aired during the family hour. It is a program, an American tradition, that can be shared with and enjoyed by the whole family.

That is until Viacom and Redstone decided that it was time to shove its sex-based cable fare down the throats of Americans. Masquerading as the halftime show was a variety of so-called singers and dancers providing nothing less than a peep show for your family.

Initially, I was fascinated with the poststunt news hubbub focusing on Janet Jackson's bare breast during family hour. In fact, the *entire* halftime production was insulting and offensive.

I knew immediately America was in for an assault when rap singer Nelly got onstage and was unable to keep his hand off his crotch. It was astounding. Here was a man on broadcast television, with millions of children watching raptly, holding on to his penis as though it were a weapon throughout his performance.

Then, of course, we get to the supposed "wardrobe malfunction," as singer (and I use that adjective with reservations) Justin Timberlake described it. Let's be honest—either these people are complete idiots or they think we are. During a song with the main refrain of "I'll have you naked by the end of this song," Timberlake managed quite aptly and exposed Jackson's breast—a breast, mind you, that looked like it had been adorned for a very special coming-out party.

Personally, and as a cultural critic, I am concerned about those who do not think this is a big deal. Let me assure you, it is. Why? Because it's reflective of Incrementalism—a slow, gradual effort at cultural change, a change that is decidedly downward. It is a change that a company like Viacom has a serious interest in accomplishing. If they can transform broadcast network television and draw that favored advertising demographic away from HBO and ESPN back to broadcast, they will see dollar signs, at the expense of you seeing your culture ripped away.

The goal of Incrementalism is to present depraved and offensive material slowly, progressively, and then more regularly over a period of time so it becomes apparently normal. That's what's happening here. Keep in mind, it's only the horrible that needs to sneak up on us. Americans always let the wonderful in the front door.

Depth Escapes Dr. Dean

If you're wondering how Incrementalism works, let's look at Howard Dean, however painful it might be. Dean, the onetime top Democrat presidential challenger, and now party chair, said the uproar over the exposure of Jackson's breast is "silly."[4]

And then, in a comment that really sums up why this man is better suited to be managing a shift at Taco Bell instead of running this great country (Yeeeaaarhhgh!), he said: "I find that to be a bit of a flap about nothing. I'm probably affected in some ways by the fact that I'm a doctor, so it's not exactly an unusual phenomenon for me."[5]

Wow! Doctors see strangers having their clothes ripped off in sexual situations in front of the children of the nation on a regular basis! Of course, he's reduced this to the sight of a breast. So, was finding Saddam the equivalent of catching some weird homeless guy? Depth seems to escape Dr. Dean.

But he didn't stop there. Dean, who does not have cable television at his home in Vermont, exemplified the moral relativism that has a stranglehold on the American Left: "I don't find it terribly shocking relative to some of the things you can find on standard cable television."

Slowly but surely we are expected to lower the bar on standards, quality, and decency. The this-is-okay-because-of-that-thing-over-there syndrome. This is the heart of Howard Dean's reasoning.

Now, let me make something clear here. I have not been possessed by the ghost of a nun who is shocked at the sight of flesh. But there is a time and place for everything. I happen to think, as I hope most of you do, that a woman's body is a beautiful thing. As adults, if we want to see a woman's breast bared on television, we have that option—late at night, when we've chosen the program, we're aware of what we're getting, and the children are tucked away.

And accepting that option is not meant as a complete abdication of what (and when) we feel certain material is appropriate. We can draw lines for the public airwaves, and we do.

I personally like films and television that challenge our notions of who we are, including our sexuality. But that's my interest as an adult, and it very well may be an interest very different from yours. The choices we make about sexuality and its imagery are and should be private choices. Viacom and its two mutant children—MTV and CBS—took that choice from us, and decided their view of sexuality would not only be forced upon us without warning, but on our children as well, contemptibly wrapped up as "family entertainment."

It's worth remembering that radio network Infinity was fined for a St. Patrick's "Sex in the Cathedral" radio stunt. Viacom, which also owns Infinity (surprise!), was told by the FCC that future violations by the company could prompt a license-revocation proceeding.

Now, isn't that a novel idea! Broadcast licenses are not granted for eternity. Licenses can be revoked or not renewed. Would it be unusual? Yes, but it's time for the unusual, including the need to take back our culture. Parents Television Council spokeswoman Lara Mahaney reminds us, "The public airwaves are given to them for free. Their licenses are a privilege, not a right."

Tearing down certain institutions that continually betray us, and reminding the cultural gatekeepers about who is really in charge, is our responsibility. That time is now.

Taking Action

1. Voice your opinions to the FCC. This agency exists to investigate your complaints about what's happening to your public airwaves. You own the mechanism that allows Viacom's Leftist Democrats to twist our culture into their image. It's time you became a player. Report offensive material by contacting the FCC. You can file a complaint electronically, by e-mail, by phone, or via snail mail. There are very specific formatic rules regarding the filing of complaints. I urge you to call the FCC at 1-888-CALL-FCC (1-888-225-5322) for more information, or go to http://www.fcc.gov/cgb/complaints.html for details. And remember, when making a complaint, context is key. There is a difference between a musician shouting the "F" word for the sake of it, and it being used in the film *Saving Private Ryan*. Context, context, context.

2. Get involved and support the Parents Television Council at www.parentstv.org. This organization is one of the most successful and prolific advocacy groups leading the way on media issues of concern to families and everyone who is concerned about the direction of mega-media corporations. They contain a wealth of information and action ideas.

3. Divest. Viacom is a publicly held company and it's possible you may hold some of its stock. Its New York Stock Exchange symbol is VIAB. Check all your stock holdings and make a statement about what's important to you by not supporting Viacom financially with your investment.

4. Do not watch any Viacom television properties. This includes CBS, MTV, VH1, and Showtime. If you currently subscribe to the cable channel Showtime, cancel your subscription. And yes, some of the most watched programs are on CBS, including one of my favorites, *CSI*, but I have stopped watching them as one way to express

my personal activism. While this disappoints me, it is a small price to pay in an effort to beat back these cultural parasites. To learn about all of Viacom's holdings, go to the *Columbia Journalism Review* at www.cjr.org. Click on the "Journalism Tools" link and then go to their "Who Owns What" project.

5. Support and get involved with the Web site action research effort www.mediaresearchcenter.org.

These are just a few steps. You may want to take more aggressive action with programming sponsors, or even branch out to not supporting other Viacom properties. Whatever you do, do it one bite at a time. Make decisions that you know you will be able to truly implement.

Whether it's one action or ten, make a commitment to do something every day that takes back our culture. And remember, even *not* watching or buying something is doing something.

The *New York Times*

In *NTP*, I wrote about how helpful the *New York Times* was to me when I was officially working for the Leftist agenda. I also detailed how they facilitated the attacks by the Gay Gestapo on my friend Dr. Laura Schlessinger. Finally, when writing *DRW*, I illustrated how the *Times* has become one of biggest Brownshirts of all,[6] leading the way to maligning Christianity and people of faith, and assaulting the basic tenets of right and wrong.

Unfortunately, between my writing that book in 2003 and now, things have only gotten worse. The time for action has come.

It was in May 2003 when the Jayson Blair scandal broke at the *Times*. Blair was the reporter who resigned after he admitted to plagiarism and faking some of his stories. Blair is black, and was mentored by then-editor Howell Raines and managing editor Gerald Boyd.

Appropriately, a great deal of the coverage of this fiasco focused on how it seemed obvious that Blair was held to a different (lower) standard because he is black. Clearly, one of the absurd problems with so-called affirmative action is the obsession with a variety of skin colors among employees. In the *Times* case, true affirmative action would focus on incorporating a diversity of ideas in their newsroom. But, as we're finding, that's not the kind of diversity they, or the Left in general, can deal with.

After the Blair incident, books and hundreds of articles flooded the marketplace, trying to explain and understand how this malfeasance could have happened. Well, it doesn't take a brain surgeon to understand that any culture steeped in groupthink would have at least one corrupt element of their culture exposed. Eventually.

Here's the bottom line about what the Blair scandal revealed: a corporate culture that is dynamically out of touch with the real world, a world that expects the simplest efforts at honesty and fairness. You see, when the corporate culture is one rife with an agenda to move a certain worldview, there is naturally less of an inclination to look at the resulting product critically. There is also more of a tendency to accept the "end justifies the means" excuse.

This sort of corruption becomes corporate culture and can only exist, of course, if the newspaper or media outlet has an "end" with which it is concerned. This is the heart of the problem with today's mainstream media—their agenda is no longer to present you the news, it is used by a few Malignant Narcissists at the top, who choose like-minded foot soldiers (reporters, editors, writers, producers) to further their cause.

Ultimately, obsessed with pushing a Leftist agenda, the Corporate Gestapo at the *Times* has also lost touch with the fact that the Paper of Record has turned into nothing more than another rag worthy of the Socialist Workers' party.

When propaganda is your strong suit, why ask questions about facts and truth?

Alexandra Marks, of the *Christian Science Monitor*, notes, "The Blair scandal is symptomatic of an overall erosion of journalistic ethics that began about 15 years ago as circulation steadily declined. . . ."[7]

While Marks is right about the decline of ethics, what she misses is that the overall mission of the *Times* is corrupt. No longer is it about bringing the news to people, it's about changing the culture. The slanting of headlines, obviously Leftist-based coverage, and setting the tone for couching opinion as "news" is at the very least intellectually dishonest and deserves an answer.

Perhaps the best example of the *Times* moving from newspaper to Leftist propaganda rag is their bizarre fixation on the Masters Golf Tournament at Augusta National. As a feminist, I support the goal of lifting restrictions on women playing at Augusta, but let's get real here. I'm a woman with a history of feminist activism. The *Times* had unabashedly and arrogantly taken up the Leftist feminist gauntlet. Their stories had nothing to do with news and everything to do with moving the Leftist agenda.

The *Times*'s Inquisition

As the 2004 election season approached, the *Times*'s hostility to Christianity and Christians became even more apparent. The newspaper has stopped even trying to mask its culture of hate for religion.

The clearest example of its anti-Christian corporate culture is found within the columns of its opinion contributors. If the *Times* had a collective head, it effectively exploded on November 3, when George W. Bush not only won reelection, but did so with more votes than any president in our nation's great history.

"The president got re-elected by dividing the country along fault lines of fear intolerance, ignorance and religious rule,"[8] whined Maureen Dowd. Her associations with the intolerant and the religious are undeniable and intentional.

"He's a radical—the leader of a coalition that deeply dislikes America as it is. . . . And thanks to a heavy turnout by evangelical Christians, Mr. Bush has four more years to advance that radical agenda,"[9] is what *Times* columnist Paul Krugman wrote about President Bush's victory. He makes it clear that the president and Christians specifically are dangerous to America.

What exactly is "that radical agenda" that threatens to destroy America? Let's see—believing marriage is between a man and a woman. Yeah, that's radical, for sure, absolutely shocking. Believing that having children should happen after marriage. Oh, my goodness, I can't believe that's even being suggested! It's good we're all sitting down.

And those pesky Ten Commandments, the most radical of all, and certainly a threat to "America as it is." Honoring thy mother and father! Gasp! Thou Shalt Not Kill. Yeah, that really puts a crimp in the Leftist culture. Thou Shalt Not Covet Thy Neighbor's Wife. Hmmm, what about Thy Neighbor's Intern? Or, for the Kennedys, how about Thy Neighbor's Party Guest? (Oops, Teddy broke two rules there, that covet thing and the death issue!)[10] Can one covet Thy Own Child's Babysitter? For Michael Kennedy, son of Robert, the answer was yes.[11]

Thou Shalt Not Commit Adultery. And Jesse Jackson "counseled" Bill Clinton during the Lewinsky scandal. What was his advice? How to get away with it?

Yeah, I see how those Christian ideals threaten to strike at this nation's greatness. Unless one, of course, reflects on the fact that those values are part and parcel of what has made this nation great. I'm afraid, however, that is not a perspective you will ever hear from the *New York Times*.

What Leftists do not understand, and what the *New York Times* maligns, is the deep desire of most Americans not to revert to a theocracy, but to return to a commonsense morality that improves the quality of our lives. On November 2, 2004, we rejected the nihilism and the death of right and wrong. We now insist on the basic common sense of decency and dignity, both of which are concepts clearly quite threatening to the culture of the *Times*.

Let Them Eat Christians

What's the best they could do? Thomas Friedman tried to be diplomatic with his standard *Times* complaint that Christians are dangerous: "My problem with the Christian fundamentalists supporting Mr. Bush is not their spiritual energy or the fact that I am of a different faith. It is the way in which he and they have used that religious energy to promote divisions and intolerance at home and abroad."

Gee, you'd think Friedman was writing about bin Laden! He has no problem with Muslims, just with how bin Laden has used that belief to promote savagery and terrorism. Frankly, Mr. Friedman should realize by now that the *Times* culture has eclipsed his Jewishness. It isn't because he's a Jew that he doesn't like Christians, he assures us. He's right. It's because he's been sucked into the Leftism of the *Times*, which doesn't like Christians.

After the Blair scandal, and the resignations of Raines and Boyd, I felt this would provide a real window into the frame of mind of Arthur Sulzberger, Jr., the publisher of the newspaper and chairman of The New York Times Company. Did he really have any intention of changing the *Times*'s culture? Who he would hire to replace the two men who resigned would speak volumes about Sulzberger's intentions, and if he realized how deep a cesspool of Leftist tripe and groupthink the *Times* had become.

What did he do? He installed columnist Bill Keller, of all people, as executive editor of the newspaper. This was especially shocking. Why? A look at his op-ed column of May 4, 2002, titled "Is the Pope Catholic," reveals this man's nature and tells you everything you need to know about him. Ultimately, his primary point to was essentially equate the Catholic Church with Stalin's Soviet Union.[12]

Yes, this is the man Sulzberger tapped to save the *Times*. In this instance there is to be no renovation, simply a rearrangement of the deck chairs.

"Go Get Your Own Newspaper"

One of the last reactions of the *Times* to the Blair scandal was their hiring of a "Public Editor," a man by the name of Daniel Okrent. Keller announced the hiring this way, in an e-mail to the *Times*' staff:

> We wanted someone with the reporting skills to figure out how decisions get made at the paper, the judgment to reach conclusions about whether and where we go astray, and the writing skills to explain all of this to our readers.[13]

Keller also noted in that e-mail that he wanted someone who was "independent." Okrent's background includes working for *Time* magazine, part of the megalith Time Warner. The editorial director at *Time* also notes that Okrent "loves the *Times* . . . loves journalists . . ."[14]

He's also a Democrat, by the way. If Keller really wanted someone independent he would have hired a Republican who's not especially fond of newspaper reporters. Then you'd have a real ombudsman, and someone who could see through the fog of being a part of the Leftist "journalist" culture as Okrent has been.

Think I'm being too harsh about the absurdity of hiring someone like Okrent to be an internal watchdog at the *Times*? Consider Okrent's own attitude.

In October 2004, C-SPAN covered a discussion sponsored by Harvard's John F. Kennedy School of Government. Okrent was the guest and was asked about the kind of e-mails he received from readers, including those that are especially critical, and even hostile. Okrent said his attitude was: "Go get your own newspaper."

Newsflash for Okrent: The *New York Times* is our newspaper!

In June 2005 Okrent left the *Times*. His replacement is Byron Calame, a retiree from the *Wall Street Journal* after forty years on the job. In other words, another newspaperman's newspaperman.

Some of you may have hope for Mr. Calame considering the fact he comes from the *Wall Street Journal*. Not too fast. Here's how he reassured readers of the *Times* that they were safe:

> A few readers have already questioned how open-minded I can be as public editor, given the well-known conservative views of *The Wall Street Journal*'s editorial page. Two points: *The Journal*'s newsroom and editorial page are separated by a thick wall, and all of my years at the paper were spent on the news side.[15]

Besides immediately giving credence to the idea that one can't be open-minded and conservative at the same time, Calame then assures everyone he had nothing to do with the conservative editorial pages. He is, all can count on, *not* a conservative.

Obviously, these hirings and the position itself are shams, a game meant to distract those of us who legitimately feel the *New York Times* needs to change dramatically.

The addition of "conservative" David Brooks to the *New York Times* editorial page is also worth noting. The fact that Brooks has long been associated with the *Weekly Standard* and the *Wall Street Journal* is what gives him his conservative credibility. He describes himself, however, as on the "leftward end" of that crowd.

New York magazine exposes why Brooks is a conservative even the *New York Times* can love:

> He lacks, he says, "militance." He is, he says, "un-angry."
> His is a kind of bashful or accidental conservatism. "I'm a

New York conservative." No doubt reassuring for the *Times*, Brooks has made a secondary career for himself on NPR's *All Things Considered* and PBS's *The Newshour with Jim Lehrer*, as a conservative for liberals."[16]

The *New York Times* hires omsbudsmen who patronize readers and love journalists, while their token "conservative" columnist is "bashful"—or dare I say ashamed—of his conservatism. Yes, indeed, how perfect, and how utterly ridiculous.

Here's the problem for the *Times:* They are not simply serving a local community with local news. They are a cultural institution that in the past has been trusted to be an actual newspaper, not a Left-wing advocacy group. They have a responsibility to this nation, to us as citizens, to approach this charge with some intellectual honesty and become a newspaper again that reports facts, not singular opinions.

It seems that people like Sulzberger and Keller are so infatuated with themselves and are convinced that everyone is out of step except them.

Perhaps they even think the demand they revert back to a real, reliable newspaper comes from a conspiracy of evangelical Christians who want to destroy this nation, sleep with their cousins, and need a dentist.

Taking Action

It's time we answer that call and show them the Great Unwashed Masses are in fact great, washed, and a collection of individuals who know they deserve better.

They will be reminded that while not everyone subscribes to the *Times*, we're all affected by the message the paper sends and the standard it sets for every other media outlet that looks to it for the Talking Points of the day.

The *Times* is also a publicly held company. Here are some details.

The New York Times Company owns nineteen newspapers, including the *Boston Globe* and the *International Herald Tribune*. It owns eight local television stations, two radio stations, has a partial stake in the Boston Red Sox, and 50 percent of the Discovery Channel.

The *Times* Web site boasts, "In 2004 the Company was ranked No. 1 in the publishing industry in Fortune's list of 'America's Most Admired Companies,' for the fourth consecutive year."

Let's change that one bite at a time.

The simplest things make a difference. Think about it—massive numbers of like-minded people are reading this book. And while there will be no big marches for television to cover or surprising visuals for the evening news, the action you take, along with so many others, can send a message to Sulzberger and all those who have lost sight of the fact that this is our culture and we care about it.

Perhaps you have been overlooked because your passion for this nation is a quiet passion. It's time to be organized with your wish to make a difference. Here's how to start:

1. If you subscribe, cancel. While the New York Times Company is huge, focus at first on one element—let's focus on the *New York Times* newspaper. Circulation is what determines advertising rates, which is what the game is all about—profit. Canceling your subscription is easy. If you buy the *Times* on a single-issue basis, stop.

If you absolutely **need** to read the *Times*, do so at the library or reread the copy that is shared at your local coffeehouse. The other option is to read it on the Internet, but even that access translates into dollars. Is this more inconvenient than getting your own paper? Yes, it is. But any effort we make to change our culture will involve breaking certain habits.

Remember, people like Sulzberger and Keller rely on your *habit* of reading their paper. They trust that you will be passive and will not be willing to change your pattern. Prove them wrong. Affecting circulation strikes at the heart of their corrupt agenda.

2. **Encourage others to cancel their subscription.** While taking action in our own lives is important, it is also vital to make your voice heard with the people around you. Let them know what you think, what you've done, and encourage them to do the same. Spread the word!

3. **Be a discerning consumer.** Do not patronize companies that advertise in the *Times*. As a second layer of your discerning consumership, make a note of who is advertising in the *Times* and do not patronize them, and tell those companies what you're doing. Let those companies know that you reject the agenda of the *Times*, and are making a point of not supporting companies that support the newspaper.

4. You don't need to read the paper itself to stay in touch with what they're doing. Brent Bozell, of the Media Research Center, has founded "Times Watch" on the Web at www.timeswatch.com. This is a Web site that deals with the coverage of the *Times*. Their site notes, "By documenting and exposing the *Times* liberal bias, Times Watch is committed to compelling the paper to provide balanced reporting, or risk forfeiting its standing as the "newspaper of record.""

5. **Divest.** As with Viacom, stop helping to fund this Leftist propaganda machine. Check any stock holdings you have and determine if you own New York Times Company stock (symbol NYT). Perhaps you have 401K investments, or mutual funds purchased by a stockbroker. Look into what you actually own, and divest. I know some activists encourage purchasing stock of companies with which you have disagreements. This is based on the presumption you'll be heard or have access as a stockholder. Don't bother. Divesting sends a larger message and reflects the more appropriate personal statement about what you want your money to support.

I know these seem like simple steps, and they are. During my time as a Left-wing organizer, I found very quickly what a difference one person can make with one phone call, one letter, one personal protest. Imagine tens of thousands of people making the same effort you are. The difference will be felt.

How is it you can make a difference? Ultimately, people like the Malignant Narcissists running Viacom and the *Times* are motivated by two things: Leftist nihilism and greed. To change the former, you need to appeal to the latter. Economic projects work and work well. Do not buy. Do not watch. Divest. Be heard. Make a ruckus. Welcome and embrace that Radical Individual in you.

Just remember, one bite at a time.

7

Know Your Enemy: Unmasking the Left

I have never made but one prayer to God, a very short one: "O Lord, make my enemies ridiculous." And God granted it.

—Voltaire

n January 2005, the world came together to raise money for relief efforts from the devastating tsunami in Southeast Asia.

Television, radio, Web sites, networks of social organizations—there was no place you could look that didn't implore you for your individual assistance. Unless, of course, you were reading the Web sites of the American feminist establishment.

For anyone who looks to Eleanor Smeal's Feminist Majority and the now painfully pathetic National Organization for Women for information about a tragedy of this magnitude, and its impact on women and children, you would have had no idea that anything of consequence had happened in Southeast Asia.

There were no stories about the disaster, no news alerts, no links. There was no reference at all—nothing about the children orphaned, the women suffering, the kidnapping and sexual molestation of children, or the notorious sex-tourism industry in the region. And you would think, of all the entities in the world, the feminist establishment would be the first to jump to the aid of women in need.

The feminist establishment Web sites did make pleas for donations during the tsunami crisis, but the pleas were for their *own* coffers.

I mention the complete moral and physical absence of the American feminist establishment during the tsunami crisis because it illustrates the moral vacuity now encompassing the Left Elite in general. The Hate America First contingent does not know what to do when a situation arises that requires basic human decency.

Instead, on January 2, 2005, one week after the tragedy, the Feminist Majority Web site touted Smeal's testimony to Congress about how the Ohio election was somehow rigged and should be thrown out.

As the world was rallying around the victims of one of the modern age's worst disasters, NOW's Web site had the usual tripe about how "abstinence only education teaches blatant lies," and "NOW remains committed to the right to marry for same-sex couples," and a link promoting an anti–George W. Bush Web site.

The inability of these organizations (and I use that term lightly these days) to respond to reality is comparable to someone driving around in 2005 with an eight-track tape player wondering why no one wants to listen to her copy of Helen Reddy's "I Am Woman."

It's Still All About the Money

At the top of the Feminist Majority's Web site you're assailed with, "Make a tax-deductible donation to the FMF today!" While NOW insists, "Support women's rights. Contribute to NOW."

Actually, I had to laugh when it dawned on me what their problem was. You see, if they promoted fund-raising for tsunami victims, *donations to their organizations would decrease.* Do not forget, I know these people and have worked with them. These are the same people who did not want to endorse Bill Clinton for president in 1992, not because he wasn't the best candidate (which even I believed at that time) but because if he won, it would affect their fund-raising.

You can imagine how surprised I was, within a year into my post as president of Los Angeles NOW, to hear that debate among national feminist leaders. It was one of the many times I was provided with a glimpse of the hypocrisy within the movement, and it was one of the many things I chose to ignore.

I was twenty-nine years old, idealistic, and gung-ho, thrilled that in Clinton we had a candidate who was great on all our issues (little did I know!). I felt that NOW and the feminist establishment could make a difference getting that man elected. You can imagine my youthful enthusiasm at the time, and the utter shock at overhearing feminist leaders more worried about their fund-raising than getting the right man into office.

Their concern? If Bill Clinton was elected, then feminists would feel the fight had been won and donations would dry up. I made a critical mistake that day (one of many in the years to come) by calling attention to the fact that it was our own fault by aligning ourselves with one party. I noted we gave the impression that we were nothing more than an extension of the Democrat party.

Molly Yard was quickest to put me in my place when she yelled, "Well, that's who we are!" It was an admonition I grew used to hearing from her, and others, through the years.

Forget about making actual progress. Forget about working to truly make a difference on the issues. Through my experience working with these women, and getting to know them personally, I discovered that the primary concern of this organization is making ·money. The danger of succeeding on the issues, of course, is you run the risk of organizing yourself out of business, and that they cannot have.

For the Feminist Elite running these organizations, generating money for the Leftist machine eclipses bringing in money to actually make a difference on the issues. Like Leftists everywhere, they are out only for themselves. The issues they tout are mere slogans.

As an example, during my tenure at NOW, direct-mail fund-raising was big at both the local and national levels for NOW and the Feminist Majority. NOW would "test" messages to see which would bring in the most dollars. Abortion rights and all its "sky is falling" rhetoric frightened people the most and hence were the biggest moneymakers. The more you could make your membership base feel as though the end of the world were approaching and women would be thrown back into the kitchen, barefoot, pregnant, and lobotomized, the more the money poured in. It didn't matter if the message was accurate or fair, or even realistic. If it made money, it would run.

You've seen it—organizations on both the Left and the Right do it. You receive a piece of mail, three pages, double-sided, with the most frightening phrases underlined. Over and over again the threat is reinforced, the rhetoric heightened, and the only solution, of course, is for you to send money.

By the time a mass mailing of tens or hundreds of thousands of pieces is sent, all the messages, all the lines, all the fear have been tested and now marketed as slogans with the specific goal of getting you to write that check.

It's rather ironic that with all the complaints the Left makes about Big Evil Corporations manipulating the public at large for the even bigger twin evils of the dollar and profit, they operate at the same level, every day and for the same reasons.

And then they have the gall to tell you *Wal-Mart* is the enemy of the working class!

Feeling Their Pain— While Convenient

Mal Nars (Malignant Narcissists) do have a remarkable knack for exploiting tragedy for their own benefit. If feminists trying to stop progress on the issues in order to make money doesn't convince you, take a gander at Bill Clinton—Missionary.

With one of the most stark examples of cashing in instead of helping out, only Clinton could find a way to make a buck while simultaneously making people think he was ministering to victims of a monumental natural disaster.

Clinton received worldwide public attention and positive press coverage when he and former president George H. W. Bush traveled in February 2005 to tsunami-wracked Asia. They were to assess the damage, meet with leaders of the afflicted nations, and deliver the personal touch of caring for the victims.

The *New York Times* reverently characterized a Clinton moment during a visit to a devastated village this way:

> Mr. Clinton's eyes watered and his voice trembled as he spoke about the trauma suffered by children in the village. "I thought about all of our religious traditions and how they all teach us how we are not really in control—but we don't really believe it until something like this happens, and it reminds us all to be a little more humble and grateful for every day," he said after his visit to the village.[1]

Within forty-eight hours of that scene, Clinton was whisked away. Most people probably think he then went to help with vaccination shots, or the delivery of food and water, or even just to sit and play with a child who is now alone in the world.

Instead, with dry eyes and a steady voice, he moved on—away from all the suffering and humbling human drama, orphaned children, and overflowing morgues—to boost sales of his memoir, *My Life*.

For a man whose people usually make sure the press know exactly where he is and what he's doing, Clinton book signings arranged in Taiwan, Hong Kong, Japan, and South Korea were kept as quiet as liaisons with an intern. The Clinton Foundation Web site[2] dutifully notes his seventy-two hours in the tsunami zone and even provides a little map where site visitors can lovingly keep track of where the ex-president will be feeling the pain of tsunami victims.

Actually, it would then have been appropriate for the Web site to provide a cash-register icon so visitors could tally up what Clinton accomplished next—for himself.

While most Americans believed Clinton was still in Asia assisting those who lost everything on earth, he was lining his pockets in Hong Kong by charging $280 for an autographed book and the thrill of shaking his hand.

While Sri Lankans were worrying about living in tents during the monsoon season, Clinton jet-setted to Taipei and the Kelly & Walsh bookstore where it's reported he signed five hundred copies of his biography.

As aid workers struggled to identify and repatriate thousands of unidentified remains, Clinton hopped over to the Kyobo bookstore in Seoul for more glad-handing, more book signings, and more public adulation.

Nowhere on the Clinton Foundation Web site, which chronicled the ex-president's tsunami travel, is there any mention of the book signings or how much money Clinton raked in. It's safe to say if his skirting off to those signings was part of his fund-raising efforts for tsunami victims, it would have been a major part of the site's reportage.

And keep in mind—Clinton leapfrogged to his book signings after the American people paid for him to get to the region—supposedly for an exclusively diplomatic and humanitarian mission.

In this instance, the "I Feel Your Pain" president surely felt nothing worse than writer's cramp and the discomfort of a fat wallet on his backside.

Striking a Pose

Probably the best example of the feminist establishment's hypocrisy is their astounding silence on the liberation of twenty-five million women and children (so far) by the United States under the leadership of George W. Bush.

Their silence on this milestone achievement for women in the Middle East makes it clear that, to them, women's issues are simply convenient slogans. Their outrage at violence against women is nothing more than the striking of a pose.

International human rights organizations documented the abuse and rape of women and girls by Saddam's inner circle. In the middle of the day, little girls were routinely pulled out of their elementary school classes for Saddam's mutant offspring, Qusay and Uday. If chosen by Saddam's sons this way, you would be repeatedly raped the rest of the day.

Even before the United States invaded Iraq, we knew a great deal about the horror that women and children faced under Saddam. And yet, here was NOW's October 2002 statement about the impending invasion and liberation:

"For Iraqi women, the war carries the danger that their nation will degenerate into an even more militarized society. We know all too well how such an extreme militarized culture in Afghanistan gave rise to a life of violence and oppression for women there. A U.S. invasion of Iraq will likely entail similar dangers to the safety and rights of Iraqi women—who currently enjoy more rights and freedoms than women in other Gulf nations, such as Saudi Arabia."[3]

In other words, the U.S. military is just like the Taliban, and our liberation of Iraq will be bad for women. And what sort of "safety and rights" had Iraqi women been "enjoying" under Saddam Hussein? Amnesty International has documented the rape of wives of opposition leaders with the violence videotaped and sent to the husbands; beheadings of women accused of prostitution; and the murder of women who criticized government corruption.[4]

In one instance, fifty women were beheaded by Saddam's henchmen, with their heads hung on doors as a warning to other women.

"Enjoying" safety and rights, indeed.

That said, the Feminist Elite continued to criticize the Bush administration for invading Iraq, even as mass graves are unearthed there, some of which were full of women and children exclusively.

And yet, after years of condemning the Bush administration, the War on Terror, and the liberation of Iraq, Eleanor Smeal seems somehow to have morphed into Rumpelstiltskin. Here is what she has to say in a December 21, 2004, press release about the not-very-surprising announcement by the Islamist Fascist Iranian government's plan to execute two women for "crimes against morality":

> "When will these barbaric acts against women stop? How can we sit by and watch innocent women brutally killed by extremist regimes around the world," demanded Eleanor Smeal, president of the Feminist Majority, asking the international community . . . to express outrage at these horrific acts.[5]

Here's a newsflash for Smeal and every woman in her wretched and hypocritical "feminist" organization—these barbaric acts against women stop *when the U.S. deposes the extremist regimes*.

Yet there was a project promoted on the Feminist Majority Web site to protest the Iraq war. While our troops were preparing to risk their lives liberating Iraq, women and children included, this is what the Feminist Elite were planning:

> Against the war in Iraq? Send Bush a tampon!

> On March 15, women all over the country are going to send President Bush a tampon that has been dyed red (with paint, food coloring, marker—anything but actual blood—that would be a biohazard . . .) along with the message: "You want blood? Have some blood."[6]

Lovely, isn't it? In what I'm sure came as a complete surprise to the Feminist Arts-and-Crafts Militia, women from all over the country did *not* send the president a tampon. Normal people were busy supporting this nation's leadership in deposing a tyrant. Obviously, Authentic Feminists have their own deposing to do these days.

The better use of Smeal's press release would have been to make it an internal memo to staff and member donors. If she and her staff, and all of her donors, were serious about stopping these "barbaric acts against women by extremist regimes around the world," she would send her organization's yearly budget as a gift to the United States Marines.

Members of the U.S. military, mostly men, many of whom are pro-life and Christian, go to these cesspools and fight and die to stop savage acts from continuing.

Smeal and her ilk complain in press releases about barbaric acts against women. Yet they consciously ignore the sacrifice our troops have made in actually ending Islamist savagery with their blood and sweat.

Ironically, if American policy reflected the Smeal/Steinem attitude, not only would Iranian women lose the hope they have with 140,000 American liberators at their border, the women of Afghanistan and Iraq would still be living lives of unimaginable hell from which the American military has freed them.

The truth of Smeal's agenda may lie in the last paragraph of the Feminist Majority's press release. What does she ask of the feminists who received this awful news about condemned and hopeless Iranian women? "DONATE to the Feminist Majority Foundation and support its work for women's rights globally."

Ah, well, there you have it. Smeal has the gall to ask for money from people because she expresses outrage at the treatment of Iranian women. Of course, they also asked for money as they sent press releases condemning the president and the liberation of Iraq.

Here's a press release for you, Feminist Elite: Your blind criticism of President Bush and the liberation of Iraq makes dealing with Iran even more complicated. The American Left's anti-Bush rhetoric and condemnation of his policy to bring democracy to the people of the world is used by our enemies. It gives aid and comfort to the very same Islamists who salivate at murdering women for "immorality." It is used to demoralize the very same people America's Left claims to represent—the hopeless and downtrodden, in this instance living under tyrants in Iran and Syria and Saudi Arabia. And it gives strength and encouragement to the Hate America First crowd who aim to weaken our military and force a worldwide American retreat.

If we were to abandon the world, our fate would belong with the Ayatollahs, the Kim Jong Ils, and the bin Ladens of the world. All because America's Left is controlled by self-obsessed Mal Nars more devoted to party politics and the empty thrill of sloganeering than to real and lasting freedom.

So, for those who wring their hands at the oppression of Iranian women, you can thank in part the Feminist Elite for making it more difficult for the United States to do what's necessary—removing another part of the Axis of Evil.

An Unnecessary War?

There used to be a day when feminists were rightfully outraged at the treatment of women around the world. Funny what happens to the principles of right and wrong when shallow hypocrites are running the show.

On International Women's Day, on March 7, 2003, several women, including the Very-Self-Important-Black-Woman-Author Alice Walker, the Not-Very-Important-Malcontent Janeane Garafalo, and NOW President Kim Gandy demonstrated at the White House to "stop this immoral and unnecessary war from happening."[7]

How horrible it is that a day meant to show support for women around the world demonstrated how selfish and cruel American feminists have become. While acknowledging that Saddam Hussein is a "maniacal tyrant, cruel and vicious," protestors bravely called for the U.S. to do nothing,[8] allowing that brutal and vicious man to torture and gas more of his own citizens, including women and children, to death.

Consider a twenty-five-year-old Iraqi woman known as Um Haydar, who, as Amnesty International reports, was beheaded in front of her children and in the street without charge or trial at the end of December 2000. Her crime? Her husband was suspected of illegal political activity. Security men took her body and the head away in a plastic bag. The fate of her children and mother-in-law, all of whom were also taken, remains unknown.[9]

It's interesting how the fate of women and children—so righteously declared as the special and unique charge of the American Leftist feminist movement—means nothing when the president is a Republican.

For Ms. Walker, Ms. Garafalo, NOW, and every other unconscious and misguided feminist who thinks that removing Saddam was "immoral," remember that Um Haydar is just one of thousands of women who have been raped, tortured, and murdered in front of their families.

Today's "liberals," including their pathetic representatives in Hollywood, don't really care about people or principles. All their braying has nothing to do with stopping war, or caring about "innocents." In reality, it's about sacrificing innocent women on the Altar of Politics. It's about slogans and partisanship and political power.

Forget about the real struggle, the real women dying, the real rape of children, the real beheadings. The pond scum of Hollywood, Leftist special-interest groups, communist traitors who give aid and comfort to our enemy with anti-U.S.A. and anti–George W. Bush rhetoric prefer to let Saddam's innocent victims struggle and die so they can make political points here at home. All because they want Republicans to look bad.

At Home with Savages

In February 2005, Bill Clinton gave a remarkable interview to PBS's Charlie Rose at the World Economic Forum held in Davos, Switzerland. The astounding thing about the interview was that Clinton named a country where he felt most ideologically at home. And it's not the United States of America.

Here's Clinton's description of the utopia he so admires:

> "It is the only country in the world that has now had six elections since the first election of [its president in 1997]. (It is) the only one with elections, including the United States, including Israel, including you name it, where the liberals, or the progressives, have won two-thirds to 70 percent of the vote in the six elections. . . . In every single election, the guys I identify with got two-thirds to 70 percent of the vote. There is no other country in the world that I can say that about, certainly not my own."

That last line drew considerable laughter from the primarily Leftist Hate America First crowd that dominated the Davos forum.

What country could he be speaking of? Perhaps Canada, or New Zealand, or maybe Sweden? Not quite. The nation with the guys Clinton identifies with is . . . the Islamic Republic of Iran.

When I first read this story, I didn't believe it. Then I heard the audiotape of the interview. Besides the rank absurdity of his description of Iranian "elections," the fact is this ex-president made these comments during the height of the nuclear standoff between Iran and the Western world.

Everyone in the free world, and the unfree world for that matter, knows that Iranian elections are as free and fair as they are in every tyranny. Saddam Hussein had "elections," too. Iraqis would go to the polls under Saddam and were handed a piece of paper with one name on it—Saddam's—and it was already checked. "Voters" were allowed to drop the ballot into the box.

Clinton, as a former president, knows that Iranian elections are meaningless. Candidates are approved by the "Supreme Guide," while, as in Egypt, no one from the opposition is allowed to run for office. Parties are banned, and if opposition leaders speak out they are imprisoned or executed.

And who are these men Clinton identifies with? He referred to the election of President Muhammad Khatami as an example of the liberal vote holding forth. This is the same President Khatami who, in the same month Clinton was praising his depraved country, declared Iran's support for Syria by declaring, "We respect the Syrians who are in the front line against the Zionist regime. . . . We support the resistance in Lebanon [led by their proxy, terrorist group Hezbollah], and all those fighting the [Israeli] occupation."

Inexplicably, Clinton insisted to Charlie Rose and the Davos audience, "Iran today is, in a sense, the only country where progressive ideas enjoy a vast constituency. It is there that the ideas that I subscribe to are defended by a majority."

And what sort of ideas are these, as represented by those elected by that incredible liberal majority in Iran? The United States government describes Iran as "one of the most active state sponsors of international terrorism."

Murdering dissidents in their own country isn't enough for Clinton's "progressives." In a trial of an Iranian for the 1992 murders of Kurdish dissidents in Berlin, the German government, not exactly a foe of the Iranians, found the government of Iran—those guys Clinton most identifies with—guilty of implementing a policy of assassinating dissidents abroad.

And perhaps the feminist establishment should remind their hero of Eleanor Smeal's complaint noted earlier about the execution of women for "morality crimes." Considering all the women's lives Clinton has personally destroyed, perhaps we shouldn't be too surprised at his affinities these days.

Clinton also admitted that during his presidency, and when Khatami was elected, he formally *apologized* to Iran on behalf of the

United States for crimes this nation had committed against Iran! The irony of this is staggering. It was Khatami's brother, Muhammad-Reza, who in 1979 led the "students" who seized the U.S. Embassy in Tehran, threatening those Americans daily with summary execution for 444 days.

Clinton apologized to the country whose agent, the terrorist group Hezbollah in Lebanon, carried out the homicide bombing of our Marines' barracks in Beirut in 1983. And now he praises the same regime that admits harboring Al Qaeda leadership and sends terrorists and more weapons into Iraq to murder innocent Iraqis and our brave troops.

Of course, the question has to be asked, Why? Why would Bill Clinton support and embrace a nation that ends its parliamentary sessions with shouts of "Death to America" as it madly scrambles to build a nuclear bomb? Why would a former president declare that he is more ideologically at home with a nation committed to wiping the nation of Israel (and all the Jews who live there) off the face of the earth?

As the United States and the world have come together to isolate and pressure Iran to back down, why would Bill Clinton give them aid and comfort? Because Bill Clinton is a classic Mal Nar and wants something for himself. And when Mal Nars want something, they'll do whatever they can to get it. They not only don't care about the impact of their actions on others, even considering other people is inconceivable to them.

What does Bill want? Most believe he is jockeying to become the next secretary general of the United Nations. We shouldn't be surprised. After all, why wouldn't Clinton be drawn to an organization where sex abuse, internal corruption, sexual harassment, and diplomatic immunity prevail?

The U.N.'s Heart of Darkness

After the world tried to commit suicide twice over in the twentieth century, the establishment of the United Nations was meant to give the world hope—hope for rational minds and decent men and women working together to make the world a better place.

Instead, and perhaps predictably, it simply became a building in New York to organize under one roof the internationalist megalomania, greed, corruption, and malignant narcissism that make the world a horrible place for so many. Today, the United Nations has proved itself to be a scourge of the world by its passive neglect and active corruption.

Since its inception it has waged a war it has yet to complete (Korea), allowed nations that sponsor terrorism and have the world's worst human rights records to sit on its Human Rights committee, admittedly done nothing about genocide, has watched sexual harassment proliferate in its offices, and, most famously, transformed the Iraq Oil-for-Food program into one of bribes, corruption, and money laundering.

That corrupt program allowed genocidal maniac Saddam Hussein to grow richer by the tens of millions. Certain U.N. Security Council member countries also benefited financially from their deal with the devil. And in 2002 and 2003, America was trying in vain to persuade countries like France, Germany, and Russia of the importance of removing Saddam Hussein.

If only we had known how big Saddam's bed actually was, it all would have made sense. Perhaps we wouldn't have given that tyrant six months' warning if we knew how many considered him their patron.

What did Saddam do with the advance warning the U.N. debate provided? Weapons inspectors agree that chemical and biological weapons still remain unaccounted for. While the search has been called off in Iraq, Syria and Lebanon are considered possible stash sites.

Knowing he could not withstand the power of the coalition military, it is now believed Saddam also took that time to design the terrorist insurgency to hunt and murder troops and civilians after his government fell.

Let me be blunt—the existence of the U.N. puts all peace- and freedom-loving people on this planet in danger. It serves to give the incompetent and malevolent a voice with which to continue worldwide misery and to delay efforts to liberate the oppressed. The U.N. is peopled with nothing more than men and women who are obsessed with themselves while cynically claiming to be the heralders of the rights of others.

The United Nations, simply put, is Mal Nar Central.

Most clear-thinking people believe the various investigations into the oil-for-food scandal have just skimmed the surface of the rot at the U.N. It is also now growing more apparent that U.N. sex scandals are not limited to their posh suites in New York.

What should be most absurd and insulting to normal people is how the U.N. describes its primary efforts: Economic and Social Development, International Peace and Security, Human Rights, Humanitarian Action, International Law, and Decolonization.[10]

All of these claims reveal how depraved they are when you consider a "Code of Conduct" rulebook the U.N. had to issue in 2002 for "peacekeepers" and staff. The message? It was a *prohibition against sexual activity between staff and children and the exchange of money or food for sex.*[11]

I think it's safe to say that at your workplace, while there should be a policy against sexual harassment, your office hasn't felt the need to have a policy forbidding the rape of children. To understand the U.N., imagine the sort of a place that *does.*

On what has been dubbed the U.N.'s "Sex-for-Food" scandal, the *London Times* reports at least 150 allegations of sex crimes by U.N. staffers in the Congo, replete with pornographic videos and photographs of U.N. staff raping little girls.[12]

In another instance, two Russian U.N. pilots paid young girls with jars of mayonnaise and jam to have sex with them. Allegations of U.N. staff in Liberia offering women sex for food or sex for jobs are commonplace.[13]

The *London Times* also reported that "U.N. 'peacekeepers' from Morocco based in Kisangani—a secluded town on the Congo River— are notorious for impregnating local women and girls. In March, an international group probing the scandal found 82 women and girls had been made pregnant by Moroccan U.N. staffers and 59 others by Uruguayan staffers. One U.N. soldier accused of rape was apparently hidden in the barracks for a year."[14]

After the initial reports of the rapes of children in Congo, the U.N. insisted the issue was an isolated incident. Now they admit they fear that sex abuse by U.N. peacekeepers is a problem *in every single one* of its sixteen missions around the world.

The *Weekly Standard* reports:

"Various U.N. reports and interviews with humanitarian groups suggest that international peacekeeping missions are creating a predatory sexual culture among vulnerable refugees—from relief workers who demand sexual favors in exchange for food to U.N. troops who rape women at gunpoint."[15]

One February 26, 2005, newswire report put it this way:

"Rocked by widespread abuse of women and girls, including gang rape, in the Democratic Republic of the Congo, the United Nations also has found sexual exploitation cases in at least four other missions— in Burundi, Liberia, Ivory Coast—as well as more recently in Haiti, they added."[16]

And what did the U.N. have to say about the bizarre systemic propensity for people associated with it to be serial child rapists and exploiters of women? "We think this will look worse before it begins to look better," Jane Holl Lute, assistant secretary-general for peace-keeping, told reporters. "We expect that more information will come from every mission on allegations. We are prepared for that."[17]

Well, isn't that nice? *They're* prepared for that. Here is an entity that is looked to for assistance from countries that are already in desperate straights. U.N. "peacekeepers" and staff establish missions where people have lost hope, where there is starvation, famine, civil wars, genocide. These are the most vulnerable among us. What is it systemically that allows a culture of rape and destruction to breed in teams of people sent specifically to help and save?

Now, courtesy of the U.N., the troubled people of the world actually have to be protected from the protectors.

If the problem were isolated, it could be explained by the probability that one freak got through a screening system. Pedophile monsters do exist. But it says something quite different when the monsters appear to be throughout a specific organization, preying on the most vulnerable, the weakest, the people who are the most desperate.

These reports, by the way, didn't just emerge. The *Weekly Standard* notes, "Allegations of sexual abuse or misconduct by U.N. staff stretch back at least a decade, to operations in Kosovo, Sierra Leone, Liberia, and Guinea."

One of the U.N.'s own reports declares, "A 2002 U.N. report characterized the sexual exploitation issue as 'a betrayal of trust as well as a catastrophic failure of protection,'" and yet nothing is done.

But then again, ignoring catastrophes is one of the U.N. Internationalists' specialties.

Somalis? Rwandans? Let's Have Another Piece of Pie!

In 1994, engaging a brutal and murderous enemy in Mogadishu, Somalia, United States soldiers suffered eighteen casualties. President Clinton's response? Withdraw the troops. What's important to remember here is that it was *Osama bin Laden* who financed the Somali warlord we were fighting and who waged a campaign of murdering journalists, U.N. troops, and innocent Somalis.

Because of Clinton's frightened-dog retreat, that Somali madman and his followers gained more support, and continued their campaign of terror. Even more important, it impressed bin Laden, who noted after that debacle that the United States was "obviously a Paper Tiger." The impression Clinton made on bin Laden no doubt contributed to that savage's confidence about being able to defeat the United States, leading to the implementation of September 11.

I bring up Bill Clinton again to remind you what led us into this discussion—Clinton angling to become U.N. secretary-general, a post now held by Kofi Annan. It's an odd job for a man to want whose inability to deal properly with international threats and problems still haunts the world.

Despite a decade of denying, it has been revealed that Clinton knew of the Hutus' "final solution" in Rwanda, and the genocide of Tutsis that took place. For years Clinton denied knowing the scope of the killing. Ten years after the 1994 genocide, it was finally revealed that his administration knew exactly the extent of the slaughter, but buried the information, justifying its inaction.

Intelligence reports obtained using the U.S. Freedom of Information Act show[18] Clinton knew of the genocide, with his senior officials privately using the word within sixteen days of the start of the killings, but chose not to acknowledge it publicly. The president, it's reported, was terrified of "another Mogadishu" and decided not to intervene.

With these reports, it appears the legacy of our first "black president" is that he chose to ignore the murderous slaughter of 800,000 actually black people.

So what could Clinton have been thinking when he chose to look away from the Rwandan genocide because he didn't want "another Mogadishu"? It's because to avoid a Mogadishu, one needs courage and a moral principle rooted in decency. Facing down murderous maniacs takes a leader who can think of someone other than himself on occasion.

Bill Clinton has never been, and will never be, that man.

Clinton's maneuver for the U.N. post could be helped by his friendship with Kofi Annan. Both men have supported each other for years. Oh, yes, guess who was head of the U.N. peacekeeping forces during the Rwandan genocide? That's right—Kofi Annan.

Both men have apologized, and Annan announced at the ten-year anniversary of the slaughter that he backed the Rwandan government's request for a world "minute of silence" to remember the victims. After confessing to not having done enough to stop the genocide, Annan then noted to the Rwandans, "Let us be united in a way we were not 10 years ago."

Well, at least he can promise that. After all, things have changed—there are *800,000 fewer Rwandans* in part because of the inaction, cowardice, and self-obsession of Clinton and Annan.

With the track record of the U.N., it makes perfect sense these two are the Internationalists' Ideal Men.

The Strategy of Hate

It's not surprising that hate would become the preferred political strategy of the Left—it is the driving emotional force of the victimized narcissist. It is a strong, survival-based emotion that is raw, simple, and easy to tap. It is also what all Leftists have in common with one another.

Hate is a bonding, familiar emotion that reinforces loyalty to the group.

Many people think that narcissism denotes "self-love." In fact, it's quite the opposite and better described as "self-obsession," specifically the belief that everything that happens happens because of you, or is about you.

While narcissism isn't curable, so to speak, it can be managed. For Leftists, however, the psychological damage of victimhood, instilled in childhood, is the cornerstone of their identities. Psychological recovery is out of the question, because eliminating victimhood threatens their very existence.

Without help to manage their narcissism, it turns malignant, with all the concomitant symptoms, the primary one being the need to transform society into their image. These damaged people work constantly to make all of society feel victimized, isolated, and hopeless.

After all, once the Leftist leaders have their supply of damaged foot soldiers marching in malignant narcissism, they realize they have to be organized and maintained.

It's worth noting that hate is not a thought, but a feeling. It is as inexplicable and amorphous as love. As feelings, both love and hate are indescribable as they, like all emotions, are not ruled by logic or reason, but spring from primitive instinct.

Many think that emotions and reason are intransigent opposites. I disagree. The emotional and rational minds are meant to work in unison. Trouble begins when one or the other operates singularly, without the benefit of the other.

The healthy individual embraces and implements both, as complementary tools to understand the world. The rational mind used without the benefit of love, understanding, or compassion is nothing more than a cold machine.

Leftists throughout the world have shown us the destruction wrought when emotions are left to their own devices, without logic or reason.

The *Oxford English Dictionary* defines "hatred" this way:

"The condition or state of relations in which one person hates another, the emotion or feeling of hate; active dislike, detestation, enmity, ill-will, malevolence." To hate is "to hold in very strong dislike; to detest; to bear malice to. The opposite of to love."

A good example of hate being used as a tool to mobilize the Left is shown by Leftist icon and mass murderer Che Guevara.

As Fidel Castro's right-hand man, Guevara was unapologetic about the mass murders he either ordered or implemented himself. While in charge of the La Cabana prison in Havana, Guevara ordered the executions of hundreds of people. As a Stalin-worshipping Communist leader, Guevara understood quite well the primary organizing tool of the Left wherever the virus took hold.

Coldly explaining his rationale, Guevara stated:

"To send men to the firing squad, judicial proof is unnecessary. These procedures are an archaic bourgeois detail. This is a revolution! And a revolutionary must become a cold killing machine motivated by pure hate."[19]

Hate as a Tool

While other Leftist leaders are either too smooth or too unconscious to articulate this strategy, Guevara was not. He admitted that hate was a strategic tool not only as an element to instill fear in the enemy but, more important, to control and direct Leftist foot soldiers:

> Hatred is an element of struggle; unbending hatred for the enemy, which pushes a human being beyond his natural limitations, making him into an effective, violent, selective, and cold-blooded killing machine—this is what our soldiers must become.[20]

There is not one Leftist "revolution" in history that was not brutal in its implementation and disastrous in result. From the French Revolution and the bloody terror that followed, to Hitler's Third Reich, to the Soviet Union, Communist China, Castro's Cuba, and Kim Jong Il's North Korea, all owe their existence and perpetuation to terror, threat, oppression, and, ultimately, genocide and mass murder.

For Marxists, epitomized by Stalin, the target for hatred was the bourgeoisie, or the capitalist, educated middle class. Terror and mass murder were the result.

For Hitler, Mussolini, and the French Vichy regime, the organizing tool of hatred was used against Jews. Terror and genocide were the result.

For the communist Chinese and North Koreans, and Castro and

Guevara's Cuba, the middle class, the educated, and the noncon-formists are hated and imprisoned or killed. Ironically, those in America who romanticize and even support these Leftist regimes are always the first to be targeted by the "tolerant" Left Elite.

Guevara's La Cabana, considered Cuba's first gulag, housed "people who have committed crimes against revolutionary morals," including dissidents, homosexuals, Jehovah's Witnesses, and even people who played loud music.[21]

Hate is the strategic tool for the Left, not just for the reasons Guevara noted, but also because it perpetuates itself once ensconced. Reinforcement and reorganizing become unnecessary once you can tap into the passive consumption of hate.

Hate embodies almost the identical symptoms of groupthink. Like driving in a circle, the hater returns again and again to thoughts of the hated. Loathing transforms into fear, and the hated becomes a threat to the hater. This fear then confirms for the hater the righteousness of their hatred, and the cycle continues.

If the rational, logical mind were to enter the picture, the absurdity of this process would be laid bare. This is why the rational mind becomes a direct threat to the cause of the Leftist. Therefore, the rational mind must be rejected by the Malignant Narcissist.

Now the concept of the "unbalanced mind" of the Leftist makes more sense, doesn't it?

I contend Leftists are indeed mentally unbalanced in their exclusive reliance on emotions, and on hate in particular. It is inevitable, however, when damage has defined you and your view of the world.

Projecting Hate

Narcissists, in their self-obsession, see themselves in everyone around them. For example, the thief thinks everyone is out to steal from him, or the liar believes everyone lies to him. Therefore, the narcissist, who is driven by hate, sees *everyone around him as driven by hate*.

Hence, one of the patent tactics of the Leftist Elite is to label as a "hater" anyone who dissents from the Leftist point of view.

By now, I'm sure even you believe that perhaps other Christians or other white men must indeed hate women, gays, and blacks. While you don't hate these groups yourself, you cannot escape the Leftist rhetoric, which has convinced almost everyone that we live in a racist, sexist, and homophobic society.

I, too, believed that. As the quintessential pro-choice, lesbian feminist establishment leader, I believed it so strongly I devoted almost two decades of my life to hating the haters. I worked to stop *their* evil agenda, which would inevitably lead to concentration camps and the extermination of people like me.

My hate was legitimate because, after all, *they* were the ones making it personal. All those evil, intolerant Christians and heterosexual Republican white men were after me, personally, and had plans to do me in. I, therefore, hatched plans of my own. I would beat them at their own game and criminalize their very thoughts.

Why? Because, as I was told, their thoughts were wrong. Their thoughts were wrong because they were hateful thoughts. The enemy hated me simply because they were full of hate for anything unlike themselves. They hated the unknown, the different, and so I would punish them and make them suffer if they dared to continue to think incorrectly, to think badly of me, to want to harm me.

Of course, once I was completely free from the Leftist establishment, and looked back on my own reasoning, I realized first with shock and then with shame that I was describing *myself* as I described the unthinking haters who wanted to punish people for being different.

The Enemy in the Mirror

It was my colleagues and I who were obsessed with people who were different from us and dared to dissent. Who was it that was hating, planning, and creating a society that punished people for thinking and behaving incorrectly? It was me. I hated not only people I had never met, but people I wasn't even sure existed.

Like good Leftists everywhere, I had constructed stereotypical bogeymen to hate, never realizing I was using myself as a template. My mind had filled in the blanks of the Bad Guy, and in my narcissism the Bad Guy was really me.

It certainly wasn't those pesky Christians who wrote hate-crimes legislation. It wasn't the straight white guy living in New Orleans, Norfolk, or Tucson who obsessed day in and day out about how to punish me and other women.

On the contrary, as most of the Leftist "enemy" were going about their business, they were committing the most serious sin of all—they weren't really thinking about women, blacks, and gays at all! Imagine my shock when I realized through talk radio that the enemy wasn't thinking day in and day out about *me*.

And, most inexplicable, they didn't hate me at all.

Oh, sure, there were frustration and irritation, mixed in with a bit of the perplexed, but with the exception of the marginalized few who still have white robes and hoods in their closets, they certainly weren't wasting their time "hating" me. But my feminist cohorts and I, on the other hand, were obsessed with them.

To this day, I think of the wasted years when I hatefully accused others of hate. I am ashamed for helping to brainwash society to the point where they don't even notice the Left has become the Cultural Gestapo—yet they still insist that conservatives are the "Fascists."

The Personal Struggle

My description to you of hate being used as a tool to manipulate and control doesn't come only from studying history and the obvious strategy of the Leftists. My personal experience within the Left is fraught with hate.

The hypocrisy was easy to see. So was the hate. One main theme that was echoed over and over again among leaders and activists in general was that we were to "trust our emotions," that our "gut feelings" were the most important thing, especially among women. I was told on scores of occasions that I was "thinking too much" when I would question certain decisions or actions.

Negative emotions, primary fear, and hate drove the Left's agenda. Virtually every feminist leadership meeting I ever attended started with the premise that we were being victimized and that we needed to destroy the oppressor. Never can I recall a gathering of any sort that was based in a progressive plan to implement an idea that would improve women's lives, or was positive in its outlook.

Hate, fear, anger, and resentment were always the order of the day, the driving force of the decisions we made and provided the bonding between street activists.

I know this because I, too, took part in the process.

While I am proud of most of my work as a feminist activist, I must remain vigilant about why I do what I do. I am always asking myself how and why I come to the decisions I make. I was effective and successful as a feminist leader partly because of the hate I fed on, the hate for the perpetual "oppressor" (always male and usually white), so I know how easy it is for me to slip into that rut.

I made my choice, and I recognized what I was becoming, and I continued, despite noticing the continuing damage, the unhappiness, the vitriol inherent in the Feminist Elite themselves.

Paranoia, distrust, jealousy and, yes, hate prevail in the feminist establishment between women and within and between organizations.

It's been fascinating for me finally to understand the difference between getting angry and doing something about it, and becoming filled with hate. I've learned the difference from the Christians and conservatives I speak with on a daily basis on my radio program. There is clarity and a focus brought to the issues when emotions are combined with logic and reason. Passion meeting the mind offers a kind of clarity not only on the issue, but on how best to make a difference.

I used to mistake hate for passion. I now can tell you I know the difference. I used hate to reinforce self-righteousness. I now use confidence and understanding to reinforce my desire to educate.

Am I free of hate? With my past, I don't think I ever will be, any more than I will be free of my own narcissism. I can tell you that my mind, as opposed to my emotions, now manages both, especially the negatives ones.

I know from my own experience that many liberals are to this day unconsciously slipping into the politics of hate without even knowing it. When you live with hate and are rewarded for it, it becomes an expected, normal part of your life. By default, hate is the emotion that infects everything you do.

I was able to recognize and reject what was happening because I was unusually lucky and became a radio talk show host. It took that sort of dynamic experience to shake me out of my trance.

I write these books and do my work to this day because I know what having access to information did for me. In addition to encouraging and supporting Authentic Conservatives and Classical Liberals, I do this work with the hope that other liberals will recognize what I did, and perhaps in the process I can save some of you five to ten years of your emotional and intellectual lives.

Taking Action

As we continue to eat the elephant, here are a few more bites we need to take for our New American Revolution. We now know that while some problems seem insurmountable, by our own actions we've seen that focus, patience, awareness, and the American spirit makes everything possible.

The Left is a very insidious force in this nation. It's not just an idea or something people feel, like hate. It has an infrastructure with people at the helm. Very few people, I might add. There are specific organizations to which we can all point that lead the rhetorical way of the Left—they perpetuate the hate, the distrust of the president, of our military, and of our own intentions as Americans.

Hasten the demise of the feminist establishment. Never discount the power of a phone call, letter, or e-mail. Contact your congressional representatives and U.S. senators. Tell them you understand that organizations like the National Organization for Women, the Feminist Majority, and Planned Parenthood receive your federal tax dollars in one way or another, and you want it to stop.

Also, tell them the nonprofit, tax-exempt status of these obviously partisan organizations should be rescinded. If enough of you send this message, it will be heard, and decent congressmen and senators may feel empowered to do something about the charade of the feminist "nonpartisan" organizations.

Go to www.senate.gov and www.house.gov to contact your representatives. You can also call Congress directly. Remember, those people work for you. You have every right to chime in and tell them what you want. **Call 202-224-3121.** The Capitol telephone operator can tell you who your senators and representatives are and connect you to their offices.

Help tear down the ACLU. One of the most damaging Leftist entities in this nation right now is the so-called American Civil Liberties Union (ACLU). This is the group recognized by thoughtful Americans everywhere as Base Camp for the Left's nihilistic agenda. For years, the ACLU has never been challenged. An organization of lawyers can be pretty intimidating, but now there are two organizations (described below) that have taken the lead to confront and reverse the impact of this enemy within.

Educate yourself about the ACLU. Clearly, this is an institution that needs to be torn down. One of the best resources you'll find with information on how you can personally make a difference and contribute to the destruction of the ACLU is Joseph Farah's Web site, www.worldnetdaily.com.

Support the Alliance Defense Fund. Founded to respond to the urgent need for the legal defense and advocacy of religious freedom, they now lead in countering the malevolent agenda of the ACLU. In addressing religious freedom and family values, the prime concern of their founders was the dramatic loss of religious freedom in America's courts. Their Web site describes their purpose to: "Aggressively defend religious liberty by empowering our allies, recognizing that together, we can accomplish far more than we can alone."

I couldn't have said it better myself.

The ADF deserves your support. If you are a lawyer, become a volunteer. As a pro-choicer, I don't agree with their entire agenda, but it's obvious that the ACLU has come dangerously close to erasing many of the things that have made this nation great and strong.

If you're pro-choice, you can feel comfortable donating money to them. Just ask them to apply your donation to a specific project, such as their work countering the ACLU.

Go to www.alliancedefensefund.org or call 800-835-5233.

Support the American Center for Law and Justice. We're lucky enough to have two organizations that are forcefully representing decent Americans through law and legislation. I can't tell you how important it is to support these organizations, which fight the ACLU on their own turf—the courtroom.

Their ACLJ Web site describes their mission:

"The American Center for Law and Justice (ACLJ) specializes in constitutional law and is based in Washington, D.C. Through our work in the courts and the legislative arena, the ACLJ is dedicated to protecting your religious and constitutional freedoms. In addition to providing its legal services at no cost to our clients, the ACLJ focuses on the issues that matter most to you—national security, protecting America's families, and protecting human life."

Most of you will support the complete agenda of the ACLJ. For those of you who don't, just ask that your donation be applied to a specific issue.

Go to www.aclj.org or call 800-296-4529.

Support the Young America's Foundation. Described as The Voice of Freedom on Campus, the Young America's Foundation (YAF) is America's largest campus outreach program. You know how the American school system, from elementary school on up, has been hijacked by Leftists.

The YAF is dedicated to making sure the marketplace of ideas actually remains so, and is committed to ensuring that increasing numbers of young Americans understand and are inspired by the ideas of individual freedom, a strong national defense, free enterprise, and traditional values. The foundation introduces thousands of American youth to these principles. They accomplish their mission by providing essential conferences, seminars, educational materials, internships, and speakers to young people across the country.

Go to www.yaf.org or call 703-318-9608 or 800-USA-1776.

Help tear down the United Nations. The U.N. is not simply irrelevant, they have become part of the problem. The Oil-for-Food scandal is only the tip of the iceberg when it comes to the corrupt nature of the organization. Sexual harassment and abuse complaints have existed for years against U.N. "peacekeepers," staff, and relief workers ostensibly helping to reconstruct poor nations.

The United States is the U.N.'s host country and primary funder. In the next year alone, the U.S. will give $490 million, at a minimum, to support those U.N. missions where a predatory sexual culture prevails. It's time our tax dollars stop being spent on an entity that is violating its own human rights declarations and is openly hostile to our nation generally and our president specifically.

What can you do?

Support Moveamericaforward.org, the organization working to kick the U.N. out of the United States: Go to www.moveamericaforward.org or call 916-441-6197. In addition to facing down the U.N., their Web site explains: "Move America Forward is a nonpartisan, not-for-profit organization committed to supporting America's efforts to defeat terrorism and supporting the brave men and women of our Armed Forces."

Stay informed and active. For thoughtful and concise news analysis and opinion, bookmark and visit daily Web sites www.news-max.com, www.frontpagemagazine.com, and www.mensnewsdaily.com.

All have a variety of views, but share the common thread of defeating the Leftists among us, and keeping this nation as great and strong as she has always been.

Fight On

Remember the words of Che Guevara, the Left's Ideal Man:

> Blind hate against the enemy creates a forceful impulse that cracks the boundaries of natural human limitations. . . . A people without hate cannot triumph against the adversary.

This is the mantra of the Left, and it's also a lie. It is the crux of the cultural and political civil war in which we are now engaged. The future will only be won by the damaged who view the world with hate if we allow it.

The optimistic, hopeful individual must be unapologetic in recognizing the superiority of hope and optimism over hate and despair. I know the Left's politics of hate can be defeated because I've been there, know how weak hate is when confronted with reality and truth, and I know *you*.

Our New American Revolution exists because Americans are different. We did not succumb to the hate and fascism of the twentieth century, and we *will* eradicate the vestiges that have crept into the twenty-first.

I've explained to you what the problems are and how they came to be. It is now time to celebrate the fact that we are better than the Left wants us to be. As we continue our New American Revolution, we can now be certain we are worthy of the ultimate sacrifice of over one million Americans in the course of our history. Throughout our history, hundreds of thousands of American heroes have suffered and died so we can continue the fight for liberty at home and abroad.

With all of us working together, I know we won't let them down.

Epilogue:
The Elephants in the Room

*A society that does not recognize that each individual
has values of his own which he is entitled to follow can
have no respect for the dignity of the individual and
cannot really know freedom.*

—F. A. HAYEK

Before we go, I'd like to address something. I debated long and hard about whether or not to write this epilogue. I am conflicted by my belief that certain issues are deeply private and, on the other hand, by my deeply held commitment to honesty. I know many of you would prefer not to be reminded that we differ on some issues, namely on my being pro-choice and homosexual.

Despite these concerns, I decided to write the epilogue. If I didn't, I felt as though I would be lying to you. After all, this is a book about individualism, and to ignore my individual elephants in the room would do none of us any good, and would make me a hypocrite.

These issues specifically do set me apart in many ways—and because I have successfully avoided discussing them with you in my two previous books and even at length on my radio program, I feel this would be the best forum to make it clear to you who I am, because in many ways this book is about doing exactly that—especially for ourselves.

My struggle with how to speak with you about these issues revealed a great deal about myself to, well, myself. Very romantically, I tell myself and others, "I am on a political island." Having left the Leftist establishment behind, I can crow, "It's nice to not have to worry about what others think. I now can speak freely and without fear."

And yet I worry about what you will think, whether you will approve or simply understand.

Here I am—the tough, seen-it-all loner who is no longer concerned about approval, no longer biting her nails wondering about the "risk" in delving into these subjects. And what is that risk? Your opinion of me, of course. I have felt quite comfortable avoiding these issues. I've done so in part because, perhaps like you, I simply preferred not to remind myself about our differences.

If I perpetually avoid meeting these issues head-on, however, it would be a personal lie that would sit square in the face of this book, and my life's work. We can only truly be Individual Americans if we explore these issues and learn a great deal about ourselves in the process.

Because I respect you, I want to make my position on issues more clear to you. I am distressed by the fact that because I'm a homosexual I am automatically thought by some to embrace the Gay Elite agenda. I do not.

While I am pro-choice, as I have aged, my opinion about the issue has grown and changed over time. And I have spoken with and listened to thoughtful people on the other side of the issue.

My experience is not unique. Our sense of who we are and what we stand for does change and grow over time. But the only way we can invite and embrace change is by being free of group politics, free of pressure, compromise, and threats to think only a certain way, or what the Left would prefer—for us to not think at all.

I finally felt comfortable writing this chapter because even though we do differ, you have made me feel safe. You extraordinary New Radical Individuals—the living legacy of the American spirit—are not only tolerant but curious.

So let's begin.

Safe to Say

There is an undeniable void of any reasonable discussion of abortion and homosexuality, let alone one led by a former Leftist whose Classical Liberal politics remain intact. Both subjects speak to the individualism at the core of this book. Now, don't get me wrong—I'm certainly not saying one needs to be pro-choice and gay to be an individual! But for me, both issues are elemental to our understanding of the concept of individualism itself, especially when it comes to government and its control over our lives.

Let me also preface this discussion with the fact that I don't have all the answers. As I've noted, one of many things I have found since my break with the Left is that I am a work in progress. At no point will I ever claim to have all the answers, nor will I promise to answer all your questions as well as they deserve to be answered.

What I strive to do, especially with difficult issues, is to be as honest as possible about my analysis and how I got there. For me, it has been an astounding personal experience to finally break free from the vicious cycle of groupthink and condemnation of those who are different from me.

At first I was afraid that if I didn't view pro-lifers, the religious, conservatives, or even heterosexuals as the enemy, my own identity would be at risk. In truth, the opposite happened. When I finally understood that thoughtful people could disagree and not be "enemies," my own personal and emotional freedom allowed me to become more myself.

For you conservatives and people of faith out there, I can already sense the hair on the back of your neck rising! Don't worry, I'm not trying to change your views. I respect religious and conservative perspectives on these issues, and it is only the groupthink Leftists who want you to think their way or not think at all.

And, of course, the heart of this book is to encourage you to own and embrace *your* opinions.

An admonition is also due to you liberals out there—don't presume because of my background and how I describe myself that you're going to hear a regurgitation of what the Left-wing establishment has to say on these issues. But stay with me, no matter how hard it is to read what I write. Liberals, I know, are not used to considering dissenting points of view.

Thoughtful People, Different Opinions

I receive hundreds of e-mails a week from listeners and readers. A great many of them come from pro-life conservatives and people of faith who note that while they disagree with me "on certain issues," they generally like what I have to say. However, most of these writers never reveal what those "certain issues" are. But I know exactly what they're referring to: the fact that I'm pro-choice and a lesbian.

Frankly, I have found this sidestepping very telling, and moving. These are the subjects that are supposed to divide Americans into two camps, one always at the throat of the other. And yet most of us would prefer to have civilized discussions, focusing on what we have in common, something I've always encouraged people to do who reach out to me. The cultural enemy camps, so relied on by the Left to keep us isolated and ignorant, must be thrown aside. In this New American Revolution, I have experienced, with very few exceptions, that all of us are keen to disagree and debate on the issues on which we differ, but ultimately it always comes back to being an American first.

A common message of mine has been that thoughtful people can and do come to different conclusions on serious social issues. I promote that message because extremists on both ends of the spectrum try to paint their opponents as evil. On the Left, those who are pro-life, very often people of faith, are made to look like ignorant, Kool-Aid–drinking bigots who hate women and live in some fantasy world reminiscent of the Stone Age.

Of course, that is a lie perpetuated by isolated ideologues who have no clue of what they speak.

Over the years, religious fundamentalists, too, have had a field day demonizing and isolating pro-choicers. The all-inclusive and unmistakable "baby killer" is a label I've heard too many times to count. It has been screamed at me, written to me and, one time, even phoned in attached to a rather specific and vile threat to kill me because of my abortion rights work.

I would guess that person never understood the irony of threatening to kill someone in defense of the pro-life position.

Pro-Choice, Not Pro-Abortion

For the record, I am pro-choice, not pro-abortion. For many politicians, this is just a statement meant to cover one's bases. Not for me. I stopped compromising and appeasing people a long time ago.

But this wasn't always the case. For a very long time I accepted an argument that abortion was actually good for women.

I accepted that argument because it was articulated by a woman I admired—a woman I wanted to impress. I didn't mind not thinking the issues through because I wanted to be accepted.

My feminist activism began back in the mid-1980s. I was young, in my twenties, and automatically considered myself pro-choice. The difference in me between then and now is that I now understand the deeper core of why the issue has always been important to me.

Ultimately, it is about the most intimate element of self-determination and individualism. How? I became active fifteen years ago because of a group called "Operation Rescue." This crowd was nothing more than bullies dressed up as religious extremists, primarily white men, traveling the country and physically blocking the entrances to women's health-care and abortion clinics.

In the name of being pro-life and wanting to "save babies," these bullies decided that the rights of a fetus eclipsed the rights of a woman. I know many of you also feel that way, but having an opinion and using physical force to coerce someone to obey your will are two different things.

My first glimpse of this group was on television outside a women's health-care clinic in New York City. At the time, working in public relations, I casually identified as a feminist and wrote the right checks to Leftist special-interest groups.

The bullies of Operation Rescue were blocking the entrance to the clinic, which provided everything from Pap smears to prenatal care to, yes, abortion services. To this day, I see a nurse-practitioner at a clinic just like the one I saw overrun by these self-righteous bullies who had decided that they knew better than the women who were seeking medical care.

There are moments in our lives when we know a transformation has taken place. That was one of those moments for me. It wasn't so much that women were not being admitted to the clinic (it certainly did irritate me, though!). It was the arrogance and message of the event itself.

For me, it was a sign of a sort of cultural totalitarianism—the manifestation of a group of people who had decided they would tell women what they could and could not do. At the time I was not able to articulate what had moved me so much, but now I know. It is an instinctual rejection of what sits at the heart of totalitarianism—a group of people with such an inviolate belief combined with a cynicism and hatred for others that they don't think twice about resorting to physical force and intimidation to get what they want.

What I knew then was that my involvement in the movement needed to move beyond writing checks. What I didn't know at that moment was that one experience would change the rest of my life.

In the years that followed, I became president of Los Angeles NOW. This was during the time, the early nineties that for feminist activists were known as the "abortion wars." Ironically, Operation Rescue became a terrific organizing tool, as it motivated thousands of activists into Leftist movements. It brought people like me into the clutches of the Left-wing establishment.

As a Left-wing leader, I knew the strategy: new recruits, who had malleable one-track minds, usually engaged in activism only on a single issue ("I am a feminist because I support a woman's right to choose," "I am a Leftist because [fill in the blank]," etc.). It was our job as establishment leaders to "connect the dots" for them. In other words, the extremism of one group such as Operation Rescue would be used to paint *all* Christians, *all* pro-lifers, and *all* conservatives as bullies who wanted nothing more than control over your very body.

I believed that message. As a young woman working in the entertainment industry, I had no contact with real Christians or the politically conservative. They were not in my world. I bought the Leftist leadership message hook, line, and sinker.

Ignoring the Questions

Personally, I simply ignored the questions I had about the issue of abortion. At first, it was easy because there was so much work to do.

But as my sense of individualism burgeoned, I realized that ignoring my questions—and ignoring the civilized discussion of the issues with rational people with divergent views—forced me to be ever more conscious about my own position and why I think what I think. In my gut I knew that groups like Operation Rescue assaulted my ability to determine my own freedom as a woman in a larger sense. But I hadn't yet owned my own beliefs and opinions. Owning these issues and being able to engage people about them speaks directly to your personal political power. And that is the last thing the Left wants you to do.

For me, being pro-choice means being determined to keep the government from dictating what I can do with my body. I realize the heart of the argument for many pro-lifers is that abortion is murder and demands the intervention of government.

The argument about when "life" begins is inherently a religious one. And while I have the utmost respect for people of faith and Christianity especially, the United States is not a theocracy. The laws we put into place should not be guided by a strongly held religious belief.

These days, people of faith have also grabbed hold of scientific and medical progress to reinforce their argument about a fetus being a separate person worthy of government protection. But let's be honest here—the antiabortion argument is one rooted in faith, and has no place being ensconced in legislation.

Ultimately, I believe legislation at the federal or state level outlawing abortion sends one message and one message only—women are so out of control and uncontrollably barbaric that we kill babies on a whim and need to be controlled by Daddy Government.

In a nation where women's decisions about their own reproductive lives are so unethical they have to be managed by the Feds, how could we trust creatures like those in a boardroom, in the halls of Congress, or in the White House?

The answer is, you don't. It also sends a message to women that we are to be "taken care of." Young women hear the message that nothing more is expected of them, they are creatures to be kept, to be handled, to be controlled. Make no mistake, the choices women make about their reproductive lives is at the core of freedom for women.

And there, my friends, is where I leave the feminist establishment and the pro-abortion Left.

The Problem of Abortion

Dear Tammy,

I caught your lecture on cable a couple of weeks ago, think it was CSPAN, and one idea really hit home with me. This is a thing that has bothered me for years and you said it so well. It was on the abortion issue. Why . . . why could it possibly be that if feminism has been successful, that abortion is still such an issue?

It has bothered me for a long time. When I was pregnant with my only child who is now 12 years old, my opinion on abortion gelled in a real way that had previously been just abstract ideas. I knew at that time that there was no way I could ever tell anyone that they could not have control of their own body.

I knew at that time that I would not support any law restricting abortion. I also knew at that time that a pregnancy is a support for another distinct and individual life, and that abortion is ending a life and that I personally would never take part in the very freedom I support.

Tammy, I am a feminist. But feminism has failed our young women at the basest levels. I really want to see a way to empower, and if young women are not empowered with their own bodies, they are not empowered at all.

Keep up the good work.

Angie

Angie is right. Empowerment is the key. Empowerment, I note, is not being able to march into an abortion clinic. Empowerment is *not having to march into that clinic in the first place.*

At every one of my speaking engagements, where many young feminists attend, I ask rhetorically if they ever wonder why abortion is still an issue in the twenty-first century.

The legacy of the modern feminist movement has been one of exploitation and abandonment. Have there been occasional successes? Absolutely. There were enough successes in the 1960s and 1970s to make the movement viable.

But then the abortion rights fight morphed into something other than a fight for women. It became a necessary cash cow for the feminist establishment that could never truly be "won." It was the key rally point within the feminist establishment. Therefore the idea of eradicating the need for abortion became anathema. In other words, the Feminist Elite pitched abortion as a good thing, as opposed to a sloppy and backward way to deal with irresponsibility, in the scientifically advanced late twentieth and twenty-first centuries.

Sexual freedom is like every other freedom we have. When it comes to our rights, we live in a nation where we can do as we please, for the most part. The lesson is this—the value of a freedom is realized only when you choose how *not* to use it. As an example, with freedom of expression we have become better people because while we can say whatever we please, we don't.

We have learned the value of words and their consequences. This personal restraint in the face of freedom to act, I believe, is at the core of what makes Americans so different. With American-style freedom, we have had the benefit of the personal growth allowed by having to struggle with choices and seeing the benefits, or the harm, of the choices we make.

You see, it's not having the choice that's the problem, it's the character of the decisions we make.

I mentioned how for a time I embraced the idea that abortion was a good thing; that women being able to abort when necessary was a right not just for convenience, but it was something singularly fundamental to women's freedom.

Fortunately, I grew up and realized that women's real power was based not on how many options we could employ to handle desperate mistakes, but on having enough understanding and love for ourselves so that we did not make those mistakes in the first place.

With sexual freedom should come responsibility. The feminist movement initially claimed to want to stop women from being sex objects. Now all you have to do is look at any women's magazine in your grocery store and the headlines scream: HOW TO BE HIS LOVE SLAVE! or BE SEXIER IN BED, or KNOW WHAT HE REALLY WANTS BE-TWEEN THE SHEETS. How can headlines like this possibly stop women from being treated like sex objects? And, worse, how can women develop a healthy, serious respect for themselves by reading that trash?

The Ultimate Feminist Betrayal

Establishment feminism has not only ignored the issue of personal responsibility, it has encouraged a cultural anarchy when it comes to how we lead our lives. Instead of lifting women up and out of sexual objectification, the abortion rights effort has forced them to condemn themselves. Feminists focus on abortion as something that women should have not just with ease, but with pride. Yet they ignore promoting sexual respect and responsibility.

The epitome of this monumental failure and condemnation of women is the fact that today abortion rights is still an issue! Any reasonable person and certainly reasonable feminist must ask, "Why, in a world where birth control is affordable and easily accessible, where Planned Parenthood has been around for almost a hundred years, are there still so-called unwanted pregnancies in the first place?"

With our modern knowledge and science, there is absolutely no reason for abortion even to be an issue in our lives.

Unless, of course, it's the only issue with which you can organize and fund-raise. Think about it—what has been the only issue you've been hearing about from the feminist establishment for the past twenty years? Abortion. It is an issue perfectly suited for the Malignant Narcissists running the depraved status quo in Leftist groups such as NOW, the Feminist Majority, and Planned Parenthood.

When presented properly, the abortion rights mantra gets money to pour in as women flock to fend off the Great Oppressor who wants women to be barefoot, pregnant, and in the kitchen.

So, you see, if sexual responsibility had been a cornerstone of the feminist movement's rhetoric, it would have saved so many women from having to endure what must be at the very least an unpleasant surgical experience and, at the very worst, a life-changing trauma.

As we have seen, however, what's best for women is the last thing on the Leftist establishment's list. Their actions are determined by what's best for their fund-raising.

The Abortion Police?

America is great because we balance freedom with decency and responsibility. At the heart of the power of American individualism is making sure that government does not get too big or too powerful—here at home in our private lives. Only then can we guarantee our lives are controlled by *our* values—not the Left's or those of anyone else invested in government as Daddy.

I note this because there is an arena where I want America's power to be second to none—and that is in our military and foreign policy. That is where the United States government, at the behest of the American people, should use its extraordinary power to quash tyranny, expose corruption, and spark freedom and democracy.

So, when we consider laws here at home, we must give thought to what the enforcement of those laws means to our lives, our trust of one another and of government itself.

Consider this: If we really do think abortion is murder, and if we are going to pass laws that restrict what a woman and her doctor can do, how are we to enforce this? I, for one, believe we should enforce our laws. We're nothing but hypocrites if we say something is important enough to command federal legislation and then do nothing about it.

So what shall we have? Uniformed Abortion Police at doctors' offices? Should women have to sign an investigation form when they go to the doctor declaring what they're there for? Should there be cameras in the examination room? What happens if your wife or daughter, God forbid, goes in for an examination during her pregnancy and then miscarries? That experience alone can be devastating. Should she now be grilled by the Abortion Police where she and her doctor would have to "prove" to the Feds what really transpired?

One of the more dramatic experiences I had during my clinic defense work was outside of a clinic during an attack. My group had organized a defensive ring around the clinic, and we were alerted by walkie-talkie whenever a patient arrived. We had the clinic call all their patients scheduled for that day, whatever their procedure, and had them park a block or two away from the clinic.

We then had a team meet the patient, and dress her up as a pro-choice clinic defender to get her through the throngs of bullies. If we did not do this, the patient would be subjected to some of the most extraordinary verbal abuse you can imagine, from people who had no idea why she was coming to see her doctor.

Remember, we were defending clinics that performed a whole variety of services for women, not just abortion.

Toward the end of the day, the bullies realized what we were doing. I was escorting a young and frightened woman into the clinic, when we were descended upon by four men. One was a man who appeared to be in his forties, the other three in their twenties. When we saw them running toward us as a pack, I and two other clinic defenders surrounded the woman as best we could to protect her. We had no idea what to expect.

When they reached us, the older man started to scream that she should be ashamed that she was having an abortion, and that she and the rest of us were baby killers. I asked this man if he really had any idea why this woman was here. He said he was told every woman coming to this clinic was having an abortion. I told him to look at the sign—for all we knew she was here for prenatal care, or a Pap smear.

He looked a little confused and then demanded she tell him what procedure she was having. The four men kept a very aggressive position against us. We in fact were unable to move as they surrounded us.

The patient began to cry, burying her head in my shoulder. He demanded again she tell him why she was there. I then asked him,

"Do you realize what you're doing? You're standing in a parking lot screaming at a total stranger to report to you why she's going to the doctor. What if this was your wife, or your daughter?" As I looked to the younger men, "Why should she have to tell you, total strangers, what her plans are in this clinic?"

I was shocked but the older man actually looked a bit pensive. So did the young men with him. He then said, "Well, let her tell you then." I told him I was as much of a stranger to her as he was and I had no business asking either.

He actually backed away and, to my complete amazement, said, "You're right. This is ridiculous." He apologized to the woman and then said, "Let's go, boys." I was to find out later that was a man and his sons who attended a local church. This man "getting it" made me realize that reason and logic could be grasped even in the heat of the moment.

Those thoughtful men, no doubt, are probably still pro-life. But at least on that day they decided not to become fascist Abortion Police.

Becoming the Mob?

I tell you this story because if we are to pass and enforce antiabortion legislation, including late-term abortion restrictions, we will be re-creating that scene in the parking lot, where strangers will be demanding of women information about why they're seeing their doctor, what their intentions are, if they're pregnant, or if they're not.

Instead of persuading people to realize how obscenely invasive this sort of mob mentality is, we will be on our way to codifying it.

Americans also seem to be a bit uncomfortable with the reality of antiabortion laws, including late-term abortion restrictions. Interestingly, laws either written or discussed call for the arrest of the doctor performing the procedure, but not of the woman involved.

Why not? I believe at our core as Americans, even on this serious an issue, we refuse to have a nation where doctors and women are under suspicion and arrested like common criminals. And yet, if we're serious, we're nothing more than hypocrites for ignoring the woman at the center of the debate! Ignoring women in that fashion actually reinforces the message that women either have no control, are easily led, or are so unhinged they cannot be held personally responsible.

No matter how you feel about when life begins, the refusal of lawmakers and Religious Right organizations to lobby for the arrest and punishment of women exposes the underlying recognition of the invasive and fascist nature of the law.

To put it in even clearer perspective, let me use an example with which I believe a great majority of us are in agreement—the impact of guns.

Owning a gun, having that power, is something the vast majority of gun owners respect and take seriously. And yet there is a small percentage of people who abuse the right and do great harm with firearms. It is that small minority of evildoers who fuel the antigun crowd with their frenzied calls for the banning of guns.

We argue against that because we know that the few should not direct a government crackdown on the majority who follow the law and handle guns responsibly.

I argue that outlawing abortion because of a few women who abuse it is also not fair or right. Should there be continuing public debate and discussion about the issue? Absolutely. As I've already noted, there *must* be an increased discussion among women about sexual responsibility.

We must work to make abortion an irrelevant argument by making abortion obsolete. Banning the practice, just like banning certain speech, will never make it go away, it will simply be driven underground. It will also stop the very necessary public argument about the failure of the feminist establishment.

Authentic Feminists and conservatives have a great deal in common, actually. True empowerment of women involves being in control of their own lives, including their reproductive lives. Having to resort to abortion means we have lost that control. Social arguments based in persuasion on the issue of personal self-esteem and empowerment linked to sexual responsibility will transform women's lives.

At the same time, imagine, if we *do* make abortion unnecessary and passé, our modern fascist feminist establishment will lose their only successful fund-raising and organizing tool. When they lose their control at maintaining abortion as an issue, it means women's lives will actually improve; more women will be free to find and embrace their true individual selves, free of the feminist bosses, and finally off the Leftist plantation that keeps so many women enslaved.

The Choice of Homosexuality

Abortion is not the only forbidden topic. Homosexuality, and how we deal with it as a marginal lifestyle, speaks directly to the American commitment to personal freedom and diversity.

Of course, I'm not speaking of the Left's version of diversity here, which requires you to become lobotomized and passive about issues. I speak of the authentic, Classically Liberal American point of view of allowing people to live their lives while expecting the same tolerance, respect, and dignity that you live by, in return.

That's hardly the case today when we speak of "gay" politics. Rarely do we have a personal discussion about the issue and its relationship with individualism, so now it's time we do so.

Perhaps the headline for this section has already given you pause. The most politically incorrect thing a homosexual can admit is that their sexuality is their choice. It is for me. The ongoing rhetoric in the "gay" community that we're "born this way" is patently absurd, primarily because the people making this claim have no clue what the truth is. They have no idea because it's forbidden to suggest we study or inquire about the nature of homosexuality.

So, instead of being curious and wanting facts, it's simply politically more manipulative to make a declaration about science without even bothering to involve science.

My readers and listeners often ask me about my homosexuality. For many of you, I may be the only lesbian you know. I think for most of you I represent one gay person whom you feel you can safely ask questions and get honest answers.

I received a very thoughtful e-mail from a gentleman, I'll call him "Robert," who asked a very smart question. He watched a presentation of mine on C-SPAN where I discussed this issue and wrote asking me to elaborate on what it actually meant for me to *choose* homosexuality. As a heterosexual, he noted that it wasn't something he chose or even thought about. It was simply, naturally, who he is.

An excellent point, and worth addressing.

You don't have to be a brain surgeon to recognize that heterosexuality is the natural order. The supermajority of people—about 95 percent or so—are heterosexual. While the majority of those people are naturally who they are, there is also a percentage of people who identify as heterosexual but are in fact attracted at times to the same sex, yet ignore it.

I suppose our sexuality is like our health—we really don't notice the norm, unless it's affected. If you're a healthy person in general and rarely get sick, your perspective about your health fades. Being well is the natural order of things. It's only when the flu throws you for a loop that you realize how wonderful good health really feels.

While I'm using a health analogy, I am in no way suggesting homosexuality or bisexuality is a sickness. It is simply the best analogy I can think of; health, like sexuality, is something that most people take for granted and almost ignore as a regular part of the daily life experience (in one way or another). Good health is a scenario that can seem automatic, and we live in it without thinking about it.

For heterosexuals who have no attraction to the same sex, there is simply no counterpoint for them to consider. That's perfectly normal.

Our health is specifically and intensely personal. How we feel and how our body behaves is unique to us and like no other. But very few people relate to themselves in this way. I can't stress enough how our sense of individualism is not just in our minds, but also in our perception and awareness of our bodies. Our sexual awareness should be on the same plane.

When someone realizes that he or she may not be exclusively heterosexual, either religious convictions or family upbringing make it a difficult snafu. It is this diversion, if you will, that makes certain people more aware of their sexuality specifically because it *does* diverge from the norm, even if it is never acted on.

Personally, I was never distressed by my sexuality. I'm lucky in that regard. Being able to be honest about myself has led me to a level of comfort about who I am. I am also not threatened by asking questions, by being challenged, or by the fact that I am indeed a minority and even live a socially marginal life because of my choices.

Why? Because I have not always been free to be myself. You know my history and the personal compromises I made while leading NOW. My individualism relied so intensely on the approval of others that I had lost touch with what really mattered to me. All that mattered in those years as a Leftist leader was pleasing others, toeing the line, and living the lie.

I now understand that true individualism requires accepting oneself, no matter how divergent our choices, as long as they are reasonable choices.

When I speak of "choices" here, I'm speaking of mature, thoughtful choices which, when it comes to sex, involve consenting adults. There is absolutely no legitimacy to the targeting of children or others who are unable to consent to a sexual relationship.

I know Leftists in our society want those lines to be blurred, but they don't have to be. We can recognize divergent sexual points of view, without having to "understand" or "tolerate" depraved acts that destroy people's lives. There is no slippery slope here—this is called common sense.

Preference, Not Orientation

Even while many of my speeches at universities have been boycotted by the gay groups on campuses, there is usually a representative cadre in the audience. Of all the things I say, the Gay Gestapo is infuriated most when I declare that my sexuality is not an "orientation," but my "preference."

Liberals are always shocked by this statement, which is tacitly forbidden in the gay community. The only "correct" position is that we are all born this way. According to the Gay Gestapo, you are to refer to homosexuality only as sexual "orientation."

Of course, the silliness of this claim reinforces the main lie in the Leftist world—that none of us are responsible for our behavior, who we are, or what we become.

If anyone dares suggest that we analyze the psychological history or development of homosexuality, it causes the hissy fit heard around the world.

I am dismayed by the lack of personal reflection in the gay community about who and what we are. Within the community itself, the Gay Gestapo has pushed along the message that any effort to gain insight about our nature is really a secret plot to "change" or "convert" us into the dreaded heterosexual. To prevent this secret plot, we have to claim that we're born this way.

This "gay from birth" angle also makes it easier to argue for special protections as a group, like a racial minority. This drive for special social protections (like hate crimes legislation, nondiscrimination laws, etc.) requires homosexuality to be an "identity" as opposed to just a sliver of who we truly are, to say nothing of it being a sliver based on *behavior*.

I'll repeat what I noted in an earlier chapter: There is *nothing* that makes homosexuals different from anyone else except *behavior choices*. Ranging from who we sleep with to behavior affectations, all of these things are *choices*. To deny this is a complete and total abdication of the individual self. Claiming a gay "identity" is nothing more than a slogan to excuse oneself from personal responsibility and personal control. It is the ultimate in individual abandonment.

Some gays argue back that sexual *attraction* is not a choice. I believe that to be true, but I personally am intensely curious about *why* my sexuality is indeed different from the norm, being attracted to both women and men. And until there is legitimate and comprehensive scientific investigation into the differences, we must consider *environment* and *choice* to be factors in the actions we take.

For the victim class, however, recognition as a special victim group is ambrosia. And the only way the Gay Gestapo can achieve this is to forbid any actual inquiry about what makes us tick, and then simply claim that there is some extended identity attached to being attracted romantically to the same sex.

For me, nothing could be further from the truth.

Deciding on Identity

For most of my young adulthood I was heterosexual. I didn't identify myself as such, it was simply a sliver of my identity then. Being homosexual for me now is a bit more complicated.

In all honesty, I have always felt an attraction to other women. While I loved men, women were inherently different creatures—I saw a beauty in women that I simply did not see in men.

I identified through my twenties as bisexual. Attracted to men and women, I eventually resolved to *decide* what I wanted and who I was going to become. Ultimately, the obvious reality of the situation was that if I were with a woman, I would be gay and if with a man, straight. Even the label "bisexual" infers a promiscuity in which I did indulge in those days. But I recognized even then that my identity was up to me. I wanted to be clear about what I wanted and, as a result, understand more of who I was.

I remember quite distinctly when I made my decision to identify as a lesbian. I realized that if I were to be with a man, I would also need a woman in my life. Yet, when I was with a woman, I did not need a man. Clearly, I had a preference and felt it important to choose. So I did.

There was also a basic but important difference for me—when with a man, I felt as if I were with a creature from another world. I was disturbed by the fact that I could never *really* know what he felt, physically and emotionally. Being with men, for me, was guesswork at many levels. I also don't want to mislead you here—I enjoyed being with men romantically, but there was always something missing, something key.

When I am with a woman, there is a complicity, a fundamental understanding of who and what we both are as women. An inherent recognition of each other, physically and emotionally. There is no guesswork there. I am simply more comfortable, more at ease, more involved with a woman.

So, you see, being a homosexual is indeed my sexual preference, not an "orientation." It is, I admit, an indulgence that for many of you is probably seen as selfish and inexplicable. I do not begrudge you your opinion, but what I can tell you is that I am committed to making sure that who I am not only does not make our world worse, but better. I do that with my work. I have made a conscious choice to discuss this issue only when relevant and when it can help explain why I do what I do.

I do thank God and the forebears of this extraordinary nation for creating an environment where I can safely be myself. I thank you for that as well. It is not lost on me that your compassion and commitment to tolerance, despite your disagreement with some of my personal choices, allow me to lead a wonderful life.

Mary Cheney Makes a Difference

The Democrats and the Leftist Elite, while mouthing slogans in support in individualism, are the worst harborers of all they decry—

racism, sexism, and especially homophobia. One of the best examples of this is a moment from the 2004 presidential campaign, a moment that decent Americans should make a note to remember.

John Kerry, thankfully shown the door by a majority of Americans, used one of the presidential debates to make a singular point about his view of homosexuality, and it wasn't what most people would have expected.

Kerry, in this grand moment, used Mary Cheney by noting she was a lesbian and then, remarkably, declaring what Mary would have to say about whether homosexuality is a choice. Turning into Miss Cleo, Kerry declared Mary would say she was "being who she was born as."

Wow, I had no idea he was so close to Mary, or could read the minds of lesbians. I better go think nice thoughts right now!

Reports from those in the auditorium indicated there was a general gasp from the mixed Republican and Democrat crowd. The gut instinct of the people in the room, and the millions watching, was that Kerry's use of Mary Cheney was more than inappropriate—it smacked of exploitation and an agenda based in something other than respect.

In reality, Kerry exposed more of the New Left strategy than he had hoped by revealing the ugly underside of the collective. Kerry made it clear: If you try to stop us, we'll come after your children.

There are plenty of gay people Democrats know of. If they really want to make a point about what the homosexual thinks, they could have their candidate refer to the very out daughter of Dick Gephardt, Chrissy Gephardt, or the very gay Senator Barney Frank, or the newly "Gay American" and former New Jersey governor, Jim McGreevy.

While the Kerry behavior seems bizarre at best, there is a method to the Left's madness.

First, Mary Cheney is hated by the Gay Elite. There are discussions and direct efforts to make life uncomfortable for her. Why? Because she dares to be different. She has made the same mistake as

I—she refuses to have her sexuality be the singular defining aspect of her identity, and she has had the gall to be her own person and not bow down to the Leftist agenda. Yes, she commits the fatal mistake of not conforming to the conformist gay agenda.

Of course, pundits have argued that you can't embarrass an openly gay person by referring to her as, well, gay. While Mary Cheney is out, she has made choices to lead a quiet private life, laden with that pesky dignity thing, and, oh yeah, she's a . . . a . . . Republican!!

Mary Cheney is a perfect example of the New Radical Individual. She is someone who is committed to being herself, with all its complexities and inevitable isolation. Mary Cheney, like each of her parents, is an American first.

Secondly, and perhaps even more revealing of how disconnected the Democrat party gang really is, they truly felt Christians would reject the Bush and Cheney families because of this issue.

In the decade-plus of my work as a radio talk show host and writer, I have spoken with thousands of Christians from across this country. What I have found, coming from the feminist establishment as I do, is that while they hold religious beliefs against homosexuality, they are the most tolerant, understanding, and kind people I have ever met.

One of the most illustrative examples of this is provided by President George W. Bush during private moments when, unbeknownst to him, he was being recorded. In 1998, just as the president was moving onto the national scene, Doug Wead secretly taped scores of private conversations between himself and then–Governor Bush.

The president recounted pressure he received by extremists to attack homosexuals. How did one of the most powerful and influential Christians respond? He insisted he was "not going to kick gays, because I'm a sinner. How can I differentiate sin?"[1]

And when recounting to Wead a report from the Christian Coalition he noted, "This crowd uses gays as the enemy. It's hard to distinguish fear of the homosexual political agenda and fear of homosexuality, however."[2]

Oh sure, there are fringe extremists on the Right, just as there are on the Left. But the hundreds of Christians and others I heard from by e-mail and on my radio program are representative of the same thoughtful, compassionate Christianity that envelops the president.

It's worth reiterating one of the president's points: There's a difference between the "gay" agenda and homosexuals. I drove this point home to you earlier in this section. The president understands the difference, and exemplifies how being against "gay" marriage has absolutely nothing to do with homophobia.

Respecting Traditional Marriage

The gay rights movement started in the sixties with a simple demand: All we wanted was to be left alone. Boy, how things have changed. Now not only do we demand bigger government, but we insist Big Daddy Government luuuuuuuuve us like no other.

Like spoiled little children, we want everything everyone else has. It's like the little kid who kicks and screams and demands the same ice cream some other little kid has. Then, when he finally gets it, he throws it on the ground.

The Gay Elite demand demonstrations of how much the rest of America loves and accepts us. And yet they also want to be different, unique, marginal, out of the mainstream, eschewing the norm and condemning tradition.

Well, except when a certain tradition will get them something— or rob others of their specialness. I'm talking about gay marriage.

The debate over the idea of gay marriage has produced arguments that it will lead to people marrying their livestock on one extreme to cries of "Homophobe!" and "Bigot!" on the other extreme.

Neither accusation is valid, so as an independent gay woman, I think it's time to make a few things clear. First of all, despite what you hear from the Gay Elite, there is *no* consensus in the gay community about this issue. We do not all operate in the cultural or political equivalent of a Vulcan mind-meld.

I am not alone in the gay community in my respect and understanding for the growing concern about the disintegration of our traditions and values. Consequently, I respect the majority of Americans and their opinion that marriage should be defined as between one man and one woman.

At the same time, as an American, I also believe that every American deserves the same rights and protections as every other. Most of you do, too. The very same polls that show how united Americans are against "gay marriage" indicate a majority approves of civil unions.

That doesn't surprise me. It is consistent with the American belief that we can have fair play and equality while recognizing the need to honor traditional institutions.

Frankly, I believe the cultural trouble and moral vapidity in our society today has sprung from the "liberation" movements of the sixties and seventies. It was then that the Left began to attack tradition in the name of liberation and equality.

Anything that would strike a pose against authority and social norms—ranging from promiscuous sex to drug abuse to adultery to riotous violence—was embraced and encouraged by the Leftist leadership. The "counterculture" was born.

Today's struggle with single-parent families, drug addiction, the epidemic of sexually transmitted diseases among the young, suicide rates, the devaluing of the family, and even the extraordinarily high divorce rate, I contend, can be traced back to the time that lionized the destruction of tradition and the elevation of moral relativism.

Despite this, American society remains committed to equality, but it's apparent that we don't like the aftermath of taking our traditions for granted. So, yes, we've decided to maintain the idea of "marriage" as it has stood, while finding another way to guarantee the rights of gay people.

Yet that's not good enough for our modern Gay Gestapo. Consider the reckless lawbreaking behavior of San Francisco Mayor

Gavin Newsom bestowing marriage licenses on gay couples. A few of my gay friends voiced their support for this action. I reminded these friends, who are also pro-choice, that Fresno, California, has a pro-life mayor. How would they feel if that mayor decided to ignore the law and keep women from accessing their legal abortion rights?

They heard me, but it was disturbing that I had to put this into perspective.

The Silly Putty Solution

In an answer to the recklessness of predictably nutty San Franciscans and Massachusetts judges who decide to legislate from the bench, President Bush's solution is to amend the U.S. Constitution.

Regardless of how you feel about gay marriage, the Constitution is not made of silly putty—to be twisted and shaped and torn apart depending on our national mood. It is written in a way that forces us to struggle with issues we face.

After all, if we are truly committed to wanting to save and not tamper with our traditional institutions, which represent the core of the American value system, doesn't the Constitution fall into that category as well?

We've been through worse, we've survived and found solutions. We'll survive this, too, but the gay community must come to terms with a few issues first.

Gays ultimately need to stop looking to government and society-at-large for unconditional love and approval of who we are. Andrew Sullivan, a political commentator and writer whom many of you know and respect, wrote a piece for *Time* magazine in which he actually equated governmental recognition of gay marriage as a necessary element to all gay people feeling accepted and wanted. He claimed that anything other than marriage will "build a wall between gay people and their own families."

While his story was personal and moving, the argument was,

frankly, nonsense, and representative of the general mentality among the Gay Elite. It also gives the government and other people's opinions far too much power over the quality of our lives and effectively eliminates our own responsibility for our happiness.

Part of the fight for gay marriage is based in Sullivan's lament— that it is only governmental recognition of who we are that will make us whole. Let's get real. The only thing that will make gay people whole is personal acceptance of ourselves by ourselves. Instead, we are still looking to Mommy or Daddy, now in the form of Society, to tell us we're Okay. To sanctify, if you will, our lives and relationships.

Society has been the benevolent parent for a very long time. It has been amazing, and a testament to the American character. Despite being a people of faith who have legitimate concerns about the gay lifestyle, Americans have made this the best place on earth for gays and lesbians, where we are free to live incomparably rich lives.

Now, when Americans have said, through polls and by voting, that they do not want to give up the meaning of marriage but support a comparable alternative, how do the Gay Elite respond? When you ask for one cultural thing to be left untouched, the Gay Gestapo emerges.

It's a very fast change from the polo shirt to the Brownshirt these days.

In classic Thought Police fashion and like children throwing a tantrum, the name-calling flies—those who oppose gay marriage are "homophobes," "haters," and the label du jour, "bigots." Once again the Left, unable to answer critics with respect, resort to name-calling only to widen the divide they need to validate their inevitable victimhood.

Marriage is worth protecting, in more ways than one. It's also worth noting the cavalier way in which heterosexuals have handled marriage has lent fuel to the fire of this issue.

How seriously can any of us take the president's vow to "protect the sanctity of marriage" when Britney Spears indulges in it for five minutes in Vegas? To say nothing of marriage actually becoming a television reality game show.

And protecting children? Before amending the Constitution, perhaps the states should make divorce a little harder to get. It's divorce that is ruining children's lives at the moment, not a couple of lesbians who want to get married (no matter how scary some of those pictures were out of San Francisco).

If President Bush is serious about "saving the institution," he has his hands full and he's running late.

Despite our differences, or illustrated by them, our Great Experiment has worked specifically because of the duality of who we are. We do love and want to protect the traditions that have made this nation great, while we remain curious and eager about change and progress. Ultimately, America is the only place on earth that has found this balance between tradition and progress.

In our New American Revolution, not only does tradition not need to capitulate to the progress, but our brilliance is in making the two work together, *even rely on each other.* I am an example of how the marginal not only do well, but thrive in our nation of ideas and hope. At the same time, I am able to indulge in being different specifically because I live in a nation where the traditions remain consistent.

I know it sounds contradictory, but it's not. Our traditions include curiosity, tolerance, compassion, creativity, and hope. Americans love the underdog, the rebellious, and, yes, the different. It is our *American culture* that ties it all together, a culture that survives the differences because our foundation is indeed one of tradition.

Our values and traditions make difference possible, but only if respect, dignity, and values survive in the mix. Only the individual fight for personal freedom and liberty makes it possible for this remarkable American Dream to continue for all of us.

Taking Action

A big part of this book is telling you how to use the power of your individualism to make a difference. And yet on these issues I am the one who has learned a tremendous lesson from you: how people can disagree on serious social issues and still respect and admire each other. I've seen something on the Right that is nonexistent on the Left—*genuine* compassion for people who are different, and a true love of ideas, personal freedom, and the American spirit.

I've learned through you that we can be free while respecting ourselves and others. I know for most of you that's probably a no-brainer, but believe me, it's a concept so lost on the Left the next time it appears it will be on a milk carton.

Personal liberty must include personal responsibility because without it we simply become slaves, again, to a Left that preys on the miserable.

I was there. I know.

If you identify as a Christian or conservative, you've most likely already taken action on these issues. How? As the New Radical Individual you stand by your beliefs, defend your principles while embracing authentic compassion and tolerance. On the Left, those words were nothing more than slogans. If you're reading this book, it means you actually take these values to heart.

For my readers who are pro-choice and/or homosexual, or leaning toward the Left and feeling a special affinity for people like yourselves, reading this book and considering my ideas already says a great deal about your open mind. I can tell you about the action I've taken, which seems to be most simple but is actually quite complicated: Americans have heard the pleas from women, gays, and other minorities to treat them with equality, dignity, and decency.

Start returning the favor and behave toward those with whom you disagree politically and socially with the same compassion and respect the Left has demanded for itself.

ACKNOWLEDGMENTS

As with all of us and our work, there are many individuals who make it possible. In my case, it is always a cadre of people who themselves challenge the system while also working within it. For many, it would be easier not to engage in the promotion of challenging ideas, but I've been lucky to find the cultural heroes—those who work with a quiet passion for ideas, communication, publishing, and broadcasting. They are at the forefront of making sure our national dialogue continues as our nation becomes an even better place.

My thanks to everyone at William Morrow, especially my editor, Mauro DiPreta. Working with Mauro has been a dream—he let me do my thing, and remained a solid, supportive influence. I can't thank him enough for making this a wonderful experience. His assistant, Joelle Yudin, was an integral member of our team, prodding me along when necessary, steady and supportive, she was always there when I needed her. Thank you Joelle.

A number of you bought this book because you got to know me through my radio program, cleverly titled, *The Tammy Bruce Show*.

Syndicated nationally by Talk Radio Network, my everlasting thanks and gratitude to Mark Masters and Bill Crawford for making it all possible. To David Ruben for opening that door, and Marcelo Carona for putting together and managing a radio team second to none. You change the world for the better every day. I'm honored to know and work with all of you.

Lastly, David Richardson, a man who has been an influence on me and my work since my first book. Now my manager, David is a young man who gives me hope for the future. He is smart and kind, and exemplifies the values that have made this nation extraordinary. What you see in all of my books is a result of David's critique of my ideas and encouragement of my work. David, "thank you" will never be enough, but I will say it always.

APPENDIX

TOOL CHEST 1:
Continuing the Revolution

Media Contact Tools

Of all the necessary actions to continue our New American Revolution, keeping the heat on the mainstream media (MSM) is first and foremost. One of my favorite Web sites to keep in touch with the shenanigans of the Leftist media is the Media Research Center at www.mediaresearch center.org.

Established in 1987, their Web site explains:

> The mission of the Media Research Center is to bring balance and responsibility to the news media. Leaders of America's conservative movement have long believed that within the national news media a strident liberal bias existed that influenced the public's understanding of critical issues. On October 1, 1987, a group of young determined conservatives set out to not only prove—through sound scientific research—that liberal bias in the media does exist and undermines traditional American values, but also to neutralize its impact on the American political scene. What they launched that fall is the now acclaimed—Media Research Center (MRC).

If you are able to stay in touch with only one Web site for information, research, and action to counter the MSM, the Media Research Center is it. I know the corporate media seem overwhelming and megalithic at times, and in a sense they are, but by now you know after reading this book that every opinion you have, every step you take, every action you implement makes a difference. The MRC is there to give you the information you need to make a difference on the front line of this continuing revolution.

Taking back mass communication in this country is indeed revolutionary. Realizing the people are in charge, not the few Media Elite who have had a free cultural ride in the past decades, is revolutionary. Realizing that you, one among many, can make a difference especially when we act in unison is revolutionary.

Part of continuing the revolution is making sure your voice continues to be heard. The following list provides contact information for major news magazines, major newspapers all across the country, news services, wire services, and television networks.

While this list is comprehensive, don't be limited by it. You may very well find your local newspaper listed here, but local television news affiliates are not. Add to this list local television and radio news and talk stations.

It's also important to remember that most of us think about writing only when we hear or read something we don't like. It is equally important to chime in with your appreciation when you see fair and balanced news coverage, or news reports, in print, radio, or television, that provide a counterpoint to the usual Leftist pabulum offered up by the MSM. So, remember, your voice is powerful when critical and when favorable.

Major News Magazines

Newsweek
251 West 57th Street
New York, NY 10019
e-mail: letters@newsweek.com
Web site: http://www.newsweek.com

Washington Bureau:
1750 Pennsylvania Avenue NW, Suite 1220
Washington, D.C. 20006

Time
Time & Life Building
Rockefeller Center
New York, NY 10020
e-mail: letters@time.com
Web site: http://time.com
Web site: http://www.pathfinder.com
(Pathfinder is the Web site portal to all of Time, Inc.'s magazines)

Washington Bureau:
1050 Connecticut Avenue NW, Suite 850
Washington, D.C. 20036

U.S. News & World Report
2400 N Street, NW
Washington, D.C. 20037
Web site: http://www.usnews.com

Major Newspapers

Arizona Republic
200 E. Van Buren Street
Phoenix, AZ 85004
e-mail: Arizona Republic
Web site: http://www.azcentral.com

Washington Bureau:
1000 National Press Building
Washington, D.C. 20045

Atlanta Journal-Constitution
72 Marietta Street NW
Atlanta, GA 30303
e-mail: conedit@ajc.com
Web site: http://www.ajc.com

Washington Bureau:
(see Cox Newspapers in next section)

Baltimore Sun
501 N. Calvert Street
Baltimore, MD 21278
e-mail: letters@baltsun.com
Web site: http://www.sunspot.net

Washington Bureau:
1627 K Street NW, Suite 1100
Washington, D.C. 20006

The Boston Globe
P.O. Box 2378
Boston, MA 02107
e-mail: letter@globe.com or news@globe.com
Web site: http://www.boston.com/globe

Washington Bureau:
1130 Connecticut Avenue NW
Washington, D.C. 20036

The Boston Herald
One Herald Square
Boston, MA 02106
e-mail: letterstoeditor@bostonherald.com
Web site: http://www.bostonherald.com

Washington Bureau:
988 National Press Building
Washington, D.C. 20045

The Charlotte Observer
600 S. Tryon Street
Charlotte, NC 28202
e-mail: opinion@charlotte.com
Web site: http://www.charlotte.com

Washington Bureau:
(see Knight-Ridder Newspapers in next section)

Chicago Sun-Times
401 N. Wabash Avenue
Chicago, IL 60611
e-mail: letters@suntimes.com
Web site: http://www.suntimes.com

Washington Bureau:
1206 National Press Building
Washington, D.C. 20045

Chicago Tribune
435 N. Michigan Avenue
Chicago, IL 60611
Web site: http://www.chicagotribune.com

Washington Bureau:
1325 G Street NW, Suite 200
Washington, D.C. 20005

Cleveland Plain Dealer
1801 Superior Avenue
Cleveland, Ohio 44114
e-mail: news@cleveland.com
Web site: http://www.plaindealer.com

Washington Bureau:
930 National Press Building
Washington, D.C. 20045

Daily Oklahoman
P.O. Box 25125
Oklahoma City, OK 73125
Web site: http://www.oklahoman.com

Washington Bureau:
914 National Press Building
Washington, D.C. 20045

Dallas Morning News
P.O. Box 655237
Dallas, TX 75265
e-mail: letterstoeditor@dallasnews.com
Web site: http://www.dallasnews.com

Washington Bureau:
1325 G. Street NW, #250
Washington, D.C. 20045

Denver Post
1560 Broadway
Denver, CO 80202
e-mail: letters@denverpost.com
Web site: http://www.denverpost.com

Washington Bureau:
1270 National Press Building
Washington, D.C. 20045

Des Moines Register
715 Locust Street
P.O. Box 957
Des Moines, IA 50304
Web site: http://www.dmregister.com

Washington Bureau:
1300 I Street NW, Suite 1010 E
Washington, D.C. 20005

Detroit Free Press
321 W. Lafayette Boulevard
Detroit, MI 48231
e-mail: business@det-freepress.com
Web site: http://www.freep.com

Washington Bureau:
700 National Press Building
Washington, D.C. 20045

Detroit News
615 Lafayette Boulevard
Detroit, MI 48226
e-mail: letter@detnews.com
Web site: http://detnews.com

Washington Bureau:
1148 National Press Building
Washington, D.C. 20045

Fort Worth Star-Telegram
P.O. Box 1870
Fort Worth, TX 76101
Web site: http://www.startext.net

Washington Bureau:
1705 DeSales Street NW, Suite 400
Washington, D.C. 20036

Houston Chronicle
801 Texas Avenue
Houston, TX 77002
e-mail: viewpoints@chron.com
Web site: http://www.chron.com

Washington Bureau:
1341 G Street NW, Suite 201
Washington, D.C. 20005

Los Angeles Times
Times Mirror Square
Los Angeles, CA 90053
e-mail: letters@latimes.com
Web site: http://www.latimes.com

Washington Bureau:
1875 I Street NW, Suite 1100
Washington, D.C. 20006

Miami Herald
1 Herald Plaza
Miami, FL 33101
e-mail: HeraldEd@herald.com
Web site: http://www.herald.com

Washington Bureau:
(see Knight-Ridder Newspapers in next section)

The Milwaukee Journal Sentinel
P.O. Box 661
Milwaukee, WI 53201
Web site: http://www.packerplus.com

Washington Bureau:
940 National Press Building
Washington, D.C. 20045

Minneapolis Star Tribune
425 Portland Avenue
Minneapolis, MN 55488
e-mail: politics@startribune.com
Web site: http://www.startribune.com

Washington Bureau:
1627 I Street NW
Washington, D.C. 20006

Newsday
235 Pinelawn Road
Melville, NY 11747
e-mail: letters@newsday.com
Web site: http://www.newsday.com

Washington Bureau:
1730 Pennsylvania Avenue NW, Suite 850
Washington, D.C. 20006

The New York Times
229 West 43rd Street
New York, New York 10036
e-mail: letters@nytimes.com
Web site: http://www.nytimes.com

Washington Bureau:
1627 I Street NW, Suite 700
Washington, D.C. 20006

The Oregonian
1320 S.W. Broadway
Portland, OR 97201
Web site: http://www.oregonian.com

Washington Bureau:
1101 Connecticut Avenue NW, #310
Washington, D.C. 20036

The Philadelphia Inquirer
Philadelphia Daily News
400 N. Broad Street
Philadelphia, PA 19101
e-mail: Inquirer.Opinion@phillynews.com
e-mail: DailyNews.Opinion@phillynews.com
Web site: http://inquirer.philly.com/
Web site: http://dailynews.philly.com/

Washington Bureau:
(see Knight-Ridder Newspapers in next section)

Pittsburgh Post-Gazette
34 Boulevard of the Allies
Pittsburgh, PA 15222
e-mail: letters@post-gazette.com
Web site: http://www.post-gazette.com

Washington Bureau:
955 National Press Building
Washington, D.C. 20045

Rocky Mountain News
400 W. Colfax Avenue
Denver, CO 80204
Web site: http://www.insidedenver.com

Washington Bureau:
(see Scripps Howard News Service in next section)

St. Louis Post-Dispatch
900 N. Tucker Boulevard
St. Louis, MO 63101
Web site: http://www.stlnet.com

Washington Bureau:
1701 Pennsylvania Avenue NW, Suite 550
Washington, D.C. 20006

San Diego Union-Tribune
350 Camino de la Reina
San Diego, CA 92108
e-mail: letters@uniontrib.com
Web site: http://www.uniontrib.com

Washington Bureau:
(see Copley News Service in next section)

San Francisco Chronicle
901 Mission Street
San Francisco, CA 94103
e-mail: chronletters@sfgate.com
Web site: http://www.sfgate.com/chronicle

Washington Bureau:
1085 National Press Building
Washington, D.C. 20045

San Francisco Examiner
110 Fifth Street
San Francisco, CA 94103
e-mail: letters@examiner.com
Web site: http://www.sfgate.com/examiner

Washington Bureau:
(see Hearst Newspapers in next section)

San Jose Mercury News
750 Ridder Park Drive
San Jose, CA 95190
e-mail: letters@sjmercury.com
Web site: http://www.sjmercury.com

Washington Bureau:
(see Knight-Ridder Newspapers in next section)

Seattle Post-Intelligencer
P.O. Box 1909
Seattle, WA 98111
e-mail: editpage@seattle-pi.com
Web site: http://www.seattle-pi.com

Washington Bureau:
(see Hearst Newspapers in next section)

Seattle Times
P.O. Box 70
Seattle, WA 98111
e-mail: opinion@seatimes.com
Web site: http://www.seattletimes.com

Washington Bureau:
245 2nd Street NE
Washington, D.C. 20002

USA Today
1000 Wilson Boulevard
Arlington, VA 22229
e-mail: editor@usatoday.com
Web site: http://www.usatoday.com

The Wall Street Journal
200 Liberty Street
New York, New York 10281
e-mail: letter.editor@edit.wsj.com
Web site: http://www.wsj.com

Washington Bureau:
1025 Connecticut Avenue NW, Suite 800
Washington, D.C. 20036

The Washington Post
1150 15th Street NW
Washington, D.C. 20071
e-mail: Letterstoed@washpost.com
Web site: http://www.washingtonpost.com

The Washington Times
3600 New York Avenue NE
Washington, D.C. 20002
e-mail: wtnews@wt.infi.net
Web site: http://www.washtimes.com

News Services/Washington Bureaus

If you see an article with a Washington dateline written by a news service or the Washington bureau of a newspaper chain, use this list to find
the best address to correspond with the reporter.

Copley News Service
1100 National Press Building
Washington, D.C. 20045

Cox Newspapers
2000 Pennsylvania Avenue NW, Suite 10000
Washington, D.C. 20006

Gannett News Service
1000 Wilson Boulevard
Arlington, VA 22229

Hearst Newspapers
1701 Pennsylvania Avenue NW, Suite 610
Washington, D.C. 20006

Knight-Ridder Newspapers
700 National Press Building
Washington, D.C. 20045

Newhouse News Service
1101 Connecticut Avenue NW, Suite 300
Washington, D.C. 20036

Scripps Howard News Service
1090 Vermont Avenue NW, Suite 1000
Washington, D.C. 20005

Wire Services

Associated Press
50 Rockefeller Plaza
New York, New York 10020

Washington Bureau:
2021 K Street NW, Room 600
Washington, D.C. 20006

Knight-Ridder/Tribune Information Services
790 National Press Building
Washington, D.C. 20045

Los Angeles Times–Washington Post News Service
1150 15th Street NW
Washington, D.C. 20071

New York Times News Service
229 W. 43rd Street, Room 943
New York, NY 10036

Washington Bureau:
1627 I Street NW
Washington, D.C. 20006

Reuters Information Services
1700 Broadway, 31st Floor
New York, New York 10019

Washington Bureau:
1333 H Street NW, Suite 410
Washington, D.C. 20005

United Press International
1510 H Street NW, #600
Washington, D.C. 20005

Television Network News and Public Affairs

ABC News
77 West 66th Street
New York, New York 10023
Web site: http://www.abcnews.com

Washington Bureau:
1717 DeSales Street NW
Washington, D.C. 20036

CBS News
524 West 57th Street
New York, New York 10019
Web site: http://cbsnews.cbs.com/

Washington Bureau:
2020 M Street NW
Washington, D.C. 20036

Cable News Network
P.O. Box 105366
One CNN Center
Atlanta, GA 30348
e-mail: feedback@cnn.com;
cnn.onair@cnn.com;
Web site: http://cnn.com

Washington Bureau:
820 First Street NE, Suite 1100
Washington, D.C. 20002

New York Bureau for CNN and CNNfn:
5 Penn Plaza, 20th Floor
New York, New York 10001

C-SPAN
400 North Capitol Street NW, Suite 650
Washington, D.C. 20001
e-mail: viewer@c-span.org
Web site: http://www.c-span.org

Fox News/Fox News Channel
1211 Avenue of the Americas
New York, New York 10036
e-mail: comments@foxnews.com
Web site: http://www.foxnews.com

Washington Bureau:
400 North Capitol Street NW, Suite 550
Washington, D.C. 20001

MSNBC and CNBC
One MSNBC Plaza
Secaucus, NJ 07094
e-mail: hardball@cnbc.com; letters@msnbc.com;
opinion@msnbc.com;
TheNews@msnbc.com;
Web site: http://www.msnbc.com
Web site: http://www.cnbc.com

Washington Bureau for Hardball:
400 North Capitol Street NW, Suite 890
Washington, D.C. 20001

NBC News
30 Rockefeller Plaza
New York, New York 10112
e-mail: dateline@news.nbc.com; nightly@news.nbc.com;
today@news.nbc.com; MTP@nbc.com
Web site: http://www.msnbc.com

Washington Bureau for NBC News and MSNBC:
4001 Nebraska Avenue NW
Washington, D.C. 20016

Westwood One/Infinity/CBS Radio News
1755 South Jefferson Davis Highway, Suite 1200
Arlington, VA 22202

National Public Radio
635 Massachusetts Avenue NW
Washington, D.C. 20001
Web site: http://www.npr.org

PBS
1320 Braddock Place
Alexandria, VA 22314
Web site: http://www.pbs.org

NewsHour with Jim Lehrer
WETA-TV
3620 South 27th Street
Arlington, VA 22206
Web site: http://www.pbs.org/newshour/

Here's also a handy list of the Web sites noted in this book and others of special importance:

www.tammybruce.com
www.defenddemocracy.com
www.discoverthenetwork.org
"A Guide to the Political Left"

www.opensecrets.org

www.cjr.org/tools.owners
"The Columbia Journalism Review's guide to what major media companies own."

www.frontpagemagazine.com

www.newsmax.com

www.worldnetdaily.com

www.steynonline.com

www.littlegreenfootballs.com

www.michellemalkin.com

www.powerlineblog.com

www.jihadwatch.com

www.redstate.org

www.realclearpolitics.com

www.jewishvirtuallibrary.org

APPENDIX

TOOL CHEST 2:
Reading into the
New American Revolution

One of the most important tools for the continuation of the New American Revolution is reading. Not just the skill, but the act itself—and not just of anything, but the reading of books specifically.

These are the days where the "entertainment room" has taken the place of a library or a quiet den in the home. Young people are more likely to have an iPod or Game Boy in their hands than a book, as adults look more often to news and other articles beamed into their cell phones or BlackBerries.

Reading the few lines of a ticker-type news report or an electronic copy of the week's latest news or entertainment magazine is not the same as engaging a book, full of complex and interconnected communication structures.

Critical thinking skills honed by language, and more specifically the written word, are atrophying in our world of Instant Messages and immediate images. Pictures cannot convey abstract ideas, nor do they invite debate. They simply "are."

Ideas expressed in writing enjoy having sprung from the mind of an individual, and require interpretation in the same fashion by another unique person. Words live only when engaged by us, with the written word being the most serious, the most personal way to learn, persuade, influence, and ultimately change the world.

It has never been more important to remind ourselves that while information itself is important, the act of reading books plays a fundamental role in our own development and ability to understand the world around us. In a world where the Left is in control of most visual mediums, *how* we get our information is now dynamically important.

Why has reading become less in vogue? Our busy lives don't leave much time to be still and concentrate. Television and even radio allow us to remain passive—we can engage in listening or watching without even necessarily being present.

Make no mistake, however. One of the questions I still hear on my radio program and in e-mails is, Why and how did we allow the Left to influence and manipulate us so much during the past few decades? We looked and then turned away as our culture, nation, and individuality were being slowly and deliberately whittled away.

Part of the answer is that staring hypnotically at television allows our passive listening to open our minds to the Leftist messages perpetuated by mainstream electronic media. We fell face-first into one-sided information mediums, which conditioned us with messages promoting the Leftist darlings of multiculturalism, political correctness and socialist politics.

Television asks us not to think, but to absorb. Reading, on the other hand, demands we sit, be quiet, and *think*. Reading is an action that requires an interaction that at its core reinforces your individualism, specifically because every message, every story requires your having a relationship with the material. It is a world that only exists when you engage it.

While newspaper and magazine reading can be enjoyable and informational, the act of reading a book is the primary venue where we must be able to follow extended arguments and comprehend the nuances and symbols involved in abstract communication.

The world of ideas in a book requires the partnership of your very sense of self, your ideas, your imagination to make it come alive. Yes, it is more involving than television, and that's the point. Our mind is the muscle that allows us to embrace, expand, and project ourselves, and like any muscle, if left unused it will become mired in habit and prone to suggestion.

And that's exactly what the Left wants.

The less you read, the less you understand yourself. The less you read and the more you watch television, the more susceptible you become to Leftist conditioning. The less you read, the critical skills of anticipating and understanding arguments, especially when an argument is vapid and depraved, become weak and are eventually forgotten.

Inside the Liberal Mind
(a Brief Journey)

While writing this analysis of reading for you, my friend Stacy McCain at the *Washington Times* sent me an e-mail with this extraordinary story. Its relevance to the issue at hand was undeniable while simultaneously exposing the inside of the liberal mind.

In December, C-SPAN's Brian Lamb hosted the final installment of "Book Notes." His guest was Mark Edmundson, a University of Virginia English professor (with a Ph.D from Yale) and the author of *Why Read?*

Discussing free speech, Edmundson explained in typical arrogant liberal fashion, why conservative ideas irritate him:

> I think a lot of the kind of angry conservative movement that rubs me the wrong me, the Rush Limbaugh kind of stuff, came about because people going to college felt, All my professors are liberal, I could never give them my reservations about the liberal line, so that those things festered and got darker and nastier. And then, you know, welcome to talk radio. . . . If they'd been listened to in a tolerant way and disagreed with in an affectionate way, we might have a little bit better civil discourse in the country.[1]

As part of this farewell episode with Edmundson, Lamb also featured video footage of past guests on the show, talking about their own favorite books. Nobel Prize–winning economist Milton Friedman was included, discussing Friedrich Hayek's *The Road to Serfdom*, which was a bestseller in 1945 and is recognized as one of the most important and influential books of the last century.

When the video clip of Friedman ended, Lamb noted: "He's talking about *Road to Serfdom*—Hayek—a bible for people on the conservative political side."

Edmundson said, "I'm glad to know about it. Until this moment, I've heard nothing about it. But I will write it down and give it a look."

At which point Lamb, seemingly stunned, asked, "So, you've never read *Road to Serfdom*?"

To which Edmundson answered: "Never. Nor heard of it, until this moment."

When Stacy sent this story to me, I burst out laughing. I thought at the very least Edmundson could have *pretended* he had a clue, but no. Like the truism that the insane have no idea they're crazy, the deeply ignorant are truly clueless and, well, have no clue about it.

The irony of the moment is remarkable, and obviously lost on Edmundson. Here is an English professor speaking about the importance of reading, while simultaneously dismissing conservative thinkers and rhetoricians as nasty and dark, all because they were never engaged, or "listened to."

Clearly, it's impossible to engage people unlike yourself when you have so little interest in different ideas that you ban them from your personal reality.

Not only are conservatives not listened to in college, the Left, embodied by Edmundson, *still* has no interest in learning about the ideas that have shaped this country and continue to make her the greatest nation on earth.

Here's a news flash for Edmundson—conservatives don't need "affection" from liberals. We need liberals to know what they're talking about *and why so many people think differently from them*. Reading is part of that framework. Writing about the importance of reading is one thing. Doing it is quite another.

As Lamb noted, *The Road to Serfdom* is indeed a bible of conservative thinkers (of Classical Liberal American thought, actually). It is a classic work of political philosophy, intellectual and cultural history, and economics. Lamb could not hide his shock that the man he had just spoken to about the importance of reading and engaging other points of view had never even *heard* of the book, one which shapes the arguments and viewpoints of the people he so casually dismissed just moments earlier.

This is an important lesson for all of us: There are many books we've heard of and have never read. We think we know them because we've heard so much about them. And then there are books that continue to shape our lives, and perhaps you've never heard of *them*.

As a salute to the New American Revolution, and commitment to the glorious renewal of our individualistic spirit, now is the time to have books play at least an equal role to television in your life, if not an even larger one. I know all of us love television, but I am personally working on spending more hours each week reading, and fewer with TV.

For those of you who are already voracious readers, I hope to expand your horizons with the following list and suggestions. As one of my readers, and getting this far indicates you're already ahead of the pack, you already enjoy reading and know the difference it can make. However, there are also ways to incorporate it as naturally into your life as it is to click on the television when you get home.

Actions

At first, **set aside television-free hours in the home,** and replace that time with reading. Whether you have a family or live alone, this applies to everyone. Gradually increase that time to a whole day (and days eventually) where television and other electronic media are banned. While I believe television and other electronic media play important roles in our lives, deliberately removing them for a designated period of time and incorporating the reading of books will change your life and how you view the world.

Start or join a book club that shares your interests. Exploring books, their messages and meanings with others is a great way to have fun, meet people in your community with similar values, and learn even more about the material you're reading. You will network, educate yourself, and have fun all at the same time.

Take bites out of the following Reading List. Looking at a list like this can be a bit daunting. Like looking at the whole elephant and being a bit overwhelmed. Just remember to approach this action in the same manner as I've noted earlier: Eat the elephant one bite at a time.

Each book is one bite, is a gem, and waits for you. Don't think of the list as a whole; look at it like a buffet that will always be there, and to which you can return at any time. Take a little at a time, and return when you're ready.

I have selected a number of books representing a variety of genres. Many of the books you know you'll enjoy, but some may represent a more difficult choice. I guarantee there are books on this list with which you will disagree, in whole or part. I've included them, however, because they're important for you to know.

Reading should never be a chore. Choose titles at first that you know for sure will be a pleasure to read. Save the more difficult ones for a time when you're ready to engage something different. There are no rules here—this is meant to inspire you. If a book is completely unfamiliar, make a point to read reviews and do a little research before you dive into it. This will be especially helpful for a classic such as Wyndham Lewis's *The Revenge for Love.*

Of course, I don't expect you to stop here. This is not, to say the least, a comprehensive list, but it is meant to inspire you. These books and ideas should lead you into creating your own list, to adding more titles, more genres, more challenging work for knowledge and growth, along with the classics and our tried and true fiction reading for pleasure and information.

I will suggest that you make a point of reading a genre you're not necessarily familiar with. As an example, I love nonfiction and history, so I make a point of including *fiction,* which has nothing to do with history, in my reading list.

Make choices that are different from what you would expect of yourself when you can. You may find some sorts of books just numb your mind—then leave them. If you continue to try something that you do not enjoy, you'll turn away from the experience, and that's the last thing I want for you. Absolutely challenge yourself, while making sure it all remains a fun, pleasurable experience.

Reading is the last *sublime* individualistic communication experience. It is part and parcel of your uniqueness and individuality, and key to your personal freedom. So, let's go!

Political Philosophy/Classics

The Road to Serfdom, F. A. Hayek
Free to Choose: A Personal Statement, Milton Friedman and Rose Friedman
The Conservative Mind: From Burke to Eliot, Russell Kirk
Nicomachean Ethics, Aristotle

Social/Political Analysis

The New Thought Police: Inside the Left's Assault on Free Speech and Free Minds, Tammy Bruce
The Death of Right and Wrong: Exposing the Left's Assault on Our Culture and Values, Tammy Bruce
The Case for Democracy: The Power of Freedom to Overcome Tyranny and Terror, Natan Sharansky
The New Anti-Semitism: The Current Crisis and What We Must Do About It, Phyllis Chesler
Scapegoat: The Jews, Israel, and Women's Liberation, Andrea Dworkin
Pornography: Men Possessing Women, Andrea Dworkin

For those interested in the abortion debate (which for the most part includes all of us), please read the actual U.S. Supreme Court *Roe v. Wade* decision. An Internet search will bring up many sources for the complete decision.

Faith

Mere Christianity, C. S. Lewis
God and Ronald Reagan: A Spiritual Life, Paul Kengor
Christianity and Culture, T. S. Eliot
The Hidden Face of God: Science Reveals the Ultimate Truth, Gerald Schroeder

Economics

Capitalism and Freedom, Milton Friedman
Basic Economics: A Citizens Guide to the Economy, Thomas Sowell
Wealth of Nations, Adam Smith

Social and Political Psychology

Groupthink: Psychological Studies of Policy Decisions and Fiascoes, Irving L. Janis
Malignant Self-Love: Narcissism Revisited, Samuel Vaknin and Lidija Rangelovska
Emotional Blackmail: When the People in Your Life Use Fear, Obligation, and Guilt to Manipulate You, Dr. Susan Forward

War on Radical Islam

Unholy Alliance: Radical Islam and the American Left, David Horowitz
The Rage and the Pride, Oriana Fallaci
The Myth of Islamic Tolerance: How Islamic Law Treats Non-Muslims, Robert Spencer (editor)
Hatred's Kingdom: How Saudi Arabia Supports the New Global Terrorism, Dore Gold
Preachers of Hate: Islam and the War on America, Kenneth Timmerman
Losing bin Laden: How Bill Clinton's Failures Unleashed Global Terror, Richard Miniter
The Trouble with Islam Today, Irshad Manji

History

Ominous Parallels: A Study of America Today and the Ominous Parallels with the Chaos of Pre-Hitler Germany, Leonard Peikoff
The American Cause, Russell Kirk
The Roots of American Order, Russell Kirk
The Age of Reagan, 1964–1980: The Fall of the Old Liberal Order, Steven F. Hayward

Scientific Theory

Relativity: The Special and the General Theory, Albert Einstein
A Brief History of Time: The Updated and Expanded Tenth Anniversary Edition, Stephen Hawking

Fiction

The Revenge for Love, Wyndham Lewis
The Fountainhead, Ayn Rand
Brave New World, Aldous Huxley
1984, George Orwell
Fahrenheit 451, Ray Bradbury

Internationalism

Our Oldest Enemy: A History of America's Disastrous Relationship with France, John J. Miller
Verdict on Vichy: Power and Prejudice in the Vichy France Regime, Michael Curtis
Anti-Americanism, Jean Francois Revel
Tower of Babble: How the United Nations Has Fueled Global Chaos, Dore Gold

Culture

The Waste Land, T. S. Eliot, (Norton Critical Editions) Michael North (editor)
The Disappearance of Childhood, Neil Postman
Amusing Ourselves to Death: Public Discourse in the Age of Show Business, Neil Postman
Black Rednecks and White Liberals: And Other Cultural and Ethnic Issues, Thomas Sowell

For Kids (and Adults!)

Gulliver's Travels, Jonathan Swift
A is for Abigail: An Almanac of Amazing American Women, Lynne Cheney
The Chronicles of Narnia, C. S. Lewis
The Phantom Tollbooth, Norton Juster
The Ugly Duckling, Hans Christian Andersen, adapted and illustrated by Jerry Pinkney
Animal Farm, George Orwell

Additional Action

Volunteer to teach reading. As Leftists gained control of our public school system, the focus of the classroom turned from teaching the basics—reading, writing, and arithmetic—to teaching "self-esteem" and "tolerance." Ironically, this feeling-centered pedagogy has turned out generations of Americans who have graduated from high school essentially illiterate, and yet are supposed to think quite highly of themselves.

More and more young Americans are finding a need to either learn to read or to improve their reading skills if they are to pass the SAT decently, or even to simply get a job. In fact, literacy experts report more than forty million adults in the United States cannot read well enough to fill out a job application, follow a bus schedule, understand a medicine label, or read to their children.

While it may be late, promoting literacy—for both adults and children—not only saves economic lives, but opens minds to new ideas, making individuals less likely to become or remain empty-headed fodder parroting the Leftist agenda.

Your local library will have volunteer resources. Also, support and volunteer with these literacy advocates:

Reach Out and Read http://www.reachoutandread.org/ (617) 629-8042
"Reach Out and Read (ROR) programs make early literacy a standard part of pediatric primary care. Pediatricians encourage parents to read aloud to their babies and infants and give books to their patients to take home at all pediatric check-ups from six months to five years of age. Parents need to know that reading aloud is the most important thing they can do to help their children love books and start school ready to learn."

Literacy Partners, Inc. www.literacypartners.org (212) 725-9200
"Literacy Partners, Inc., a not-for-profit organization, provides free community-based adult and family literacy programs to ensure that all adults have the access to quality education needed to fully realize their potential as individuals, parents, and citizens."

NOTES

Chapter 1

1. Littlegreenfootballs.com provides the most complete index of documents and coverage of the CBS Memogate scandal. You can access it here: http://littlegreenfootballs.com/weblog/?entry=12582_CBS_Killian_Document_Index&only. For CBS's version of events, see: http: www.cbsnews.com/stories 2005/01/10/national/main665727.shtml.

2. For the most comprehensive coverage of the problem that is Ward Churchill, please visit a blog dedicated to the issue: www.pirateballerina.com.

3. Ryan Deuel, "Hinchey: Rove may be behind fake documents," *Binghamton Press & Sun-Bulletin*, 22 February 2005, 5B.

4. http://transcripts.cnn.com/TRANSCRIPTS/0410/29/lkl.01.html.

5. Eason Jordan, "The News We Kept to Ourselves," *New York Times*, April 11, 2003, Op-Ed.

6. http://www.thesmokinggun.com/archive/1027042harris1.html.

7. Ibid.
8. "Three Arrested in GOP Vandalism," *USA Today,* 6 November 2004.
9. Linda Blumenfeld, "Soros's Deep Pockets vs. Bush," *Washington Post,* 11 November 2003.
10. Ibid.
11. Harvey Shapiro, "Advocating an Open Society," *Hemispheres,* March 1996.
12. For more details about Soros's funding of the Left, research his name at: www.opensecrets.org and specifically http://www.open secrets.org/527s/527indivsdetail.asp?ID=11001147458&Cycle=2004. For detailed background, see http://discoverthenetwork.org/individual profile.asp?indid=977.
13. Uriel Heilman, "In Rare Jewish Appearance, George Soros Says Jews and Israel Cause Anti-Semitism," *Jewish Telegraph Agency,* 9 November 2003. Also at: http://www.jta.org/page_view_story.asp?in tarticleid=13428&intcategoryid=4.
14. Ibid.
15. Ibid.
16. For articles offering the most complete analysis of Soros, see Rachel Ehrenfeld and Shawn Macomber, "The Man Who Would Be King-maker," frontpagemagazine.com, at http://www.frontpagemag.com/articles/readarticle.asp?ID=15710&p=1 and http://www.frontpage mag.com/articles/ReadArticle.asp?ID=15736. Also see their article "The Soros-Kerry Nexus," also at frontpagemagazine.com.
17. David Ignatius, "Beirut's Berlin Wall," *Washington Post,* 23 February 2005.

Chapter 2

1. Bettijane Levine, "Seizing the Day: NOW Leader Tammy Bruce Has Done What O.J. Prosecutors Couldn't: Put Domestic Violence Upfront," *Los Angeles Times,* 18 October 1995.
2. John Kendall, "Deaths of Three Women Following Abortions Spur Clinic Probes," *Los Angeles Times,* 23 February 1988, 4.
3. Ibid.
4. Tina Daunt, "Doctor's License Is Suspended for 1 Year by Medical Board Abortion: A women's group says the penalty is too lenient for

physician charged with incompetence in two deaths," *Los Angeles Times*, 15 August 1994.

5. Douglas P. Shuit, "Doctor Tied to 2 Deaths Loses License Abortions," *Los Angeles Times*, 25 May 1995.

6. Julie Marquis, "Handful of Abortion Clinics Put Poor at Risk," *Los Angeles Times*, 5 April 1998.

Chapter 3

1. Thomas Paine, *The Thomas Paine Reader*, eds. Isaac Kramnick and Michael Foot (New York, NY: Penguin USA, 1987), 66–67.

2. http://www.fordham.edu/halsall/mod/mussolini-fascism.html.

Chapter 4

1. Beth Fouhy, "The Red Carpet for the Clintons," Associated Press, 28 June 2004.

2. Jere Longman, *Among the Heroes* (New York: HarperCollins, 2002).

3. www.adcouncil.org.

4. Larry Elliott and David Teather, "Bush Opens Push for Democracy-3-Point Plan to Reshape Region," *The Guardian*, 10 June 2004. Also available at www.guardian.co.uk/israel/story/0%2C2763%2C1235377%2C00.html.

5. Ibid.

6. Ralf Beste and Stefan Simons, "Bush's New Conciliatory Approach," *Der Spiegel*, 14 June 2004.

Chapter 5

1. http://www.nraila.org/Issues/FactSheets/Read.aspx?ID=52.

2. Joyce Lee Malcolm, *Guns and Violence: The English Experience* (Cambridge: Harvard University Press, 2002).

3. Paul Craig Roberts, "Guns and Violence," NewsMax.com, 29 July 2002.

4. Rone Tempest, "For Well-Armed Citizenry—Handguns Are a Big Issue," *Los Angeles Times*, 9 August 2004, A1.

5. Ibid.

6. John R. Lott, Jr., "Assault Weapons Ban Was Useless Anyway," *Los Angeles Times*, 10 September 2004, commentary.

7. www.handgunfree.org/HFAMain/resources/quotes.htm.

8. http://www.nrapublications.org/tar/index.asp.

9. "Mr. Cuomo's Good Start on Guns," *New York Times,* 21 December 1993, editorial, A26.

10. Deroy Murdoch, "Say Goodnight Jesse," *National Review Online,* 9 February 2001, http://www.nationalreview.com/murdock/murdock-print020901.html.

11. Charles Krauthammer, "Disarm the Citizenry," *Washington Post,* 16 April 1996.

12. http://www.nraila.org/CurrentLegislation/Read.aspx?ID=1117.

13. Ibid.

14. http://www.nraila.org/Issues/FactSheets/Read.aspx?ID=78.

15. Michael L. Betsch, "Pro Gun Group Wants to Arm Parents and Teachers," NewsMax.com, http://www.newsmax.com/archives/articles/2002/10/10/124303.shtml.

16. John Biemer, "Md. Candidate Unveils Gun Control Ad," Associated Press, 11 October 2002.

Chapter 6

1. Richard Huff, "Fear Over 'Private' Parts," *New York Daily News,* 11 November 2004.

2. http://www.frontpagemagazine.com/Articles/ReadArticle.asp?ID=10580.

3. http://opinionjournal.com/politicaldiary/?id=110004198.

4. "Dean Call FCC Probe of Breast Incident 'Silly,'" Reuters, 2 February 2004.

5. Ibid.

6. Tammy Bruce, *The Death of Right and Wrong* (New York: Prima Forum, 2003), 256.

7. Alexandra Marks, "New York Times Resignations Signal Industry Turmoil," *Christian Science Monitor,* 6 June 2003, Society & Culture.

8. Maureen Dowd, "The Red Zone," *New York Times,* 4 November 2004.

9. Paul Krugman, "No Surrender," *New York Times,* 5 November 2004.

10. http://en.wikipedia.org/wiki/Kopechne.

11. Tom Kenworthy, "Michael Kennedy Dies in Accident on Aspen Slopes," *Washington Post,* 1 January 1998, A1.

12. Bruce, 46–49.

13. Jacques Steinberg, "The Times Chooses Veteran of Magazines and Publishing as Its First Public Editor," *New York Times*, 27 October 2003.
14. Ibid.
15. Bryon Calane, "The Public Editor; The New Public Editor: Toward Greater Transparency," *New York Times*, 5 June 2005.
16. Michael Wolff, "Right Timesman," *New York* newyorkmetro.com http://www.newyorkmetro.com/nymetro/news/media/columns/medialife/n_9749/.

Chapter 7

1. "Bush and Clinton in Thailand, Start Tour of Tsunami Region," *New York Times*, 20 February 2005.
2. www.clintonfoundation.org.
3. http://www.now.org/press/10-02/10-10.html.
4. "Iraq: Systematic Torture of Political Prisoners," http://web.amnesty.org/library/Index/engMDE140082001?OpenDocument&of=COUN-TRIESIRAQ.
5. "Iran to Execute Two Women for 'Morality' Crimes," Feminist Daily News Wire, 21 December 2004.
6. http://www.feminist.org/calendar/cal_details.asp?idSchedule=2400.
7. http://story.news.yahoo.com/news?tmpl=story2&cid=578&ncid=578&e=8&u=/nm/20030309/ts_nm/iraq_usa_demonstration_dc.
8. http://www.now.org/press/03-03/03-08.html.
9. http://web.amnesty.org/802568F7005C4453/0/167B2399A6F1C6BF80256AA8003BF823?Open&Highlight=2,Haydar.
10. www.un.org.
11. Joseph Loconte, "The U.N. Sex Scandal: Exploitation, Abuse and Other Humanitarian Efforts," *Weekly Standard*, 3 January 2005. Also at http://www.weeklystandard.com/Content/Public/Articles/000/000/005/081zxelz.asp.
12. "The New World Disorder: U.N. Shuffles on Rape Cases," WorldNetDaily.com, 1 March 2005. Also at http://www.worldnetdaily.com/news/printerfriendly.asp?ARTICLE_ID=43089.
13. Ibid.
14. Ibid.
15. Loconte.

16. "U.N. Fears Peacekeepers Commit Sex Abuse Worldwide," Reuters, 26 February 2005.

17. Ibid.

18. http://www.smh.com.au/articles/2004/03/31/1080544556703.html.

19. Humberto Fontova, "Che Guevara: Assassin and Bumbler," News-Max.com, 24 February 2004.

20. Ibid.

21. Christopher Tookey, "The Motorcycle Diaries," *The Daily Mail*, 27 August 2004.

Epilogue

1. David Kirkpatrick, "In Secretly Taped Conversations, Glimpses of the Future President," *New York Times*, 20 February 2005.

2. Ibid.

Appendix: Tool Chest 2

1. For video and a transcript of the interview, go to: http://www.booknotes.org/Program/?ProgramID=1809.

INDEX

abandonment, fear of, 52–53
ABC, 157, 158–61
ABC Evening News, 157
abortion:
    author's views on, 28, 29–30, 51, 54–58, 76–77, 106, 155–57, 206, 215–16, 219–30
    clinics, 55, 219–21, 223, 226–28
    feminist position on, 29–30, 54–58, 155–57, 186, 219–28
    organized opposition to, 28, 29–30, 51, 54–58, 106, 155–57, 191, 206, 215–16, 219–30
    as religious issue, 191, 219–21, 222, 229
advertising, 109–10, 166, 181
Advertising Council, 109–10
affirmative action, 173
Afghanistan, 33, 34, 191
African Americans, 47, 85, 103, 110, 172–73, 176
agnosticism, 124
AIDS, 162–64
Ailes, Roger, 10, 15
Alliance Defense Fund, 211
All Things Considered, 179

Al Qaeda, 15, 18–19, 30, 136–37, 196
Alterman, Eric, 25
"America Coming Together," 25
American Center for Law and Justice (ACLJ), 211
American Civil Liberties Union (ACLU), 36, 108, 139, 150, 155, 210–11
American Dream, 4, 75, 94–97, 102, 242
American Nationalism, 34–35, 108–17, 119, 122
American Rifleman Magazine, 137
Amnesty International, 189, 193
Andrus, Cecil, 155, 157
Angie (correspondent), 222–23
Animal Farm (Orwell), 66
Annan, Kofi, 201–2
antiabortion laws, 226–30
anti-Semitism, 16, 26–27
Apple Computers, 71
Arabs, 32–33
Arafat, Yassir, 116
armed forces, U.S., 7, 72, 191, 196, 226
arms control, 120–23
artists, 94–95

Ashcroft, John, 18–19
assault weapons bans, 135–36
atheism, 27–28, 124
Authentic Feminists, 190–91
Avanti, 81
Axis of Evil, 192

Beamer, Todd, 106–7
behavior choices, 233–34
Beltway snipers, 144–45
Bernadine (correspondent), 104–5
Beslan school massacre (2004), 17, 30
Big Lie, 108, 117
Bill of Rights, 124, 125, 126
bin Laden, Osama, 6, 14, 30–31, 37, 79,
    114, 176, 192, 200–201
biological weapons, 197
birth control, 225–26
bisexuality, 231, 234–35
Black Elite, 103
Blair, Jayson, 172–73, 176
bloggers, 15–16
Bloomberg, Michael, 141
bodyguards, 141
book clubs, 267
"Book Notes," 265–67
Boston Globe, 180
Boston Red Sox, 180
Boyd, Gerald, 172–73, 176
Bozell, Brent, 181
Bradshaw, Phil, 107
Bradshaw, Sandy, 107
Brian (correspondent), 127
bribery, 197
broadcast television, 166–69
    contact information for, 259–62
    standards in, 166–70
    see also mainstream media
Brolin, James, 163
Brooks, David, 178–79
Bruce, Tammy:
    armed forces supported by, 72, 191
    Bush as viewed by, 28–31, 34
    celebrity of, 46–47
    conservatism as viewed by, 39, 51,
        66–67, 74–75, 90–91, 215–43
    as Democrat, 18–20, 28–29, 73, 74, 75,
        76–80, 91, 104
    as feminist, 28, 29–30, 34, 42, 43–44,
        52, 53–58, 62–63, 77, 100–102, 104,

    106, 151, 153–57, 174, 185, 206,
        219–21, 226–28, 232
    as former Leftist, 206–8, 217–18
    as gun owner, 39, 121–23, 129, 229
    individualism of, 39–40, 52–53, 75–76,
        121, 221, 232, 238, 268
    as lesbian, 34, 58–61, 64, 76–77, 106,
        206, 215–16, 234–35, 237–38
    as Los Angeles NOW president, 151,
        153–57, 185, 220–21, 232
    mail received by, 18–20, 50–54, 74–77,
        78, 127, 218, 222–23
    personal honesty of, 62, 215–43
    as pro-choice, 28, 29–30, 51, 54–58, 77,
        106, 155–57, 206, 215–16, 219–30
    radio program of, 18, 47, 126, 129, 138,
        160, 208–9, 215, 218, 238
    religious beliefs of, 28, 72
    Republican agenda as viewed by, 74–77
    as television commentator, 18, 46,
        222–23
    writings of, 3–4, 18, 26, 39–40, 46, 50,
        59–60, 104–6, 172, 209, 215, 218
Burnett, Tom, 107
Burundi, 199
Bush, George H. W., 187
Bush, George W.:
    anti-terrorism campaign of, 18–19, 90,
        197, 200–203
    author's views on, 8, 28–31, 34
    CBS News investigation of, 13–14, 148
    as compassionate conservative, 68–69
    Democratic attacks on, 18–19, 24–25,
        26, 79
    domestic agenda of, 34, 99
    election campaign of (2000), 3
    election campaign of (2004), 3, 8–9,
        19–20, 22, 148, 159, 167, 174, 176,
        184
    foreign policy of, 24–25, 31–33
    Hitler compared with, 26, 166
    homosexuals as viewed by, 237
    international reaction to, 31–33
    Iraq policy of, 11, 33, 34, 111, 114, 115,
        119, 149, 188–93
    leadership of, 10, 31–35, 192–93
    Leftist opposition to, 8–10, 18–19,
        24–25, 26, 79, 116, 149, 167, 192–93
    marriage as viewed by, 242
    media coverage of, 148, 149, 174–75

popular support for, 3, 28–31
religious beliefs of, 28, 237
tax cuts of, 98–99
business, big, 70–71

cable television, 166, 171–72
Calame, Byron, 178
California Medical Center, 55
Canada, 116, 142, 144
capitalism, 4, 32–33, 41, 68, 70, 71, 93,
    102, 103, 112
capital punishment, 25
Carabillo, Toni, 101
Carter, Jimmy, 69–70, 80, 89, 116, 143
Castro, Fidel, 15, 86, 116, 123, 165–66,
    203, 204–5
Catholic Church, 176–77
CBS, 8, 13–14, 148, 155, 161, 163–64,
    166–67, 170, 171
CBS News, 8, 13–14, 148, 155
Center for American Progress, 25
chemical weapons, 197
Cheney, Dick, 10, 22
Cheney, Elizabeth, 10
Cheney, Lynn, 10
Cheney, Mary, 10, 235–38
children, 30, 38, 48, 168–69, 170, 183,
    188, 189, 198–200, 202, 242, 272
China, 84, 123, 146, 204–5
Chiraq, Jacques, 7, 8, 114–17
Chomsky, Noam, 11
Christian, Marc, 163–64
Christian Coalition, 237
Christians:
    abortion opposed by, 191, 219–21, 222
    evangelical, 167, 174–76, 217, 219–21,
        222, 237–38, 243
    gay rights as viewed by, 217, 237–38
    Leftist attacks against, 27–28, 37, 167,
        174–77, 206, 207
    moral values of, 25, 27–28, 38, 149,
        167, 174–77, 207, 208, 211, 237
    political influence of, 28, 38, 45, 73,
        111, 207, 229
Christian Science Monitor, 174
Churchill, Ward, 11
Cisco Systems, 71
civil rights, 138–39, 166
Classical Liberals, 29, 34, 69–73, 77, 85,
    89–90, 91, 117, 209, 217, 230, 266

class system, 85
Clinton, Bill:
    anti-terrorism measures of, 30–31,
        200–201
    book signings by, 186–88
    as Democratic president, 30–31, 84,
        165, 195–96
    gun control supported by, 141
    Iran as viewed by, 194–96
    Lewinsky scandal of, 6, 30–31, 76, 175
    liberal values of, 6, 88
    media coverage of, 186–88, 194–96
    popular opinion on, 3, 30–31, 195–96
    presidential campaign of, 184–85
Clinton, Hillary Rodham, 71, 79, 80, 84,
    98–99, 162, 184
Clinton Foundation, 187–88
"Clinton Sleepovers," 165
CNN, 15
"Code of Conduct" rulebook, 198
Cold War, 113
Cole, Raymond, 159–61
collective victimization, 70
collectivism, 85, 113
colonization, 116
Columbia Journalism Review, 172
commercialism, 117
common good, 98–100
common sense, 25, 175–76
Common Sense (Paine), 71–72
communism, 89, 92, 123, 124, 193
Communist Party, 83
community churches, 72
compassion, 66–69, 237–38, 243
compassionate conservative, 66–69,
    237–38, 243
competition, 68, 94–95, 96
conforming nonconformists, 73–76
Congo, 198, 199
conservatism:
    authentic, 51, 90–91, 209
    author's views on, 39, 51, 66–67, 74–75,
        90–91, 215–43
    compassionate, 66–69, 237–38, 243
    definition of, 86–91
    fascism and, 9, 24–25, 80, 92, 207
    feminism and, 226–30
    gay rights and, 77, 217, 232, 237–38
    individualism of, 34–35, 39–40, 48–49,
        52–53, 68–69

conservatism (*cont.*)
  in mainstream media (MSM), 44,
    152–53, 157, 158, 178–79
  moral values of, 3–4, 68–69, 90–91
  neo-, 89–90
  religious, *see* Christians
  stereotypes of, 64–65, 73–74, 87–91
  women's rights and, 226–30
conspiracy theories, 13–17, 101–3
Constitution, U.S., 36, 121, 124, 125, 126,
    127, 134, 139, 144, 145, 146, 211,
    240, 242
consumer-based activism, 155–56
corruption, 173, 196
creative genius, 94–95
crime, 142–43, 146, 233
  guns and, 129–35
critical thinking skills, 263–65
Cronkite, Walter, 14–15
CSI, 171–72
C-Span, 177–78, 222, 231
Cuba, 15, 84, 86, 95, 116, 123, 165–66,
    203–5
Cultural Axis of Evil, 150, 152
Cultural Gestapo, 207
culture wars, 5–6, 37–42, 93, 108, 150,
    152, 158–59, 168–69, 207, 218, 220

Daschle, Tom, 165
Davis, Judy, 164
Dean, Howard, 8, 11, 12, 36, 79, 169–70
death, 107–8
Death of Right and Wrong, The (Bruce),
    3–4, 26, 39–40, 51, 59–60, 172
Declaration of Independence, 85, 125–26
DeGeneres, Ellen, 47, 64
democracy:
  as American ideal, 6, 70, 72, 114–17
  capitalism and, 32–33, 41, 68, 93, 103,
    112
  as cultural process, 7, 115–17
  dissemination of, 114–17, 191–92
  freedom in, 3, 4, 6, 10, 21, 25, 30–38,
    49, 65, 70, 72–73, 85, 89, 93, 110–13,
    116–17, 119, 242
  in Middle East, 32–33, 89, 114–15,
    118–19, 189, 194–96
  personal participation in, 151–52
  terrorists opposition to, 197, 203–4

Democratic Congressional Campaign
    Committee, 165
Democratic Party:
  authentic members of, 18–20, 71, 77, 91
  author as member of, 28–29, 73, 74, 75,
    76–80, 91, 104
  Classical Liberalism and, 29, 34, 69–73,
    77, 85, 89–90, 91, 117, 209, 217, 230,
    266
  gay rights supported by, 236–37
  hostile tactics of, 11–13, 18–23, 202–9
  leadership of, 11–12, 18–19, 20, 22, 23,
    25, 30–31, 84, 165, 195–96
  Nazism and, 9, 20–21, 24–25, 80,
    81–82, 97, 116–17, 127, 204
  Republicans attacked by, 11–13, 20–23,
    28–29, 66, 74, 80, 98
  socialist influence on, 4, 6, 49, 69–70,
    77, 79–80, 98–100
  traditional values of, 76–80
Diaz, Cameron, 8
dictatorships, 165–66
diplomacy, 6
diplomatic immunity, 196
direct-mail fundraising, 186
Discovery Channel, 180
Disraeli, Benjamin, 118
divorce rate, 239
doctor-assisted suicide, 25
domestic violence, 104
Dowd, Maureen, 174–75
drug legalization, 25
Dugger, Lonnie, 138
Dunblane massacre (1996), 143
"Dykes on Bikes," 64

economy, state control of, 80, 83, 86
Edmonton Journal, 143
Edmundson, Mark, 265–67
education, 272
Egypt, 33, 195
Ehrenfeld, Rachel, 27*n*
Ehrlich, Bob, 144–45
Eichmann, Adolf, 11
Einstein, Albert, 92, 118
El-Baradei, Mohammad, 8
elections:
  of 1992, 184–85
  of 2000, 3

of 2004, 1, 3, 8–9, 19–20, 22, 28, 98,
    148, 159, 167, 174, 176, 184, 236
Emerson, Ralph Waldo, 148
equality, 40–41, 72, 84, 85, 86
equal opportunity, 85–86
Equal Rights Amendment, 100
ESPN, 169
Etheridge, Melissa, 64
ethnicity, 110
Europe, 1, 31–33, 93–94, 96, 112, 116–17
    see also specific countries

Fahrenheit 911, 8
family values, 38, 211
Farah, Joseph, 210
"Farewell Address" (Washington), 1
fascism:
    conservatives and, 9, 24–25, 80, 92, 207
    individuality achievement opposed by,
        98, 100, 123
    Leftists influenced by, 10–13, 20–21,
        43, 77, 79–83, 84, 204, 213
    socialism compared with, 81–82, 92, 97
Federal Bureau of Investigation (FBI),
    135
Federal Communications Commission
    (FCC), 148, 159, 170, 171
Federal Election Commission, 142
Feinstein, Dianne, 142
felons, 25, 133
Feminist Majority, 62, 100–102, 155,
    183–86, 191, 210, 225
feminist movement:
    abortion rights supported by, 29–30,
        54–58, 155–57, 186, 219–28
    author as member of, 28, 29–30, 34, 42,
        43–44, 52, 53–58, 62–63, 77,
        100–102, 104, 106, 151, 153–57, 174,
        185, 206, 219–21, 226–28, 232
    conservatism and, 226–30
    elite of, 43–44, 54–58, 62–63, 100–102,
        155, 183–86, 189–91, 206, 210, 222,
        223–26, 230
    fundraising by, 185–86, 225
    Iraq War opposed by, 189–93
    media as used by, 155–57, 167, 174
    opposition to, 210, 225–26
    political agenda of, 54–58, 155–57,
        225–26

see also National Organization for Women
feudalism, 97
Finding Nemo, 46
firing squads, 203–4
Fortune, 180
Founding Fathers, 61, 124, 126, 139
401(k) investments, 181
Fox News Channel, 10, 18, 46, 76, 104,
    157
France, 83, 96, 116, 204
Franco Francisco, 81
freedom:
    freedom:
        as ideal, 3, 4, 6, 10, 21, 25, 30–38, 49,
            65, 69, 70, 72–73, 85, 89, 93, 110–13,
            116–17, 119, 242
        of religion, 27–28, 38, 73, 111, 175–76,
            211
        sexual, 224–25
        of speech, 265–67
    see also liberty
Freedom of Information Act (FOIA), 201
Fresno, Calif., 240
Fresno Bee, 138
Freston, Tom, 161–62, 165–66
Friedman, Milton, 265
fundraising, 12, 185–86, 191, 225

Gallatin County, Mont., 22
Gandy, Kim, 192–93
gang rape, 199
Garafalo, Janeane, 192–93
Gay Elite, 64–65, 100, 172, 216, 236–41
Gay Gestapo, 172, 233–34
gay marriage, 29, 239–42
gay rights:
    conservatism and, 77
    Democrat support for, 236–37
    establishment for, 64–65, 100, 172, 216,
        233–42
    media coverage of, 46–48
    political influence and, 63–66, 110, 230,
        235–38
    see also homosexuality
genocide, 28, 80, 197, 200–204
Gephardt, Chrissy, 236
Gephardt, Dick, 236
Germany, 20–21, 24–25, 80, 81–82, 97,
    116–17, 127, 195, 204

Gibson, Mel, 10
GLAAD, 108, 120
"Global Government," 25–26
God, 45, 59, 60, 124–26
Gore, Al, 3
government:
    distrust of, 126–29
    limited, 71–72, 123–24
    regulation by, 222, 226, 238
    social influence of, 222, 226, 238,
        240–41
    totalitarian, 79–80, 85, 116, 123–24,
        128, 139–40
grassroots movements, 152
Great Britain, 118, 142
group identity, 76
Group of Eight, 114–15
groupthink, 20, 67, 76, 100, 152, 157–58,
    173, 217, 232
Guevara, Che, 203–5, 213
Guinea, 200
Gun Owners of America, 146
guns:
    assault weapons bans and, 135–36
    crime rate and, 129–35
    ownership rights and, 25, 36–37,
        120–26, 127, 129–47, 165, 229
Guns and Violence (Malcolm), 133

Haiti, 199
Handgun Control, Inc., 133, 165
handicapped individuals, 46
Hannity, Sean, 104
happiness, pursuit of, 111
Harrington, Michael, 89–90
Harris, Katherine, 21–22
Hate American First contingent, 184, 192,
    194
hate-crimes legislation, 207, 233
Haydar, Um, 193
Hayek, Friedrich A., 215, 265–67
Hazard, Lillian, 138
HBO, 169
health, physical, 231–32
health care, 75
health-care clinics, 55, 219–21, 223,
    226–28
Hemispheres, 25
Her Medical Clinic, 55
heroism, 106–7, 214

heterosexuality, 231–32, 234
Hezbollah, 195
Hinchley, Maurice, 13–14
Hitler, Adolf, 9, 18, 20, 24, 26, 80, 81,
    112, 166, 204
Hitler: The Rise of Evil, 166
Hollywood liberals, 117, 193
Homeland Security, 48, 136, 137
homophobia, 74, 101, 102, 148, 152,
    162–64, 165, 206, 235–36, 238, 241
homosexuality:
    Bush's views on, 237
    laws against, 73
    Leftist advocacy of, 172, 216, 232,
        233–34, 236–41
    marriage and, 239–42
    media coverage of, 46–48
    as sexual preference, 58–61, 230–34
    see also gay rights
Hong Kong, 188
Horowitz, David, 10, 66, 90
Howell, Kevin, 23
Hudson, Rock, 163–64
Human Events, 158
human rights, 72–73, 110, 125–26, 189,
    193, 196, 197
Hussein, Qusay, 189
Hussein, Saddam, 15, 86, 115, 116, 169,
    189, 192–93, 194
Hussein, Uday, 189
Hutus, 201
hyphenated identities, 109–10

"I Am an American" advertising cam-
    paign, 109–10
"I Am Woman," 184
IBM, 71
Idaho, 155–57
Ideal Man, 10–13, 202, 213
Identity Politics, 64–65, 92–93, 103, 106,
    108–10, 113, 217, 233–34
Ignatius, David, 33
Igor (correspondent), 77
immigration, 25
imperialism, 92, 111, 118
Incrementalism, 139–41, 168–70
Independent, The, 27, 33
individualism:
    authentic, 34–35, 39–40, 43, 52–53, 61,
        69, 106, 122–23, 215, 242

author's views on, 39–40, 52–53, 75–76,
    121, 221, 232, 238, 268
    in Classical Liberalism, 71–72
    competition and, 94–95
    in conservatism, 100
    gun rights and, 121, 145–46
    homosexuality and, 230–32
    Leftist opposition to, 2–3, 24, 39–40,
        42–43, 48–49, 69
    in New American Revolution, 34–35,
        39–40, 48–49, 52–53, 68–69, 122–23,
        215
    reading and, 267–68
    socialism opposed to, 75–76, 80–86,
        96–97, 113
International Herald Tribune, 179
Internet, 12–13, 20, 25, 158, 172, 180, 181,
    184, 187–88, 190, 210–13, 246, 262
Iran, 191, 192, 194–96
Iraq, Oil-for-Food program in, 197, 198,
    212
Iraq War, 11, 33, 34, 111, 114, 115, 119, 149
    feminist opposition to, 188–93
Ireland, Patricia, 62
Islamic fundamentalists:
    as fascists, 7, 36–37, 103, 113
    freedom opposed by, 37–38
    as terrorists, 2, 7, 16–19, 30–31, 90,
        135–39, 145, 180, 197, 200–204
isolationism, 7, 9
Israel, 26, 119, 195
"Is the Pope Catholic?" (Keller), 176–77
Italy, 112, 116
Ivory Coast, 199

Jackson, Janet, 159, 160, 167–70
Jackson, Jesse, 8, 47, 71, 142, 175
Jaime (correspondent), 74–75
James (correspondent), 50–53, 58, 61
Japan, 9, 116
Jefferson, Thomas, 70, 120, 126
Jesus Christ, 10, 28
Jewish Funders Network, 26
Jewish Virtual Library, 21n
Jews, 16, 21, 26–27, 176, 196, 204
jingoism, 92, 118
John, Elton, 8
John F. Kennedy School of Government,
    177–78
Jordan, Eason, 15

journalism, 172–82
    see also mainstream media
judgment, Leftist opposition to, 56
"Julie" (pseudonym), 129–32, 134
Jumblatt, Walid, 33
Justice Department, U.S., 134

Keller, Bill, 176–77, 179, 180
Kelly & Walsh bookstore, 188
Ken (correspondent), 59–61
Kenneally, Leo F., 55–58
Kennedy, Edward M., 10, 165, 175
Kennedy, John F., 29, 79, 80
Kennedy, Michael, 175
Kennedy, Robert F., 145
Kerry, John, 8, 165, 236
Khatami, Muhammad, 195–96
Khatami, Muhammad-Reza, 196
Khrushchev, Nikita, 83, 84
Kim Jong Il, 86, 116, 192, 204
King, Larry, 14
Kisangani, 199
Korean War, 113, 138, 197
Kosovo, 200
Krauthammer, Charles, 142–43, 144
Kristallnacht, 21
Kristol, Irving, 90
Krugman, Paul, 175
Kurds, 195
Kuwait, 33, 114
Kyobo bookstore, 188

labor unions, 71, 95
La Cabana prison, 203–4, 205
Lamb, Brian, 265–66
Larry King Live, 14
law, rule of, 25
Lebanon, 33, 114, 195, 196, 197
Leftists:
    anti-terrorism efforts opposed by, 18–19
    beliefs of, 43–44
    Bush opposed by, 8–10, 18–19, 24–25,
        26, 79, 116, 149, 167, 192–93
    Christians attacked by, 27–28, 37, 167,
        174–77, 206, 207
    conspiracy theories of, 13–17, 101–3
    depravity of, 2, 4–5, 26–27
    elite of, 11–12, 37, 42–43, 63–65, 67,
        82–83, 88, 93, 205–9, 217–18, 221,
        235–36

Leftists (cont.)
    fascist influence on, 10–13, 20–21, 43,
        77, 79–83, 84, 204, 213
    foreign policy and, 1, 24–25, 31–33
    groupthink of, 20, 67, 76, 100, 152,
        157–58, 173, 217, 232
    homosexuality promoted by, 172, 216,
        232, 233–34, 236–41
    Ideal Man of, 10–13, 202, 213
    individualism opposed by, 2–3, 24,
        39–40, 42–43, 48–49, 56, 69
    leadership of, 20–23, 62–63, 155–56
    marginalization by, 38, 45–48, 127–28
    mediocrity encouraged by, 39–42,
        98–100
    moral values opposed by, 38–39, 60,
        66–67, 74
    negativity used by, 26–28, 41–42, 49,
        97, 98, 102, 112, 149, 151, 153, 186,
        192, 196, 197, 202–9, 225
    politics of hate employed by, 5, 18–20,
        24, 38, 202–9
    power of, 128–29, 154–59, 172–82
    practical action against, 146–47,
        179–82, 209–14
    self-loathing of, 2–3, 5, 26–27, 28,
        41–42, 48–49
    tolerance espoused by, 205, 243
    see also liberalism
Lenin, V. I., 83, 84, 91
lesbians, 34, 47, 58–61, 64, 76–77, 106,
    206, 215–16, 234–35, 237–38
Levine, Bettijane, 53, 57
Lewinsky, Monica, 6, 30–31, 76, 175
Lewis, Wyndham, 268
liberalism:
    author's disavowal of, 206–8, 217–18
    classical, 29, 34, 69–73, 77, 85, 89–90,
        91, 117, 209, 217, 230, 266
    definition of, 86–89
    Hollywood, 117, 193
    in mainstream media (MSM), 13–15,
        41, 60, 109–10, 132, 148, 149, 151,
        152–69, 172–82, 186–88, 193,
        194–96, 264–67
    see also Leftists
Liberia, 199, 200
Libertarian Party, 76
liberty:
    as ideal, 110, 111, 112, 119, 243

    "sufficient margin" of, 79–82
    see also freedom
Liberty Belles, 147
Limbaugh, Rush, 265
Literacy Partners, Inc., 272
Liz (correspondent), 76–77, 78
Locke, John, 70
Los Angeles, Calif., 151, 153–57, 185,
    220–21, 232
Los Angeles County, Calif., 134–35
Los Angeles Times, 55, 135, 157
loyalty, 83
Lute, Jane Holl, 199
L Word, The, 47

McCain, Stacy, 265, 266
McDonald's, 111
Macomber, Shawn, 27n
Madison, James, 70
Madrid train bombings (2004), 17, 119
Mahaney, Lara, 170
Maher, Bill, 2, 11
mainstream media (MSM):
    alternatives to, 157–58, 179–82
    conservative influence on, 44, 152–53,
        157, 158, 178–79
    corporate control of, 148–50, 152–53,
        158, 161–70, 171, 173, 176, 179–80,
        181, 182
    liberal influence on, 13–15, 41, 60,
        109–10, 132, 148, 149, 151, 152–69,
        172–82, 186–88, 193, 194–96, 264–67
    network news in, 8, 13–14, 138, 155,
        157, 161, 163–64, 166–67, 170, 171
    power of, 154–59, 172–82
    violence in, 157–61
    see also specific media sources
majority, tyranny of, 101–2
Malcolm, Joyce Lee, 133
Malignant Narcissists (Mal Narsy), 8,
    26–28, 41–42, 49, 97, 98, 102, 112,
    149, 151, 153, 186, 192, 196, 197,
    202–9, 225
Malkin, Michelle, 10
Malvo, Lee Boyd, 144
Mapes, Mary, 8
marginalization, 38, 45–48, 127–28
Marine Corps, U.S., 7, 191, 196
    Beirut barracks bombing of, 196
Marks, Alexandra, 174

marriage, 175, 238–42
Marx, Karl, 91
Marxism, 6, 165–66, 204
Massachusetts, 240
mass media, *see* mainstream media
mass murders, 80, 107, 200–204
Masters Golf Tournament, 174
media:
   contact tools, 246–62
   see also mainstream media; specific
      media outlets
Media Minutemen, 15–16
Media Research Center (MRC), 246–47
medical research, 95
mediocrity, 39–42, 98–100
Men of the DNC Calendar, 25
Microsoft Corp., 71
Middle East, 32–33, 89, 111, 114–15,
   118–19, 189, 194–96
Mill, John Stuart, 62
Miller, Zel, 13
minority rights, 71, 233, 243
Misery Merchants, 93, 100, 108
Mix, Bruce, 134, 135
Modern Liberals, 89
Modesto, Calif., 138
Modoc County, Calif., 134–35
Mogadishu, Somalia, 200–201
Mondale, Walter, 143
Monde, Le 33
money laundering, 197
Moonves, Leslie, 161–62, 163, 165–66
Moore, Michael, 2, 8, 10, 89
morality:
   Christian, 25, 27–28, 38, 149, 167,
      174–77, 207, 208, 211, 237
   conservative, 3–4, 68–69, 90–91
   Leftist opposition to, 38–39, 56, 60,
      66–67, 74
   relative, 4–5, 169–70, 176, 195
   in U.S. society, 3–4, 85–86, 110–12, 240
"morality crimes," 195
Morocco, 199
Move America Forward, 212–13
MoveOn.org, 12–13, 20, 25
MTV, 160, 167, 170, 171
Mubarak, Hosni, 33
Muhammad, John Allen, 144
multiculturalism, 4–5, 7, 92, 110
Murder Capital, Washington D.C., 134

Music Behind Bars, 148, 162
Mussolini, Benito, 80–82, 112, 204
My Life (Clinton), 186–88

NARAL, 155
National Association for the Advancement
   of Colored People (NAACP), 108
nationalism, 25, 34–35, 108–19, 122
National Organization for Women
   (NOW), 52, 55–58, 62, 65, 75–76, 77,
      100–101, 104, 108, 186, 192–93, 210
   author as president of LA, 151, 153–57,
      185, 220–21, 232
National Party No More, A (Miller), 13
National Review, 178
National Rifle Association (NRA), 146
"Nazi," as label, 80
Nazi Germany, 9, 20–21, 24–25, 81, 82,
   97, 116–17, 127, 204
NBC, 157
Nelly (rap singer), 168
neoconservatives, 89–90
neoliberals, 90
neosocialists, 93
network news, 8, 13–14, 138, 155, 157,
   161, 163–64, 166–67, 170, 171,
   259–62
New American Revolution:
   agenda of, 209–14, 243
   Bush's leadership of, 10, 31–35, 192–93
   cultural influence of, 5–6, 37–42, 108,
      150, 152, 158–59, 168–69, 207, 218,
      220
   individualism in, 34–35, 39–40, 43,
      48–49, 52–53, 61, 68–69, 122–23, 215
   moral values of, 4, 68–69, 90–91
   patriotism in, 92–94, 121, 128, 158–61,
      164, 218
   reading list for, 267–72
   September 11th as catalyst for, 1–2, 4,
      6, 104–6
   "tool chests" for, 246–62
"New Normal," 2
New Radical Individuals, 29, 31–33,
   36–39, 45–49, 59, 83, 98, 99, 106,
   120–21, 150, 216, 237, 243
NewsHour With Jim Lehrer, The, 179
news magazines, 247–48, 264
   contact information for, 247–48
Newsom, Gavin, 239–40

newspapers, 140, 149–50, 152, 155, 158,
   163, 164, 172–82, 187, 248–57, 264
   contact information for, 248–57
news services, 257–58
New Thought Police, The (Bruce), 3–4,
   39–40, 59, 100, 104–6, 172
New York, 178–79
New York Stock Exchange, 171
New York Times, 140–41, 149–50, 152,
   155, 158, 163, 164, 172–82, 187
New York Times Company, 176, 179–80,
   181, 182
Night of the Living Dead, 66
Night Stalker, 129–32
nihilism, 128, 148–49, 166, 182, 225
nonconformists, 204–5
nondiscrimination laws, 233
North Atlantic Treaty Organization
   (NATO), 115, 120
North Carolina, 23
North Korea, 84, 95, 123, 138, 146, 204–5
Not by Politics Alone (Lenin), 83
NPR, 179
nuclear proliferation, 194

Oakland Tribune, 138
Ohio, 184
Oil-for-Food program, 197, 198, 212
Okrent, Daniel, 177–78
"open societies," 24–25
Operation Rescue, 219–21
optimism, 96–97, 100, 152–53
Orlando, Fla., 22
Orwell, George, 66
Ottoman Empire, 118
Oxford American Writer's Thesaurus,
   87–88
Oxford English Dictionary, 203

Paine, Thomas, 70, 71–72
Palestinians, 25
paranoia, 98
Parents Television Council, 170, 171
Pariser, Eli, 12–13
party affiliation, 8–9, 110
patriotism, 1, 92–94, 121, 128, 158–61,
   164, 218
PBS, 179, 194
peacekeepers, U.N., 198–200, 212
pediatrics, 272

Penn, Sean, 2
personal responsibility, 82, 90
pessimism, 96
plagiarism, 172–73
Planned Parenthood, 210, 225
Plato, 86
pledge of allegiance, 110
Podesta, John, 25
Podhoretz, Norman, 90
politics:
   authenticity in, 18–20, 39–40, 51,
      52–53, 71, 77, 90–91, 106, 122–23,
      190–91, 209, 215
   Christian influence in, 38, 45, 73, 111,
      207, 229
   group, 152, 157–58, 173, 232
   of hate, 5, 18–20, 24, 38, 202–9
   identity, 64–65, 92–93, 103, 106,
      108–10, 113, 217, 233–34
   leadership in, 10, 31–35
   moral relativism in, 4, 169–70, 176, 195
   party affiliation in, 8–9, 110
   see also Democratic Party; Republican
      Party
Politics of Bad Faith, The (Horowitz), 90
Pol Pot, 86
Ponte, Lowell, 165
pornography, 167
power, 128–29, 154–59, 172–82
prenatal care, 226–28
privacy, 72–73
pro-choice movement, 28, 29–30, 51,
   54–58, 77, 106, 155–57, 206, 215–16,
   219–30
profit, 86
Prohibition, 145
pro-life movement, 191, 217
propaganda, 166
property, private, 70, 71, 86
public school system, 272

racism, 47, 74, 101, 102, 103, 104, 110,
   118, 152, 173, 206, 235–36
radio, 18, 47, 126, 138, 160, 208–9, 215,
   218, 238, 264
Rainbow/Pu$h Coalition, 142
Raines, Howell, 172–73, 176
Ramirez, Richard, 129–32
Rand, Ayn, 70
rape, 199

Rather, Dan, 8, 14, 148
Reach Out and Read (ROR), 272
reading list, 267–72
Reagan, Nancy, 148, 162–65
Reagan, Ronald, 31–33, 39, 88, 89, 96,
    128, 148, 149, 162–65
Reagans, The, 148, 162–65, 166
Red Dawn, 136
Reddy, Helen, 184
"redneck," 87, 88, 89
Redstone, Sumner, 148–49, 161–62, 164,
    165–67, 168
religion, freedom of, 27–28, 38, 73, 111,
    124–26, 175–76, 211
Religious Right, *see* Christians
Republican Party:
    big business and, 70–71
    Christian support for, 38, 73, 111, 207,
        229
    Democratic attacks on, 11–13, 20–23,
        29, 66, 74–77, 80, 98
    gay rights and, 235–38
    moderate element in, 12, 72
    white male support for, 206
Restoration Weekend, 66–67
retirement, 75
Revenge for Love, The (Lewis), 268
reward, 94–95
Reynolds, Mel, 142
Rice, Condoleezza, 10
Ridge, Tom, 137, 141
Road to Serfdom, The (Hayek), 265–67
robberies, 143–44
Robert (correspondent), 18–20
"Robert" (pseudonym), 231
Roe v. Wade, 155–57
Roosevelt, Eleanor, 36
Roosevelt, Franklin D., 29
Rose, Charlie, 194, 195
Rove, Karl, 13–16
Russia, 118, 198–99
    see also Soviet Union
Rwanda, 82, 201–2

SafeStreetsDC.com, 134
St. Patrick's Cathedral, 148, 170
same-sex civil unions, 29, 239–42
San Diego Union-Tribune, 138
San Francisco, Calif., 239–40
SAT scores, 272

Saudi Arabia, 33, 114, 115, 189, 192
Saving Private Ryan, 158–61, 171
Schlessinger, Laura, 172
Schumer, Charles, 135–36, 141
Schwarzenegger, Arnold, 46–47
Second Amendment, 121, 125, 127, 134,
    139, 144, 145, 146
Security Council, UN, 197
self-identity, 73–74
self-loathing, 2–3, 5, 26–27, 28, 41–42,
    48–49, 202
Seltzer, Barry M., 21–22
senior citizens, 75
September 11th, 2001, terrorist attacks,
    1–2, 4, 5, 6, 29, 31, 33, 34, 48, 92–94,
    104–8, 135–36, 162, 164, 166, 201
serial killers, 129–32, 146
"Sex-for-Food" scandal, 198–200, 212
"Sex in the Cathedral" radio stunt, 148,
    170
Sex in the City, 47
sexism, 74, 101, 102, 152, 235–36
sex-tourism industry, 183–84
sexual abuse, 183, 196, 197, 198–200, 212,
    224–25
sexual freedom, 224–25, 239
sexually-transmitted diseases, 239
sexual preferences, 58–61, 230–34
Showtime channel, 166–67, 171
Sierra Leone, 200
Simpson, O. J., 53, 104
Six Feet Under, 47
slavery, 85, 103
Sleeping Beauty, pre-9/11 America as, 93
Smeal, Eleanor, 62, 65, 100, 102–4, 183,
    184, 190–91, 195
Smith, Adam, 70
snipers, 144–45
Snuffy (author's gun), 39, 121, 123
socialism:
    collectivism in, 85, 113
    Democrats influenced by, 4, 6, 49,
        69–70, 77, 79–80, 98–100
    economic control in, 80, 83, 86
    fascism compared with, 81–82, 92, 97
    identity prescribed by, 90–91
    individualism opposed to, 76, 80–86,
        96–97, 113
    neo-, 93
    state control in, 80, 83

socialism (*cont.*)
  totalitarianism and, 79–80, 85, 128, 139–40
social-service plans, 72
Somalia, 200–201
Soros, George, 8, 12–13, 20, 24–28
Soviet Union, 25, 28, 31, 84, 95, 128, 136, 177, 204
  see also Russia
Sowell, Thomas, 10
Spain, 17, 81, 119
Spears, Britney, 241–42
special-interest groups, 19–20, 39, 51–52, 103, 105, 112, 154
speech, freedom of, 265–67
Spiegel, Der, 33
Sri Lanka, 188
Stalin, Joseph, 16, 28, 80, 86, 91, 97, 177
  standards in, 166–70
Starbucks, 71
status quo, 88–89
Steinem, Gloria, 191
Steinhardt, Michael, 26–27
stereotypes, 63, 64–65, 73–74, 87–91, 108–9
Stewart, Lynne, 13
Steyn, Mark, 10
stock divestment, 171, 181, 182
Streisand, Barbra, 163, 164
"sufficient margin of liberty," 80–82
Sullivan, Andrew, 240–41
Sulzberger, Arthur, Jr., 176, 177, 179, 180
Superbowl, 159, 167–70
Supreme Court, U.S., 125, 155, 160
Syria, 195, 197

Taipei, 188
Taliban, 189
Tall Poppy Syndrome, 98–100
Tancredo, Tom, 10
taxation, 98–99, 210
television, 46, 166–69, 171–72, 222–23, 259–62, 264, 267
Ten Commandments, 175
terrorism:
  appeasement of, 1–2, 16–17
  causes of, 2, 7
  gun control and, 135–39, 145
  Islamic fundamentalism and, 2, 7, 16–19, 30–31, 90, 135–39, 145, 180, 197, 200–204

  state-sponsored, 197, 203–4
  war on, 18–19, 90, 180, 197, 200–203
Thatcher, Margaret, 89
theocracies, 175
Thought Police, 4–5, 39, 42–44, 74, 80, 150, 152, 167–68, 241
Tillman, Pat, 10
Timberlake, Justin, 160, 167–69
Time, 240
Times (London), 198, 199
"Times Watch," 181
Time Warner, 177
Today, 157
tolerance, 70, 205, 243
"tool chests," 246–62
totalitarianism, 79–80, 85, 116, 123–24, 128, 139–40
"total state," 81
Touched by an Angel, 167
Townsend, Kathleen Kennedy, 144–45
trauma, 98
Truman, Harry S, 79, 80
tsunami relief efforts (2004), 183–84, 186–89
TV Guide, 166
tyranny, 93–94, 101–2

United Flight 93 hijacking, 106–7
United Nations, 103, 196, 197–202, 212, 213
  Security Council of, 197
United States:
  armed forces of, 72, 191, 226
  Bush's leadership of, 10, 31–35
  democratic ideal of, 6, 70, 72, 114–17
  domestic policies of, 34
  European relations of, 1, 31–33, 93–94, 96
  foreign policy of, 1, 24–25, 31–33, 226
  global role of, 1–2, 6–7, 31–35
  immigration to, 25
  institutions of, 153
  moral values of, 4, 85–86, 110–12, 240, 242
  nationalism in, 25, 34–35, 108–19, 122
  popular culture of, 5–6, 37–42, 45–48, 93
  religious freedom in, 27–28, 38, 73, 111, 175–76, 211
  social change in, 53–54

sovereignty of, 123
traditions of, 239–42
as UN contributor, 212
United States v. Cruickshank, 125, 126
universal suffrage, 72
unlawful searches, 125
Uruguay, 199
USA Today, 84

Veterans' Day, 158–59
VH1 channel, 148, 162, 171
Viacom, Inc., 148–50, 152–53, 158,
    161–72, 181, 182
Vichy France, 204
Vietnam War, 106, 113, 138
violence, 157–60
Voltaire, 183
volunteer literacy programs, 272
voting rights, 85

Walker, Alice, 192–93
Wall Street Journal, 178
Wal-Mart, 186
"wardrobe malfunction," 167–69
war on terror, 18–19, 90, 197, 200–203
Washington, D.C., 133–35, 142, 146
Washington, George, 1
Washington Post, 24–25
Washington Times, 158
Waters, Maxine, 47, 71, 80
Wead, Doug, 237

wealth, redistribution of, 80, 83, 86
weapons of mass destruction, 149, 197
websites, 12–13, 20, 25, 158, 172, 180,
    181, 184, 187–88, 190, 210–13, 246,
    262
Weekly Standard, 157, 158, 178, 199, 200
welfare state, 83, 90
Western Civilization, 103
West Virginia, 22
Why Read? (Edmundson), 265
Will & Grace, 46
wire services, 258–59
Wolf, Ginni, 144
women:
    abuse of, 183–84, 195, 196, 197,
        198–200, 212, 224–25
    clinics for, 219–21, 223, 226–28
    equality of, 72, 74, 101, 102, 152, 218,
        224, 226–30, 235–36
    gun rights and, 122, 129–32
    Iraqi, 34, 114, 115, 188, 189, 191–92
    sexual freedom of, 224–25
workers, 71, 95
working class, 186
World Economic Forum (2005), 15, 194
World War I, 2, 112
World War II, 2, 4, 7, 9, 93, 112–13,
    116–17, 158–61

Yard, Molly, 185
Young America's Foundation (YAF), 212